T0301391

Caught in the Machinery

Caught in the Machinery

Workplace Accidents and Injured Workers
in Nineteenth-Century Britain

Jamie L. Bronstein

Stanford University Press
Stanford, California
2008

Stanford University Press

Stanford, California

©2008 by the Board of Trustees of the Leland Stanford Junior University. All rights reserved.

Printed in the United States of America on acid-free, archival-quality paper

Library of Congress Cataloging-in-Publication Data

Bronstein, Jamie L.

Caught in the machinery : workplace accidents and injured workers in nineteenth-century Britain / Jamie L. Bronstein.

    p. cm.

    Includes bibliographical references and index.

    ISBN 978-0-8047-0008-5 (cloth : alk. paper)

    1. Industrial accidents—Great Britain—History—19th century. 2. Workers' compensation—Great Britain—History. 3. Workers' compensation—United States—History. I. Title.

HD7262.5.G7B76 2008

363.110941'09034—dc22

                                        2007003972

Typeset by Thompson Type in 10/14 Minion

For Mike and Evan

Contents

Acknowledgments

THIS PROJECT BEGAN IN THE LATE 1990S as I did my research for my first book—on land reform. As I read nineteenth-century newspapers in search of news of the Chartist Land Company and the American National Reformers, I could not help but be impressed by the gothic stories of workplace accidents and injured workers that could often be found there. Why were the newspapers so florid in their descriptions of the carnage? How did these injured workers cope? How did Britain, and later the United States, move from that scenario to a bureaucratized system of workers' compensation? I have sought to answer these questions and others and have been surprised at the way in which what I found tends to subvert the traditional narrative about nineteenth-century progress.

There are many people who need to be thanked for their support and particular contributions to my work. Roger Huffman arranged a trip to Cobre Mine, and librarian Jim Knox supplied a bibliography on industrial accidents early in the process. My fellow participants in the 1998 National Endowment for the Humanities Seminar on the history of death in America engaged me in many enlightening conversations. The staffs at many libraries were extremely helpful: they included the British Library, the Guildhall Library in London, the Warwick Modern Records Centre; the Glasgow University Business Archive; and especially the Hagley Museum and Library, whose directors kindly arranged for me to stay on the museum's grounds for a month as I immersed myself in their archive. I also thank the Hagley Museum for allowing me to search the Du Pont's private graveyard for signs of their employees' graves.

The long-suffering staff of the interlibrary loan department at New Mexico State University were essential to the success of this project.

Fellow historians who gave me helpful advice at one point or another in the preparation of this project included Peter Stansky, Christopher Clark, Kevin Rosario, Randy Bergstrom, Elisabeth Cawthon, Simon Cordery, Michael Ashley Stein, and especially John Witt, who was kind enough to send me his unpublished manuscript before his book emerged in print. My colleagues in the history department at New Mexico State University heard parts of this work at our "History Sandwiched In" program and also workshopped a chapter with me; thanks in particular to Margaret Jacobs, Joan Jensen, and Marsha Weisiger for substantive written commentary. Parts of this work were given as papers at the North American Conference on British Studies, the Society for the History of the Early American Republic Conference, North American Labor History Conference, the Social Science History Association Conference, and the Western Conference on British Studies, and I would like to thank all of the commentators and fellow panelists on those panels for nudging the project along in many ways. In the final stages of the project, I am grateful to both the anonymous and nonanonymous readers who read my work for Stanford University Press; to my editors Norris Pope, Emily-Jane Cohen, and John Feneron; and to production manager Margaret Pinette.

An early version of what would become Chapter 3 was published under the title "Caught in the Machinery: Workplace Accidents and Injured Workers in Nineteenth-Century Britain and the United States," in the *Maryland Historical Magazine*, vol. 96 no. 2, pp. 163–184, in the summer of 2001.

Financially, this project was supported by a minigrant provided by the College of Arts and Sciences of New Mexico State University and by a fellowship from the National Endowment for the Humanities. It was also supported by Ronald and Susan Bronstein and Mike Zigmond, whom I thank for their encouragement, willingness to hear about this topic ad nauseam, to read chapters, and—in the case of my father, who has held the Victorian title of "Master of the Inns of Court in Workers' Compensation"—to share his experiences with the modern system of workers' compensation. Finally, I would like to thank Evan Zigmond for increasing my ability to imagine the plight of nineteenth-century working families and for reminding me of the importance of concentrating on the present as well as the past.

Caught in the Machinery

Introduction: Not Your Typical Day at the Office

PHINEAS GAGE, A SUBCONTRACTOR working for the Burlington and Northern Railroad, surely had little reason to think that going to work on that September day in 1848 would change his life. The day had been routine enough until that point, as he and his fellow workers prepared the ground to receive the railroad track. He was using a pointed rod—a tamping iron—to tamp down some gunpowder in preparation for blasting. In a moment of inattention, he assumed that the man working next to him had prepared the hole and that it was safe to tamp. When Gage's tamping iron hit the black powder, exploding it, the iron shot into his skull just below the eye, emerged from the top of his head, and landed some distance away, carrying with it a good quantity of blood and brains. Gage was loaded onto a cart and carried to the nearest doctor, who, despite the limitations of nineteenth-century medicine, managed to save his life. Even with his devastating injury, Gage would survive for another twelve years before dying of epilepsy.

Gage's story is familiar to students of introductory psychology, as he has often been misinterpreted as the inspiration for twentieth-century operations to remove part of the brain. But Gage also embodies another phenomenon: the uncompensated toll that workplace dangers took on the worker's body in the nineteenth-century workplace. Although his accident was somewhat fantastic, its aftermath was not unrepresentative. Gage received good, attentive medical care, which was most likely subsidized by his employer. However, unlike many injured railroad workers, Gage was not hired back by the same company in the role of a watchman or cleaner—the psychological changes from his brain injury were just too acute. So instead of being able to support himself on the railroad, Gage led a more peripatetic existence. He is rumored to have exhibited himself in Barnum's museum, with his tamping iron, and to have begged on the steps of the Harvard Medical School. More certain is that he spent a long period of time working as a stagecoach driver in Chile and then worked on farms in California. He never married or had children. Like many nineteenth-century workers, Gage suffered a workplace accident that had a major impact on his life.[1]

Of course, workplace accidents have always been a feature of human existence; surely some of the first hunter-gatherers misjudged their distance from wild animals or got a little too close to the cooking fire. But the advent of streamlined production in the nineteenth century, the increasing demand for fuel to power industrialization, and the mechanized transport of goods racheted up the pace by which workers were injured. The steam press, and its offspring the penny newspaper, enable us to know more about the dangers of the transatlantic workplace, and the Victorian positivist penchant for collecting and categorizing information means that historians who study the nineteenth century have some of the first government-collected data on this issue. This evidence suggests that fatal or devastating workplace accidents were distressingly common in the nineteenth century, particularly in fields like mining and railroad work, but they were not limited to these fields. Even traditional industries like farming and construction consumed lives and limbs. Factory production, while creating fewer fatal accidents than mining, created large numbers of industrial amputations, particularly of fingers. But the moral of that story may not be what we think.

A lost limb is a lost limb—but the cultural and social meaning of that injury has everything to do with the multiple contexts in which it is experienced, and these issues have not been looked at closely before.[2] How did working people interpret and categorize their painful experiences on the job? What kind of a culture of workplace injury did they create, and how did it differ from the presentation of workplace injury and death constructed by the press and by employers? In the more practical realm, where did workers turn for financial help when all the certainties of daily life were disrupted by pain, and what kind of help could they expect? And why, in such a seemingly stable system that lasted until 1880, was social responsibility for workplace accidents finally reallocated? These are some of the questions that this work will address, with its primary focus on Great Britain but using the American experience for comparative purposes.

While British workers were the first to suffer the bodily consequences of industrialization, there was more to the determination of that experience than national boundaries, as comparison with American sources tends to show. Like Phineas Gage, workers injured in both nineteenth-century Britain and the United States bore the majority of the cost of workplace accidents. Workers' compensation legislation was unknown in either country until 1880. Once injured, nineteenth-century workers faced an unfriendly legal regime. Due to a combination of common-law defenses, the fellow-servant rule, contributory negligence, and assumption of risk, neither British nor American workers could successfully collect compensation from employers through the legal system. As a result, as Chapter 2 illustrates, the social cost of workplace accidents was more widely, although not more fairly, distributed than it is today. Employers, particularly those presiding over more dangerous employments, often compensated employees when injured, either by finding them alternative employment, covering part of their medical costs, or employing members of their families. Employees themselves attempted to provide for such contingencies through benefit societies, and expressed their mutuality through informal collections for injured colleagues. Finally, the general public absorbed some of the social cost of workplace accidents, through public subscriptions and benefit performances.

If newspapers and Parliamentary Select Committees are any indication, nineteenth-century readers focused intensely on the way in which workplaces posed a danger to their inhabitants. They did refer to such mishaps as "accidents" rather than seeing them as an integral part of the system of management and production. Nor did they demand that employers take full responsibility for the toll of accidents, as would finally happen in the twentieth century.[3] Nonetheless, the consuming classes—those who rode the railroads, wore the textiles, and were warmed by the coal that had come at such a high cost—did not see workers as expendable.[4] Rather, as Chapter 3 shows, middle-class observers usually described workplace accidents compassionately, deploying one of a small number of literary genres. Accidents could be seen melodramatically, which presumed a focus on the families left wretched by the death or injury of their breadwinner. They could be seen religiously, as a punishment for sin, either on the part of the individual or the community. They could be seen as heroic stories, as workers sacrificed their own lives to bring injured brother workers out of the mine. All of these ways of looking at accidents humanized and individualized a working class that was often portrayed facelessly and collectively in other places.

While middle-class observers played up the emotional side of workplace accidents, workers themselves were more reserved. Their actions in the midst of disaster showed that, contrary to middle-class belief, they did suffer emotional torment and physical pain through accidents. But for workers, stories of workplace accidents were also stories of financial hardship and the questioning of masculine identity.

The experience of workplace accidents was contingent upon many things: the nature of the injury; the level of wage and skill that a worker had obtained; the degree to which a worker's family depended upon the injured party for survival; and the degree to which a worker's employer was paternalistic or charitable, among other things. But the identity of the worker within the larger system of employment could also play a role in determining the outcome. In Britain, where protective legislation already existed to shield women and children from the worst excesses of unregulated capitalism, young and female workers, particularly in the textile industry, had other means of pursuing their employers for compensation. In the United States, the owners of slaves who were contracted out and injured on the job were entitled to compensation, for similar reasons. Slaves, children, and female workers all lay outside the definition of workers under common law, since they were all unable, in various ways, to safeguard their own welfare. In contrast, white male workers were defined as free agents, able to take advantage of freedom of contract to avoid overly dangerous work situations (whether or not this freedom actually existed). The argument that women and children were entitled to special protection as a result of their inferior status cut across class, disabling male workers from advocating strongly for themselves. In contrast with recent scholarship suggesting that the "free labor" ideal was limited to American workers, where it evolved in juxtaposition to slavery, this study suggests that the free labor ideal was a transatlantic phenomenon that retarded the growth of workers' compensation in Britain also.[5]

Utilitarian thinkers and kind-hearted reformers in Britain proposed no-fault compensation and regulation of worker safety beginning in the 1830s. These proposals were followed, over the next several decades, by safety legislation that made a concrete difference in the lives of young and female workers. Parliament introduced mine safety legislation and a system of inspection in the 1840s and 1850s, in response to well-documented mine disasters. At the same time, workers in high-skill industries, who were better organized than their American counterparts, agitated for employers' liability legislation.

While the issue was shunted again and again to Select Committees, seemingly as a way of removing the issue from the table, limited employers' liability legislation was finally passed by the Disraeli ministry; not because it would benefit employers and employees equally, but as part of a wider campaign to address the social welfare of the working classes. The centralization of British politics meant that debates about, and solutions for, workers' compensation could be national.

In the United States, in contrast, little could be done at the federal government level, given the understanding, after the Civil War, that the legitimate aims and duties of the federal government had to remain limited. Even in the coal industry, which featured some of the most devastating disasters in human terms, federal regulation was not forthcoming until 1910. States' reactions to workplace accidents varied, with Massachusetts being the state most likely to introduce regulation for worker welfare; but even in Massachusetts, the timetable for reform was well behind that in Britain. American workers found themselves more fragmented than their British counterparts; even the labor unions that did exist prioritized reforms like a shortened work day and higher wages over systemic safety reform. Freedom of contract was a cornerstone of American politics—as Eric Foner has shown, it was one of the founding propositions of the ruling Republican Party—so that regulation of the workplace was anathema.[6]

This is not to suggest, however, that the picture for American workers who were injured was necessarily worse than it was for British workers. In fact, in many states, it was better. Compelled by Christian humanitarianism and a concern for equity, which sometimes overrode their penchant for following common-law precedents, judges in some American states created opportunities for workers to prevail against their employers in tort claims. When given the opportunity to decide in favor of injured workers, juries could be very generous. The injustice of the British system was patent, supporting calls for change; the justice of the American system was uneven, postponing calls for change. Thus in the United States, as contrasted with Great Britain, a combination of employers, labor unions, and insurance companies sought to restore predictability to the system by instituting no-fault workers' compensation legislation.

Although this narrative is primarily about the British experience, looking at workplace accidents in a transnational framework has the potential to illuminate aspects of the experiences of injured workers that have not been touched on before. The shared cultural inheritance of language, law, and the structure of labor systems on both sides of the Atlantic meant that the first industrialized nation was not alone in its experiences of the dangers of the workplace. Injury and death on the job site were common on both sides of the Atlantic, as were onlookers' reactions and workers' reactions. The categories of workers protected by legislation or judicial discretion were also the same. Britain and the United States shared a rhetoric of "free labor" concerning workers' responsibility for accidents on the job. As this book will show, what distinguished Britain in the nineteenth century were not the accidents themselves, nor the options open to workers under the legal system, the compassion or lack of compassion of employers, or the reaction of the press. Rather, what was different was the process by which the claims of injured workers were asserted and acknowledged. As a result of a combination of public sympathy, trade union activism, and political responsibility assumed by governing classes without a specific financial interest, an Employer's Liability Act was achieved in 1880—a symptom of a new way of thinking about social responsibility and social cost.

The Perils of the Workplace

WERE WORKPLACE ACCIDENTS INCREASING over the course of the nineteenth century, becoming more common as industrialization intensified? The data that historians can look at to answer this question is both incomplete and in a certain sense ambiguous. It is clear that certain industries that didn't exist before the Industrial Revolution—the railroads, for example—were dangerous at first. The railroads were constructed in the early Victorian era, when the ethics of personal responsibility and freedom of contract between the worker and the employer were at their strongest. As a result, the demands of railroads and textile factories for coal led to a significant expansion in coal production in the period in which ventilation was still dubious underground, miners were not paid for the timbering work that held the roofs up in their working places, and second shafts that might serve as emergency exits from mines were not required. Even when innovations like the Davy lamp and new methods of railway signaling were introduced, the expansion of production and transportation that they enabled, along with overconfident reliance on the new technology, might cause the number of accidents experienced to increase, thus offsetting the number of accidents prevented.[1]

We certainly know more about the incidence of accidents in the nineteenth century than in the eighteenth, as the steam press made possible the proliferation of provincial newspapers whose reports of accidents have survived to tell us about them. And as burgeoning states began to grow and to take on more responsibility to regulate industries, bureaucrats began to compile centralized records on accidents. But the reach of the bureaucrats was limited to certain industries, and spotty newspaper coverage enables us only to extrapolate. So, it is very hard to know whether the number of accidents increased, indicating that the industrialized workplace was truly more dangerous, or whether social knowledge about (and preoccupation with) accidents, and their prevention, increased. The early nineteenth century was, after all, an era marked by many different kinds of humanitarianism, including attempts to protect children, animals, and slaves. If the number of accidents did increase, it is impossible to say with certainty whether the workplace itself became more dangerous or whether the expansion of industry simply expanded the number of man hours, thus expanding the number of workers who might be injured or killed in an accident. The same problems plague historians of crime in early nineteenth-century Britain for the same reasons.[2]

The conclusions that can be drawn from the existing data suggest that contemporaries had at least some concrete reason for being more concerned about workplace accidents. Looking at friendly society data for the late nineteenth century, James C. Riley has noted that during the period known as the "mortality decline" (1870–1900), British workers' life spans increased, but they took off more time with illness than did workers earlier in the century. Riley notes that an increased incidence of workplace accidents or occupational disease may be to blame for this higher morbidity (although there are also other possible explanations).[3] Examination of the dangers of individual industries shows that, although it is hard to measure change over time, it is clear that the workplace posed large and predictable dangers to its inhabitants, and that, except in textiles, little substantive reform appeared before the advent of employers' liability legislation in the 1880s. In contrast, in the United States, the big jump in the number and severity of accidents and the likelihood of lawsuits came after the Civil War.[4]

The Railroads

Historians who have studied the dangers of the workplace in the early nineteenth century have tended to focus on a few, high-profile industries in which disasters were common. The railways, representing a new technology in the nineteenth century, have thus attracted well-founded attention. Construction of the railroads was an extremely hazardous activity for the lives and limbs of workers, especially those involved in tunneling. Construction work on a single stretch of railway line over a six-year period resulted in 32 deaths, 23 compound fractures, 74 simple fractures, and 140 "severe cases," including blast burns, severe bruises, cuts, and dislocations. Many of those injured suffered from multiple injuries. This was in addition to 400 cases of minor accidents: trapped and broken fingers, seven of which had to be amputated; injuries to the feet, lacerations of the scalp, bruises, and broken shins.[5] Similarly, a Select Committee of the House of Commons investigating accidents to railway laborers in 1846 found that in one tunnel on a 2.5-mile-long stretch of railroad, in the course of two years, four men were killed by the bursting of a drift mine, another was killed when a rope broke and he fell down a shaft, another fell from a house which was being demolished so that the railroad could be built, and another fell out of a bucket while being drawn up a shaft.[6] And the sheer spectacle of railway accidents could garner attention; Phineas Gage was not the only railroad worker to have his head impaled by a tamping iron, although he was probably the luckiest. According to Henry Lacy Pomfret, another worker was not so lucky: "one man had drilled a hole vertically in the rock, and in putting the powder into this hole, he used a iron stemmer, and this ignited the powder, and the stemmer was driven through a fellow-workman's head, and killed him on the spot."[7]

Railway construction had serious social as well as physical costs, as railway companies shifted the costs for care of their injured men from themselves to charitable institutions. Between 1835 and 1839, during the period of the construction of the London and Birmingham Railway, the General Infirmary in Northampton treated 121 accident victims, mostly for fractures. Railway workmen spent a combined total of 852 weeks and six days in the infirmary, and while £597 had been spent on their treatment, the railroad had only subscribed £115 10s., with contractors and railway workers subscribing other small sums.[8] The Salisbury infirmary admitted 52 railway workmen in 1845–46, and spent £177 on their care, while the company and contractors together had only contributed £11 6s.[9]

Once the lines themselves were built, the railroads continued to subject their workers to dangers. Many of these were caused by structural features: long stretches of single track required train conductors to time the passage of trains carefully while others sat in sidings. Even where there was double track, close scheduling and uncertainty about train schedules meant that trains that had to stop for some reason were always in imminent danger of being telescoped from behind.[10] Until the advent of automatic braking, brakemen had to climb on top of cars to set train brakes by hand, and also had to couple trains by hand, setting themselves in imminent risk between heavy cars. Returns collected by the British government testify to this risk, showing that between July and December of 1855, out of a total at-risk workforce of approximately 22,300 men, 63 railway servants were killed on the job, and an additional

54 were injured: one serious accident for every 190 workers.[11] P. W. Kingsford's statistics on railway accidents that showed that the incidence of accidents decreased from 1 worker in 250 in 1847, to 1 in 1,125 in 1870, but registered a sudden spike again to 1 in 167 a mere six years later. The increase in accidents recorded in 1876 may have something to do with the fact that the Amalgamated Society of Railway Servants was founded in 1872; unions had more motivation for collecting accident statistics than did railroad companies.[12]

Nor was railroad danger limited to Britain, with its dense geographic concentration of railway lines. While comprehensive accident information for railroads in the United States is unavailable for the period before 1889, when the Interstate Commerce Commission began to compile statistics, Walter Licht's research has shown that safety was poor in the early years. A profusion of single track necessitated that trains use sidings, but primitive signaling mechanisms made this system hazardous. Boilers exploded, steam engines emitted flying sparks and smoke, and rain and ice made track and train cars slippery.[13] As in Britain, coupling and braking were the most hazardous activities to workers' health. In his study of the railroad safety movement in the United States, C. Clark found that 52 percent of injuries to workers stemmed from braking and coupling accidents. State commissions empowered to study the figures expressed anxiety about the regularity of coupling-related injuries. Ironically, state railway safety commissions blamed the carelessness of the railroad workers in the same breath as they discussed the need for automatic coupling mechanisms.[14]

Coal Mining

While accidents to railway employees were common, railway workers got less sympathy from the general public than did coal miners, and safety legislation was slow in coming for this group. The widespread tendency to blame railway workmen for train wrecks may go some way to explain the lack of outcry for better compensation programs. After all, the most spectacular accidents— derailments, head-on collisions, rear-endings, bridge disasters, telescoping of cars, fires, broken axles, runaway trains, crossing accidents, and boiler explosions—killed passengers as well as workmen. The most costly train wrecks received much publicity, with gory scenes reproduced in illustrated newspapers, and even pictureless accounts being rife with the gory detail endemic to the Victorian press. With innocent lives at stake, those of workmen who could perhaps have prevented the accidents in question were of little account.[15]

Coal mining was a very different story. At least on the local level, coal mine explosions received the greatest amount of attention of all the mid-nineteenth-century work-related accidents. They were unexpected, they were generally impressive in their destructive power, and they acted as the great levelers within the mine, taking one miner and sparing another with no regard for age or level of experience. They killed mostly by stealth—the largest number of casualties in mine explosions were not the men directly injured by flying debris, but those who had quietly suffocated from "choke damp," the unbreatheable gas produced by the incineration of flammable methane. In the counties of Tyne and Wear alone, between 1710 and 1849, at least 120 explosions killed a total of 1,813 miners. As John Phillips, who compiled this data, pointed out, neither the development of the Davy lamp nor advances in ventilation appeared to stem this continuous tide of fatalities.[16] Another student of mine explosions collected information on 90 major colliery explosions throughout Great Britain between 1846 and 1852, which killed a total of 1,084 people, an average of 12 per accident.[17]

While mine explosions caused great harm to numerous families, they did not represent the "normal" work-related accident for the miner. James Mather found that 2,143 miners were killed in Britain in a two-year period from 1850 to 1852. Of these, only 645 had died in explosions compared with 744 in roof falls, 457 in shaft accidents, and 297 from other causes.[18] Analysis of figures presented in one of many Select Committee reports in the mid-nineteenth century bears out the assumption that the coal itself posed the greatest danger to a British collier working underground—but by falling rather than exploding. Of 234 injuries incurred at the Haswell and East Holywell collieries over the period 1849–51, no fewer than 177 were directly related to falls of coal or stone or to contact injuries with the coal. Underground conveyances injured the next greatest number of miners. The dangerous moving parts underground included the trams, the tubs full of coal, the rolleys (trucks without sides which were used to carry corves along underground horse roads or upon rails to the shaft), and the horses, all of which taken together accounted for only 36 injuries. None of the listed injuries was caused by the more high-profile fires, inundations, or explosions. A similar situation obtained at the Ince Hall Coal and Cannel Works in Wigan. Explosions accounted for only 4 of 44 accidents which had occurred over the period 1850–52; roof falls and crushing by tubs accounted for all but 6 of the remaining 40 accidents.[19]

Nor did these dangers disappear with the advent of mine inspections in 1850. Between September 1862 and July 1863, editor John Towers recorded

277 separate incidents of death or serious injury in the coal mines. Of these, two workers were thrown from wagons or ponies, one was blown down the pit, two died in boiler explosions, five fell from the cage, two were crushed by the cage, one caught glanders from his pit pony, one was dragged to death by a coal train, and three drowned. A more significant 7 percent (n = 20) were crushed under wagons or tubs. Forty-six percent (n = 127) died in mine explosions, a figure that was enhanced by the great loss of life in the Edmund's Main explosion of December 1862. Fourteen percent (n = 40) died from falls down the shaft, while 18 percent (n = 51) were crushed by falling roofs. Five men fell prey to other types of falls. One man broke his arm when the "gin went amain," one was killed by a fall of timber. Six were poisoned by gas (the number was probably actually higher, since some of the Edmund's Main rescuers were no doubt killed by choke damp), and three men were "somewhat injured" when they were struck by a drum. Finally, four were injured by unknown causes.[20] The picture that emerges is one of a diversity of underground dangers, many of which were hidden from the nonmining public.

Nonfatal injuries were much more common than either spectacular disasters or individual fatal injuries (perhaps by a factor of one hundred), but lack of press attention to this issue meant that they almost escaped public notice.[21] Bodily extremities faced the highest risk. Analysis of accident reports from the Haswell and East Holywell mines reveals that legs were more likely to be injured than arms. Broken legs were particularly serious; miners who broke legs took an average of 139.5 days to recover. While the actual incidence of injuries per miner could not be computed without information about the number of men working underground at the mines in question, 17 percent of the 182 miners listed were injured more than once during the two-year period examined.[22]

Workplace injuries had serious financial as well as physical consequences for miners. Durham and Northumberland District Factory Commissioner J. R. Leifchild examined the list of men who were receiving compensation for injuries and estimated that at the East Holywell colliery, the average male worker lost one day's work out of every fifty-two to workplace accidents, while for boys the average lost was one out of every seventy-seven. At Earsdon colliery, men lost one day of work out of every forty-seven to accidents, while boys lost one day out of every fifty-seven. The surgeon at Hetton colliery, also on the Tyne and Wear, compiled records that reveal that 6.5 percent of workers would suffer an accident in any given six-month period.[23]

The rule that prevailed in Britain also seems to have held true in the United States—the accidents that were the most spectacular and costly to human life garnered the most attention, distracting observers from the multiple small safety problems most likely to injure individuals. This was true even though mine explosions in the United States were quite rare.[24] Most famous was the Avondale, Pennsylvania, disaster, which occurred on Monday, September 6, 1869. Two months after the miners conducted a failed strike, fire broke out underground. Although built in 1867, five years after a widely publicized English coal mine disaster directly related to the mine's single shaft, the Avondale mine had one shaft, so that when the subterranean fire began and debris fell into the shaft, the miners were cut off. Sightseers who flocked to the site found a very picture of hell: flames rising one hundred feet into the air and carried by the wind to a 45-degree angle. Multiple volunteer rescue parties were sent down but met with suffocating gases and were unable to retrieve the bodies of the miners until three days had passed.[25] The Avondale disaster spawned a popular ballad that was printed on broadsides and sung in coalfields as far away as Canada. It did not, however, spawn reform at the federal level.

While headline-grabbing mine explosions were rare in the United States, deaths and injuries were not rare. Anthony Wallace attempted to estimate the number of mine accidents that occurred in one mine community, the Pennsylvania community of St. Clair, and came up with a fatality rate between 2 and 9 percent and an injury rate between 9 and 41 percent.[26] As in Britain, the majority of deaths and injuries were individual and prosaic. In the Pottsville, Pennsylvania, area alone, the *Miners' Journal* reported about twenty deaths a year in the early 1850s. Of the twenty fatalities for 1853, eleven were due to falls of coal, two men fell down shafts, three were killed in premature blasts, two asphyxiated by fire damp, one was crushed by machinery, and one fell into the coal breaker.[27]

Whether they were claimed by spectacular disasters like Avondale or the more daily roof falls and underground traffic accidents that dotted the pages of the nineteenth-century press, it was disproportionately young workers who were affected.[28] Because the mining industry employed a large number of young boys as trappers (opening and closing ventilation doors) and wagon drivers, young workers were particularly exposed to danger, and their relative experience seems to have increased the risk. Of ninety-four mining deaths reported in Northumberland and Durham, England, in 1840, fifty claimed the lives of workers or children of workers under twenty-five; only two of these were described in the returns as deaths by natural causes.[29] Similarly, although boys aged between ten and fifteen constituted only one-ninth of the South Wales workforce in the early 1850s, they suffered more than one-fifth of all fatalities.[30]

What was responsible for the steady drumbeat of deaths and injuries in nineteenth-century mines? There were many structural factors involved. When employers required that miners set their own timber to prevent falls of roof, they pitted men's concern for their own safety after men's concern for their wages, paid as they were by the full tub of coal. Workers who were forced to consider every moment underground precious might cross pit bottoms rather than using dedicated walkways.[31] Miners working in single-shift mines might labor as long as twelve hours a day, incurring casualties at many times the rate of miners in double-shift collieries.[32] Finally, it should be noted that "accidents" were not the only cause of death in mines. By the mid-nineteenth century, doctors were just starting to recognize the occupational diseases like silicosis, black lung, and eye problems that miners faced.[33]

Textile Mills and Other Trades

Railroads and mines were not the only dangerous workplaces that attracted public attention in the nineteenth century. Much has been written on the subject of textile mills as the preeminent example of proletarianization in both nineteenth-century Britain and the United States. Accidents in textile factories were fairly common, although not as much a feature of the work as they were in coal mining or railroad work. Nonetheless, because they were caused by new machinery, and because they often afflicted women and children, cotton mill accidents attracted disproportionate attention from the public, as Chapter 3 shows in detail. Cotton production involved machinery that was particularly dangerous when unguarded. The picker, which extracted impurities from the raw cotton, was one such culprit; the carding machine, with its rollers full of sharp metal spikes moving in against each other, was another.[34] Pinched fingers, resulting in the amputation of one or several joints, were common.

Whether the motive power in a textile mill was steam or water, the power was transmitted to the machinery through spinning shafts and unguarded belts. Some of the most devastating injuries to textile workers occurred when long hair or a bit of clothing caught between a belt and a shaft, catching the worker in the machinery. Sharp-pointed shuttles could fly from a loom, catching a worker in the face.[35] The young "scavengers," children who cleaned the floor under spinning mules, faced a special danger. Because the mules alternately opened and shut like giant metal jaws, a boy who became trapped between them might, like Patrick Noon of Staleybridge, get caught in between them. Noon's head was trapped in a space only four inches wide, and as a result the skin was flayed from his head, revealing the bone.[36] Many cotton factory workers fell prey to occupational illnesses. The "kissing shuttle," which was threaded by a weaver who placed his lips to the threading hole and sucked in, became a vector for all kinds of respiratory diseases. Cotton workers also suffered bronchitis, indigestion, varicose veins, and deafness—brought on by their cotton-fluff-filled environments, long periods of standing, and the noisy clacking together of carriages and slapping of shuttles.

While the rate of injury in textile production was nothing like that in coal mining, accidents were fairly frequent, especially in the years before safety devices covered all dangerous parts of mill gearing. Many witnesses before the 1833 Royal Commission that considered work by children in factories described accidents that they considered trifling: loss of a finger here, a flesh wound there, a toll punctuated by the occasional death or large-scale industrial amputation that stuck in the mind.[37] Factory children also tended to have misshapen knees from habitually stopping machinery with their knees rather than their hands, and were noticeably shorter than other children, although it is possible that malnutrition as much as the rigors of the job was to blame.[38] The evidence is more than just impressionistic: in one six-month period in 1849, English and Scottish factory commissioners reported 1,114 accidents caused by machinery and 907 other accidents, resulting in twenty-two deaths and 109 amputations.[39] A parliamentary return in 1870 noted that in the cotton industry the rate was 1 accident to 176 employed; in the woollen, 1 in 230; in the worsted, 1 in 433; in the flax, 1 in 190; and in the silk industry, 1 in 1,074; thus, certain sectors of the textile industry had a similar accident rate to that experienced on the railroad, although in general textile mill injuries were less serious.[40] Using modern statistical techniques, P. W. J. Bartrip and P. T. Fenn determined that the rate of accidents varied with the business cycle; when output per worker was high, so was the accident rate.[41]

Although mining, the railroads, and the textile mills were common sites of accidents in the nineteenth century, almost no trade was completely immune to workplace accidents. Power was particularly responsible for accidents, not only in textiles, but also, not surprisingly, in sawmills, paper mills, and grist mills, in which articles of clothing might be drawn into the bands which drove the machinery, or parts of the body drawn into precarious positions.[42] Leonard Horner, a British Factory Inspector who would become a particular tribune of working people, in 1859 documented 1,097 accidents to working people caused by machinery, compared with forty-one injuries by causes other than machinery. Sixteen workers had been killed, many of them children or young people and often because they or their clothing had been drawn into the machinery and twirled around shafts until they were beaten to death.[43] Steam boilers were also particular sources of danger; in just one five-year period in the 1860s, 875 people were killed by exploding boilers.[44]

Workplace accidents continued to occur in traditional trades on both sides of the Atlantic. During the period of construction on canals, blasting mishaps and construction cave-ins claimed many lives.[45] In his analysis of the workplace accidents that occurred in New York City in 1870, Randolph Bergstrom showed that only fourteen out of ninety-two accidents had been caused by machinery. The majority of the remainder were caused by falls or crushing, in such traditional trades as construction, brewing, butchering, farming, and cooperage.[46] The shipping trade was a perennial supplier of accidental drownings arising in the course of employment.[47] A brewer might fall into a mash tub full of hot liquor, scalding the skin from his bones.[48] A carpenter might have his eye put out by a flying woodchip.[49] A shipwright might be crushed by a falling beam.[50] Sawmill workers were killed by falling logs or fell into the machinery and were sawn in two.[51] Construction workers rather often plunged to the ground, or into rivers, when their scaffolding was faulty or the dam upon which they were working broke. If they were especially unlucky, the wood and tools with which they had been working fell on top of them.[52] In one such case noted by the *Times,* construction workers who were cheering because they had finished building a chimney managed to knock the work down through their celebration and were desperately wounded.[53] Injuries from falling objects occurred even in emerging industries; one chemical worker wheeling a barrow full of caustic substance along a narrow gangway was killed when he fell fifteen feet to the ground, only to have the barrow fall on top of him. He died of burns rather than from the fall.[54] Even farm workers might cut themselves severely on sharp implements, be drawn into threshing machines by their clothes, or be thrown from and then run over by reaping machines.[55] Fire was a constant enemy of nineteenth-century clothing, and women working in the home were never safe from conflagration at the hearthside, but they were not alone. A twenty-year-old ballerina burned to death in 1862 when her skirt caught fire from a gas jet while she performed in a pantomime.[56]

Workers in other industries were killed slowly, by occupational illnesses that stemmed from the very materials they worked with. Cutlery makers and others who ground metal were noted to suffer from a lung disease that caused them to cough up black masses the size of a pea; such workers took walks in the country specifically for the purpose of coughing up this material.[57] Potters were also reported to suffer from a bronchitislike illness that turned the insides of their lungs black; the inhalation of fine clay dust was thought to be the culprit.[58]

The editor of the *British Miner and Workman's Advocate* in 1862 and 1863 printed news of every work-related accident that came to his attention. Between September 1862 and July 1863 alone, he reported twelve serious or fatal accidents in construction (seven of which had occurred at the site of a mill collapse in Accrington), three in chainmaking, and two in the chemical industry. Nine farm laborers, all under the age of twenty-three, were killed when the boiler of an engine used to thresh corn exploded in Alnwick.[59] Foundry work claimed eleven lives and seriously injured fourteen workers, with a boiler explosion at Holytown being responsible for most of the casualties.[60] The gunpowder industry claimed seven lives, and quarrying and sawmilling each claimed one. Thirteen men were killed or injured on the railroad, and two succumbed to the hazards of soapmaking when their sugar pans exploded.[61]

Admittedly, this evidence of the prevalence and importance of accidents in the nineteenth-century workplace is anecdotal rather than statistical. But a brief foray into the workplace testifies not only to the absence of the safeguards that are present in the modern workplace, but also to the absence of the ideology that safety could or should be engineered into the workplace. In contrast with the workplaces of the twentieth century, which were designed to eliminate risk and avoid injury, the nineteenth-century workplace by its nature featured elements of risk and placed the burden of vigilance on the individual worker. In many cases, the structure of production and the payment of piece rates encouraged workers to choose between their own safety and the ability to earn a sufficient wage.

Railroading and mining were the public face of the age of steam, but it was not necessary for an industry to be mechanized or its labor divided or rationalized in any way for accidents to be distressingly common. For all but the most sedentary and skilled professions, each task had its own danger or drawback, and the lack of safety apparatus, inspections, and safety rules was matched by an absence of government infrastructure to deal with the impact of workplace accidents. Despite all this, nineteenth-century workers living in the age before the Employers' Liability Act were not at all destitute of options. As the next chapter will show, while the tort system blocked most workers from prevailing against their employers in court, injured workers and their relatives living in this age of voluntarism were able to deploy a series of inter-locking options. Drawing on their own resources, those of their friends and relatives, an often compassionate public, and employers exercising paternal-ism and discretion, workers injured in the workplace encouraged other groups to share the responsibility for the bodily toll of production.

2 | The Options for Injured Workers

IN BRITAIN, THERE IS A PREDICTABLE METHOD for settling compensation claims, and employers are required to indemnify against claims with Employers' Liability Insurance policies of not less than five million pounds.[1] Employers, employees, and the general public may express dissatisfaction with the current system and call for reform, but at least it can be said that most workers injured on the job today have a predictable path to follow to compensation. Similarly, in the United States today, participation in the workers' compensation insurance program is compulsory in all states except Texas and Wyoming, although some states allow certain employers to waive participation in the case of small businesses or agricultural or domestic employment. Employers carry workers' compensation insurance, which is sometimes underwritten by a state insurance fund, and sometimes by a private carrier. Workers who are injured and file a claim receive full medical care in forty-five states, and may receive a weekly payment while injured and off work. In return for this predictable scenario, workers have lost their right to sue their employers in the tort system.[2]

The opposite was true before 1880. Due to the absence of workmen's compensation or employers' liability laws in the Anglo-American workplace before 1880, a worker injured on the job and wishing to collect a judgment from his employer had to hire a lawyer and sue in the civil courts. Beginning in the 1840s, such tort claims were almost completely blocked by a trio of common-law defenses: contributory negligence, assumption of risk, and the fellow-servant rule. Over time, Britain and the United States grew apart from each other, with British courts hewing more strictly to common-law constructions, while American courts, particularly those in southern and western states, turned to Christianity to craft what Peter Karsten has called a "jurisprudence of the heart."[3] But in neither system were the results predictable.

As a result of the difficulty of receiving and then maintaining a compensation award through the appeal process, injured workers or the families of workers who had been killed on the job were forced to cobble together a compensation package from several different sources. As this chapter will show, as long as paternalism and deference existed in the workplace, charitable employers could be appealed to for medical assistance or disability pay. An interested and compassionate public often subscribed donations for victims of the more spectacular workplace disasters. And finally, mutual aid, individual thrift, and the exertions of family members filled in the gaps. Although the violence that constituted workplace accidents centered on the job site, its repercussions were felt and absorbed by employers, consumers, and working families alike.

The tort regime in which these alternatives developed was initiated between 1837 and 1842 largely as a result of two legal cases, *Priestley v. Fowler* and *Farwell v. Boston and Worcester Railroad*. Both of these cases are worth looking at in detail for the way in which, together, they grew from an ideology of worker free agency and personal responsibility that, fully developed, would prevent workers from achieving compensation reform. The first case concerned a young butcher's assistant, Charles Priestley, who was injured in May 1835 when an overloaded cart broke down, spilling heavy cuts of meat on top of him and breaking his thigh.[4] Priestley received medical care, and his father Brown Priestley then sued Thomas Fowler, the butcher, at the next assizes, in 1836. During that hearing, much was made of the fact that by the rules of common humanity an injured workman should not have to sue his employer to get compensated for employment-related medical bills at all. Priestley was awarded £100—twice the cost of his bills—by a sympathetic jury. The case was reheard in 1837 on a technicality, at which time the Chief Baron, Lord Abinger, reversed the original decision.

It is ironic that *Priestley v. Fowler* would be the test case later cited as having set out a "fellow servant rule," since none of the testimony in the case had invoked any fellow servants at all, dealing strictly with the issue of whether Fowler owed any particular duty of care to his employee. Abinger, without precedent to rely on, had to decide the case as a matter of public policy, and thus infused his decision with his political beliefs. His short opinion in the

case introduced the idea of fellow servants by citing several examples of terrible miscarriages of justice that would be inflicted on employers should one
worker injure another and the master be held responsible for the medical bills
of the injured party.[5] In all of the cases cited by Abinger, one domestic employee was guilty of knowingly endangering another—a state of affairs far
removed from what happened to young Priestley. Abinger painted a picture
of below-stairs help completely careless of each other's welfare, but also far removed from the supervision of the homeowner. Abinger's own political opinions have been ignored or downplayed by legal scholars writing on this issue,
but he would soon become notorious for the fact that he felt workers should be
politically deferential to their social superiors. He presided over the trials of
many Chartists on charges of sedition, and his comments about the Chartists
were so extreme that Thomas Slingsby Duncombe, the radical Member of Parliament (MP) for Finsbury, sought to have him censured by Parliament.[6]

The *Priestley* case was not particularly well reasoned and should not have
been seen as establishing any kind of precedent. It would become important,
however, because it was the cornerstone of the judge's decision in an American
case, *Farwell vs. the Boston and Worcester Railroad.* Although this was a Massachusetts decision, Justice Charles Shaw, who wrote the opinion in the case,
was an extremely prolific and prestigious judge, and thus most English judges
picked up on Shaw's opinion thereafter.[7] Nicholas Farwell, a railroad engineer,
had his right hand crushed by the wheels of a derailed train car on October 30,
1837, when a switchman put an iron rail across the tracks.[8] In court, Farwell's
lawyer, G. G. Loring, argued that if the case had been a common carrier case,
and Farwell a passenger rather than an employee, the railroad would be liable.
He also argued that Farwell was not a switcher, and so was not a fellow servant
with Whitcomb, the switcher at fault. As Loring explained, Farwell could not
have prevented the accident by any means under his power. Loring did not try
to deny that Farwell and the man who caused his injury worked for the same
railroad, but rather emphasized that the two men were not engaged in the
same branch of industry. He maintained that only where two workers had sufficient knowledge of each others' activities to be able to prevent such accidents
was the fellow-servant rule just.

The railroad's attorneys responded that a decision in favor of the plaintiff in the case would make the railroads unsafe for passengers by depriving
railroad workers of their main impetus to take sufficient care in their dangerous jobs. They contended that workers assumed the ordinary risks of the job.

Furthermore, the implied contract that a common carrier would use ordinary precautions in order to prevent accidents only held true for passengers. In making their argument, the railroad's attorneys pointed at both *Priestley v. Fowler* and another case, *Murray v. South Carolina Railroad,* and argued that these two cases indicated the direction of the common law—that workers could collect nothing from their employers for injuries suffered on the job. Finally, they denied that Whitcomb and Farwell can be considered to have been in separate employments since "they both were acting to the same end, although they had different parts to perform."

Justice Shaw ruled against Farwell on a number of grounds. First of all, Shaw reasoned, in no previous case had an employer been held responsible for an injury to a worker; he clearly agreed with the defendant's attorneys that the direction of the common law was becoming clear. Second, Shaw endorsed the assumption of risk doctrine suggested by the defendant's attorneys, noting that "all such risks and perils as the employer and the servant respectively intend to assume and bear may be regulated by the express or implied contract between them, and which, in contemplation of law, must be presumed to be thus regulated."[9]

Shaw went on to expand the fellow-servant rule to include not only other manual workers but also managers, noting that just because the negligent party is an agent of the master does not prove that the master is responsible for the worker's injury. He agreed with the defendant's attorneys that safety was better secured by giving employees an incentive to be vigilant than by granting them the ability to sue their employers. He did not, however, address the fact that Farwell and his switcher could not work together to promote safety since neither knew what the other was doing.[10] In fact, Shaw denied that the two workers were in different departments since they worked for the same end, but noted that even if they did work in different departments, employers had no responsibility for workplace injuries unless there were some express or implied contract to indicate it.

Shaw's decision did leave the door slightly ajar for future lawsuits by limiting the decision to the particular case. He allowed that there might be grounds for a case if an employer had provided faulty or insufficient working materials. "In the present case, the claim of the plaintiff is not put in the ground that the defendants did not furnish a sufficient engine, a proper rail road track, a well-constructed switch, and a person of suitable skill and experience to attend it."[11] Thus, the Farwell decision established two caveats to the general principle of nonliability of the master for acts of his servant against another servant. First, liability arose if the master employed the injuring servant knowing him to be incapable. Second, the master was not protected if he exposed his servant to unreasonable risks by providing him with faulty materials and equipment.[12]

There is much to criticize in Shaw's reading of the facts. Shaw claimed on one hand that the employee was automatically part of an implied contract to accept the ordinary risks of the job, but he also claimed that there was no implied contract between employer and employee that would protect the employee against workplace injuries. If an implied contract is left to the understanding of both parties, who is to say that a particular implied contract does or does not exist? Shaw also accepted the argument that the purpose of the fellow servant rule was to ensure employees were vigilant and guarded against injuries, yet expected this premise to function even when workers had no direct oversight over each other's activities.[13] As Leonard Levy has pointed out, the fellow-servant rule as created by Shaw detracted from safety by shifting the burden of safety from companies (some of them, like railroads, exceedingly complex in their organization) to workers, who were often ill-placed to see or correct safety violations.[14]

The picture painted by *Priestley* and *Farwell* was one of workers as free agents, fully informed about the dangers of their workplaces and able to use their own powers of reason to avoid danger, either by correcting workplace conditions or by walking away from the job. The discrepancy between the ideal world described in the legal opinions and actual practice made the new fellow-servant rule something of a hard sell, however. Because it was such an ambiguous doctrine, leaving workers at a disadvantage relative to other groups (like bystanders and passengers), the fellow-servant rule was not accepted instantly in all jurisdictions in either Britain or the United States. At first, Scottish jurists continued to provide a legal remedy for injured workers, until their line of precedent was swept away in *Bartonshill v. Reid*.[15] Later, there were attempts made to restrict the doctrine to those clearly in common employment or to those working with a common object in view. When that gambit failed, attempts were made to hold owners responsible for the actions of their "vice-principals," the managers to whom responsibility was usually delegated in large industrial concerns.

Some American judges rejected the fellow-servant rule on the grounds that it left workers without a remedy. This is clear in the case of *Little Miami v. Stevens*. In August 1846, engineer John Stevens was driving his train, and was accustomed to pass another train going in the opposite direction. On the day of the accident, the oncoming train's schedule had been changed, but Stevens was not informed, and the two trains crashed into each other. As a result, Stevens was "greatly scalded, bruised, lacerated, hurt and wounded, and in consequence thereof became and was sick, sore, lame and disordered, and so remained." Stevens sued his employers in a jury trial, the jury awarded him $3,700, and the railroad directors appealed the decision to the state Supreme Court.[16]

In court, the attorneys for the railroad cited a whole series of fellow-servant cases, calling it "well settled that the master is not liable for injuries sustained by one workman or servant by the careless or negligent or unskillful act of another workman or servant." But more than this, they argued, if the engineer could be shown to have deviated from his duty, he was the only liable one, no matter what his employer did to precipitate his injury. Stevens's lawyers disagreed, claiming that employer misconduct was the very exception to the fellow-servant rule that had been outlined in *Priestley* and *Farwell*. They argued that the Little Miami railroad had erred specifically in failing to give Stevens a new time card reflecting the changes in the oncoming train's schedule. Furthermore, the Little Miami railroad was unable to prove that they had selected a prudent, experienced, and careful servant as conductor (this was important since a conductor directed an engineer when to start and stop a train). Although Stevens perhaps contributed to his injuries through his own negligence in driving fast around the curves on the day of his accident, he should still collect damages unless he could have avoided the consequences of the defendant's negligence by using ordinary care. His attorneys also pointed out that unless John Stevens could collect from his employer, he was without a legal remedy.

It was this last element of the multifaceted legal argument that moved Justice Caldwell, who ruled on the case. Caldwell noted that it was a rule of universal application in torts that the party that could have done something to prevent an accident, and yet failed to do so, should be held liable. He denied that the implied contract of employment included anything more than ordinary risks: The employer "had paid Stevens no money for the right to break his legs, or as in this case, to empty on him the contents of a boiler of scalding water." Caldwell doubted that workers would be careless of their lives and persons or property, merely because they might have a right of action to recover for the damage they might prove they had sustained. The liability of

The Options for Injured Workers   25

the employers would be the best possible check on accidents. "It is a matter of universal observation, that in any extensive business, where many persons are employed, the care and prudence of the employer is the surest guaranty against mismanagement of any kind. The employer would, we think, be much more likely to be careless of the persons of those in his employ, since his own safety is not endangered by any accident, when he would understand that he was not pecuniarily liable for the careless conduct of his agents." Caldwell called the fellow-servant cases contrary to the general principles of law and justice, and refused to follow them as precedents.

If Justice Caldwell's reasoning attempted to seek equity behind the fellow-servant rule, Justice Spalding's reasoning, in his dissent, more closely followed the developing common law. Witnesses had testified that the conductor on Stevens's train, one George Smith, had been given a card to give to Stevens but had failed to do so. The conductor's failure to complete his task had led to the accident, thus putting the case squarely within the field of fellow-servant cases, which Spalding then proceeded to defend. He explained that there was indeed a double standard when it came to injuries to workers and members of the public, but that this double standard was logical. There was no implied contract between employers and injured innocent bystanders, so a remedy in law was necessary. In the employment relation, in contrast, there was an implied contract that the servant accepted the risks involved with a particular job. Like Justice Shaw, Spalding thought that workmen ought to be given an incentive to be careful and that the prospect of collecting damages for injury would be a financial disincentive to take care. "If we are to teach each agent, that for the negligence of the others, resulting in injury to himself he can grasp the treasures of the company, and procure a competency for life, he ceases his vigilance over those with whom he co-operates—a bribe is held out to him to incur personal risks." Caldwell was able to find in favor of the defendant, John Stevens, because he was able to imagine himself in Stevens's situation. In contrast, Justice Spalding saw Stevens and other workers as willing to endure pain and injury for the tenuous prospect of material gains from an employer.

The empathy that some American jurists seemed to feel for English workers was one major factor distinguishing the American tort regime from its English counterpart.[17] As Peter Karsten has shown, American judges deployed a discourse of Christian humanitarianism to support legal fictions (like the attractive nuisance doctrine) that promoted greater equity under the law.[18] Humanitarianism enabled American courts to resist the application of the fellow-servant rule in some serious accident cases in which only the employer was capable of providing adequate compensation. Lawyers attempted to distinguish their cases rather than overturn the rule.[19] Judges, particularly in the West, where the social hierarchy was malleable, saw the inequities produced by the fellow-servant doctrine and attempted to fashion loopholes by making railroads liable for damages suffered by employees or calling fellow servants "supervisors" in order to exempt injured employees from the strictures of the fellow-servant rule.[20]

While some American courts worked to short-circuit the fellow-servant rule, over the course of the nineteenth century British courts extended the rule to the largest possible number of situations. For example, an employee who worked with incompetent fellow servants, and too few of those to do his work safely, was nonsuited on the grounds that his continuing to work there meant that he had assumed a new level of risk.[21] The result of this erosion was that workers could only collect compensation in court under two circumstances: if they had been injured by a clearly malicious fellow worker or by the employer himself.[22] Not until the 1870s did English judges begin to limit the scope of the fellow-servant doctrine.[23]

English jurists codified their version of the fellow-servant rule using an authoritative legal language that masked the political nature of these decisions. In *Bartonshill v. Reid,* the case that applied the English fellow-servant rule to Scotland, the Lord Chancellor stated that it was impossible for England and Scotland to have different laws on this key issue, since the principles of common law were not made but rather discovered. The English decisions were not capricious; they were based on a deeply rooted and immutable structure. "The decisions upon the subject in both countries are of recent date, but the law cannot be considered to be so. The principles upon which these decisions depend must have been lying deep in each system, ready to be applied when the occasion called them forth."[24]

The development of the fellow-servant rule has received a great deal of attention from modern historians. Those writing in the Marxist tradition have tended to characterize the rule as a particular injustice, which departed from previous paternalistic practice.[25] Some evidence does bear this out; in his book tracing the evolution of the nineteenth-century idea of "free labor," Robert Steinfeld has argued that before the nineteenth century employers had an acknowledged responsibility to care for their sick or injured servants. This care of the body correlated with the amount of physical discipline that masters could exercise over their workers' bodies. While in the eighteenth century masters had to provide for their servants who lived within the household, even in cases of sickness or injury, in turn, the servant had to submit to correction and consider himself dependent, much like the wife and children in the household. As workers began to be recognized as having recognizance over their own bodies, they were increasingly construed as being responsible for themselves in times of illness or accident. According to Steinfeld, the English and the American systems of labor compulsion were different—in the United States, due to the growth of slavery, it was asserted sooner that white adults were neither under the thrall of a master, nor able to expect maintenance from a master.[26] Christopher Tomlins has also shown that before the turn of the nineteenth century, employers of servants who were injured or became ill shifted the responsibility for their cure to the parish. Free laborers, unlike slaves, were explicitly to provide for their own care.[27]

A. W. B. Simpson argues that, while there was no evidence that, before *Priestley,* employers were legally responsible to their servants in tort for workplace injuries, there was an earlier and well-documented tradition for masters to provide for their ill servants who were engaged for a year at a time. Where this did not apply, workers of all kinds had to fall back on the parish as members of the casual poor. Until the passage of the 1834 Poor Law Amendment Act, parishes of all kinds retained doctors, and even those working people who were otherwise squeamish about accepting charity would see these doctors if they were in some kind of an accident. The mode of paying for this medical care would be that, if it were expensive enough, the parish that paid would seek repayment from the parish where the person had a settlement, or otherwise, from the employer.[28]

The viewpoint that the fellow-servant rule did *not* disturb an older, paternalistic legal regime is a minority viewpoint. Legal historian Richard Epstein has argued that the absence of any known legal cases addressing employers' liability indicates that there was no way a worker had ever been able to collect anything from his employer. In other words, the *Priestley* and *Farwell* cases re-stated a longstanding reality rather than marking a reaction to changes in workplace relations. "The utter dearth of cases upon the subject indicates, clearer than any judicial opinion could proclaim, an ironclad rule of breathtaking simplicity: no employee could ever recover from any employer for any workplace accident—period."[29]

It is quite possible to reconcile the absence of cases before *Priestley* with both sets of views because, as this chapter will show, the *Priestley* decision did not cause employers instantly to shift their behavior, from caring for their employees to writing them off as careless fellow servants. Rather, as the level of compulsion and protection that workers experienced in the workplace declined, older understandings about the employer's humanitarian responsibility for injured workers receded. Free laborers were expected to provide for themselves in the case of illness or injury, and to demonstrate the manly virtue of thrift; but they could also become independent actors in the courts. The transition from domestic labor that was cared for within the employer's home, to "free labor" centered around the wage nexus, was accompanied by a number of cultural changes: reevaluations of the roles of family members, and more strident demands for political representation, along with attempts to reconcile all this in the judicial realm.

The fellow-servant rule has received the most attention from historians, and clearly, its implications were dire for injured workers seeking compensation for work-related injuries. But it was not the only fateful change to the compensation regime during the 1840s. The middle of that decade also marked a transformation in the chances for the families of English workers who were killed on the job. In that year, the 1846 Fatal Accidents Act, also known as Lord Campbell's Act, was passed, specifying a tort claim as the only possible legal response to a fatal accident. Although the Act benefited workers by specifying that the cause of legal action did not die with the person who had been killed, it also deprived workers' families of an alternate source of compensation that did not depend on being able to prove the negligence of an employer. Before 1846, coroners' juries could identify the thing that was instrumental in bringing about a person's death—be it a faulty piece of equipment or a balky animal. This thing, or a sum equivalent to the thing, was ceded to the Royal Almoner as a "deodand." Sometimes this fine—which could range from a shilling to several pounds—was given to the relatives of the deceased.[30] Because negligence did not have to be established and was in fact immaterial to the case, it was much easier to secure a deodand for a relative who had been killed on the job than it would later be to prove negligence and collect anything under the tort system.

The decline of the deodand was accompanied by the desire to reallocate responsibility for workplace accidents. If a worker were injured at work but no fellow servant was implicated in the incident, employers might claim that some negligence on the worker's part led to the injury. Contributory negligence did not have to be gross negligence; it might consist of failure to stop, look, and listen before crossing a railroad track. Getting clobbered was prima facie evidence of being negligent. A parent who allowed a minor child to continue working in a situation that the parent knew to be dangerous was negligent; so was a worker who failed to take the safest route possible when accomplishing some workplace task and (for example) fell into an unguarded hole.[31]

Unlike the fellow-servant rule, the doctrine of contributory negligence struck a balance between the legal responsibility of the worker and that of the employer. Workers were required to make a good faith effort to extricate themselves from dangerous employment and were occasionally given the benefit of the doubt when attempting to do this. Thus, British courts held employers responsible when miners refusing to work underground were injured while being raised out of the pit.[32] Nor did the worker's responsibility to take due care absolve the employer of all responsibility; in *Mellors v. Shaw* (1862), the Court of Queen's Bench decided that an employer was liable if he knew that the machinery was unsafe, and notwithstanding, sanctioned its use.[33] The deciding factor in the case of dangerous machinery was an employer's promise to repair it. If the employer promised to repair something and failed to do so, he was negligent; if the employer made no such promise, the employee now had to leave the dangerous employment.[34] Finally, in any industry in which employers were mandated by statute rather than common law to protect employees against dangerous machinery, workers could not be held contributorily negligent for their willingness to enter dangerous areas.[35]

The final legal doctrine in the triumvirate that effectively blocked most tort claims against employers was assumption of risk. Courts assumed that employers paid employees in dangerous jobs a wage premium in order to compensate them for assuming all risks likely to be encountered on the job.[36] The wage premium was linked to the fellow-servant rule; as a British court claimed in 1865, workers were considered to be in common employment so long as "the risk of injury from the negligence of the one is so much a natural and necessary consequence of the employment which the other accepts, that it must be included in the risks which are to be considered in his wages."[37] Modern economists can perform regression analyses and claim that wage premiums for risk existed in the nineteenth century. But it is unclear that many workers—or even employers—understood this was the trade-off they were making (gunpowder manufacturers excepted). The industries that were most dangerous in the nineteenth century were also those largely populated by male workers, because they were thought to require more muscle and especially more skill—and it is possible that the so-called "wage premium" was as much compensation for the perceived skill of adult male workers as for perceived risk.[38]

The assumption of risk doctrine was based on the idea that an employer owed an employee a certain duty of care. Over the course of the nineteenth century, however, the lines of this employer responsibility were ambiguous. In *Farwell,* Justice Shaw had noted that an employer had a responsibility to provide a safe workplace and proper tools for the job, but over the course of the nineteenth century, this dictum was eroded. Except in the most dangerous industries, it was not necessary that employers provide the safest or newest possible equipment—only that they follow common usage for their particular trades.[39] Even in a case in which an employer's works were so unsafe that they contravened some statute, in most American states (Kansas excepted) and in England, if a workman continued to work in the unsafe atmosphere, he was considered to have consented to the arrangement—the new level of risk had been assumed.[40]

The assumption of risk could also extend to fellow workers as well as to the general work environment. While the hiring of competent servants was one of the few positive responsibilities charged to an employer, any worker who noticed that his co-worker was incompetent and failed to inform the employer of this incompetence was presumed to acquiesce in the incompetent's retention.[41] The employer assumed responsibility for the worker's safety only if the worker informed his employer about unsafe conditions, and also the employer promised to repair them and failed to do so within a reasonable amount of time. Logically, it was not in the employer's interest to make any such promise; and since many employees could not afford to leave a workplace simply because it was unsafe, when an accident occurred, it was wholly the worker's problem.[42]

The impact of the common law triumvirate of the fellow-servant rule, assumption of risk, and contributory negligence was to deprive many plaintiffs of any legal remedy in the case of the death or serious injury of a worker—even in cases where common decency dictated that there must be a remedy. But just in case that were not enough, there were also potent structural barriers that prevented workers from pursuing their aims in court. In Britain, legal proceedings were expensive, and poor workers could seek redress as paupers only if they had no more than £5 in assets. Plaintiffs were also responsible for almost £5 in legal costs if they lost. Finally, the possibility of being blacklisted for taking one's employer to court was palpable.[43] In the United States, as Lawrence Friedman has noted, the entire system for approaching industrial accidents gently steered workers away from exercising their very weak legal option. Some of the parts of this system included unscrupulous lawyers who drummed up claims, company agents who chased down and dissuaded injured workers from suing, and railroad hospitals, where workers were treated as long as they promised not to sue. Furthermore, employees who didn't sue had a better expectation of another kind of job for the same company.[44] Upon being injured, workers might be pressured to sign a release designed to preclude further legal action in return for some small sum. Delay in the legal system, and the propensity of fellow workers to testify for the company in fear of losing their jobs, worked against the injured party.[45] Rules barred testimony by key witnesses, and prohibited some of the most relevant oral testimony because it occurred before rather than after an accident.[46] Plaintiffs might be nonsuited on any number of legal technicalities before their cases ever reached a possibly empathetic jury.[47]

The best thing that a worker seeking redress on either side of the Atlantic could hope for was a jury trial, since juries occasionally showed great sympathy for injured workers.[48] Unfortunately, this natural sympathy on the part of jurors could be undercut by judges, who their did their best to counteract this proworker bias by being extremely specific in their jury instructions.[49] James Armsworth fell from a railroad truck and was run over; his widow sued the railroad company. In his charge to the jury in the case of *Armsworth v. Southeastern Railway Company*, Justice Parke emphasized that it would be difficult for that particular jury, without the benefit of any other decisions, to put a monetary value on the life of a man. It would be so much easier just to find the company not guilty of negligence. Lest the facts of the case stir up unwanted sympathy in the jurors, Parke urged them to imagine a slightly different scenario:

> There is always a little temptation to juries to exceed the law and be blinded by matters of feeling, when the defendants in actions like the present are very rich and the plaintiffs are very poor; and I cannot for my own part help saying that in the minds of juries the consideration of such circumstances may lead to an improper mode of administering justice under this statute. I therefore advise you to dismiss from your minds who the parties in this case are, and look at it as if the conductor of the engine which caused the accident had been conducting it on his account for his own profit, and that the deceased instead of meeting with death had only been wounded.

In defiance of Parke's instructions to completely disregard the facts of the case, the jury returned a £100 award.

It is clear that the legal barriers to collecting compensation for work-place accidents were formidable. They were so formidable, in fact, that one must ask why workers' families chose to participate actively in inquests or sought jury trials. Why would they bother? R. W. Kostal suggests that the legal arena could serve as a kind of public theater, in which injured workers' families could at least attempt to tarnish employers' reputations or to seek community recognition and sympathy. Working through inquests and jury trials enabled witnesses publicly to reconstruct the scenes of accidents, and unlike other options, including violence, legal channels had the sanction of higher authorities.[50] For most workers' families this legal theater was hardly worth the effort, and so it was abandoned in favor of the elements of the pre-1880 compensation regime that were more likely to bear fruit: the charity of the public or their employers, the financial power of their fellow workers, or their own exertions.

The Cold Hand of Charity

It is not surprising, in a legal regime which focused attention on workers' contributory negligence and on the actions of fellow servants in the work-place, that employers blamed their employees for workplace accidents.[51] In the words of ninetenth-century industrial hygiene expert J. T. Arlidge, "it requires no very lengthened acquaintance with workmen to discover their reckless-ness in dangerous occupations, their neglect of cleanliness, their refusal to adopt preventive measures against evident evils, and above all, their wide-spread habit of intemperance."[52] Colliery owners and managers often wrote into their trade journals to opine that accidents in mines were the fault of the men. One asked,

> How many [deaths by accident] could be *directly* traced to acts of thoughtless-ness, ignorance, carelessness, or recklessness on the part of the men them-selves who were thus killed—acts which no *ordinary* care on the part of a manager or underviewer could have prevented. I believe such deaths, judging from my own experience, would be found to bear a very large proportion to the whole. I have never known a death from accident amongst miners which has come under my own especial notice which could not be directly traced to one or the other of these causes.[53]

Another correspondent thought that "many miners, for the want of better knowledge of things, cause their own deaths; it would therefore be a great injustice to compel by law mine proprietors to recompense the families of whose who may be killed by such means."[54] Even within the privacy of his own diary, colliery viewer Matthias Dunn commented on the "incautious-ness" of a man who stumbled underground with a naked candle and was badly burnt as a result (the management's choice to use naked candles in a coal mine escaped comment).[55] Employers sometimes went so far as to allege that workers felt that they could afford to take risks, since the property they destroyed on the job was not their own. The main mining newspaper aimed at colliery owners, the *Colliery Guardian,* seemed to express this attitude when its reporter noted in the wake of one accident supposedly caused by a worker's imprudence around gunpowder.

> The unfortunate lad was dreadfully burnt, his flesh hanging in shreds from his body. His companion also was much burnt, but not to the extent of rendering life hopeless. Near, also, to where the explosion took place, a fine horse, which had recently been bought for £30, was dreadfully burnt all over. Since the accident, the horse has been dressed with oil, in the hope of preserving him. As for Dorsett [the burnt man], very grave doubts are entertained of his recovery.[56]

Attributing all accidents to their employees' shortcomings allowed managers conveniently to avoid the question of whether structural changes or better education might make accidents more rare.

Although it may seem contradictory, the widespread attitude that workers were usually contributorily negligent coexisted with willingness on the part of many employers to absorb some of the social cost of workplace accidents. This was particularly true in dangerous industries. Employers at the Du Pont powder company uniformly expressed regret at the loss of life occasioned by explosions, as well as the loss of property.[57] They even recorded their grief, and implicitly accepted blame, when writing to clients to inform them that explosions would delay promised shipments. Given the prevailing view of workers' habits at the time, one might have expected the Du Ponts to lay more blame.[58] Instead, they eulogized the deaths of particularly loyal or skilled workers; one was described as "a most worthy and faithful hand, he had been with us 25 years, had attained the head of the list, being the oldest hand in the mills and was much respected by all persons acquainted with him."[59] The Du Ponts may have been more sympathetic to workers' troubles than were most employers, since they lived on the outskirts of the powder yards and were never free from the sights of wrecked buildings, human carnage, and community-wide grief which these explosions precipitated. Nor was their concern about human loss completely disinterested; if the death toll from a particular explosion were too high, workers might leave, and finding another contingent of men willing to risk their lives might be difficult.[60] Nonetheless, their grief appears to have been sincere.

What explains this conflict between blame and remorse, between dodging responsibility in the courtroom and sometimes accepting it in the counting-house? The early nineteenth century marked an age of competitive capitalism in both Britain and the United States, but it also marked a moment in which evangelical Christianity prompted great consideration for the "deserving poor." The families of injured workers, and more particularly of workers who had been killed, fell into this category, as long as charity was given as a privilege rather than demanded as a right.[61] Later in the century, once the evangelical movement had receded, corporations, which had never operated on this paternalistic model, were much less likely to give compensation.[62]

Payments by employers to employees after workplace accidents were nothing like a certainty. An extensive survey of the textile establishments in the northeast of England in 1833 revealed that employers provided varying degrees of medical care and monetary compensation for their workers injured on the job. Out of 294 mills surveyed, 100, or about one-third, professed to provide full or half wages to employees injured in mill accidents, although the duration of these payments is unknown. An additional 27 reported paying wages in some cases—when employees were perceived as being particularly deserving or when they were children paid by the week rather than adults paid by the piece, for example. In addition, 23 of the employers who did not provide wages for their injured workers did pay for medical care, meaning that about half of injured textile workers in Yorkshire could expect to be provided for in some (albeit insufficient) way for injuries incurred on the job.[63]

Relief was not systematic, even for the youngest workers. Rather, it reflected the degree to which individual business owners felt they could afford to bear some of the economic burden of workplace accidents.[64] Expectations varied even within a single factory. Young Joseph Hebergam broke his arm while working at Frith's mill in Leeds, and his master's doctor set the arm for him. As Hebergam explained,

> the other boy who got his arm broke by the same machine was Haley Stocks; his arm was nearly taken off, but the doctor set it again, and his bill came to £5. Mr. Frith said as it was so much his father must pay for it. His father wouldn't,

and his brother Joseph was turned away . . . I had a part of my wages while I was getting well. His was much longer, and I don't think he will ever be able to work at his own business again.[65]

Masters were likely to pay medical expenses perceived as affordable to employees perceived as grateful. Employees were encouraged to accept what they were given without attempting to set conditions or to take political or group action. Thus, John Horsfall of Leeds reported that he had made it a practice to pay the workmen their regular wages when sick or injured, whether they received money from benefit societies or not, until about a year previous. At that time, "a subsequent general combination among the workmen, enforcing higher wages, having been formed, and having been obliged to submit to vexatious proceedings, independent of wages, on their part, I have since discontinued this practice, except in particular cases."[66]

According to P. W. Kingsford, many British railroad companies shared Horsfall's outlook, contributing to employee benefit societies and infirmaries and compensating individual employees as long as not compelled by law to do so.[67] Rather than pursue cases into court, disabled railroad workers adopted less active work, or were given pensions of one-third of wages, or supplied with free medical care or artificial limbs. Railroads also made a token payment of between £3 and £25 to widows and children of killed workers, the amount depending on the man's grade, number of dependents, and degree of responsibility for his own death as judged by the company. Employers often paid some of a person's funeral expenses and made a policy of hiring widows or orphans.[68] But even within this single industry, compensation was uncertain. One railroad failed to pay the surgical expenses of a longtime worker killed in the line of service, telling the landlord at the inn where he was brought, fatally injured, that he should apply to his widow for reimbursement for having called a surgeon to the scene.[69] In another case, when a man was killed on the job, his widow did not receive his full pay for the day on which his accident occurred since, the railway management argued, "the man only worked a few hours before he was killed, and they should not pay him for the day."[70]

As Walter Licht has documented, American railways could also be generous to their injured employees, given the right conditions. The Boston and Worcester Railroad paid full wages to its workers who were injured in the 1830s and 1840s. Other lines, seeking to discourage malingering, offered partial pay plus medical costs. Companies provided less demanding tasks for disabled workers, occasionally paid medical and burial fees to widows and families, hired the children of men killed in accidents, and may even have bought prosthetics in bulk for their employees missing arms or legs.[71] Even Nicholas Farwell, plaintiff in the key 1842 court case just described, received $720 in expenses, wages, and medical care paid from his employer.[72] The increasing complexity of the railroads included their own medical organizations, with doctors on staff to aid injured employees and passengers.[73]

Ultimately the fate of each worker depended on the capriciousness of his employers. As an undated rulebook of the Louisville, New Orleans and Texas Railroad Company stated: "The regular compensation of employees covers all risks or liability to accident. When disabled, from sickness or other cause, the right to claim compensation will not be recognized. Allowances in such cases will be a gratuity justified by the circumstances of the case and previous good conduct."[74] Compensation might depend on such factors as the length of service, previous conduct, and grade of the laborer involved.[75] The power, and the ability to determine an employee's fate, rested in the hands of the employers, since the same railroad doctors who treated injured workers could also short-circuit tort claims through their expert testimony.[76]

More than most other fields of employment, English collieries in the nineteenth century maintained a coercive work environment. Colliery masters considered occasional workplace accidents an inextricable part of mining and opposed legislative interference or even inspection of their premises.[77] The *Colliery Guardian*, an industry newspaper, poked fun at philanthropic efforts to aid injured miners, noting that "the number of fatal casualties is deplorable but they are not likely to be diminished by the interference of Cockney philanthropists."[78] But even in this hardscrabble field of employment, employers recognized a duty to shoulder some of the social costs of workplace accidents. In the coalfields of Durham and Northumberland, miners who were injured on the job were sent to the company surgeon, who certified that they were entitled to "smart money."[79] This allowance from their employers ranged from 2s. per day given to deputies down to 4d. a day to underground cart drivers. Smart money might be received for as little time as a week for a bruised back or foot to as long as two months for a broken leg or the loss of an eye.[80] In the coalfields of South Staffordshire, a poor law union auditor reported in 1843, there was an almost universal custom among the mine owners—enforced by magistrates—of allowing 6s. a week to those wounded in workplace accidents, and 1s. 6d. a week to the widow of any man killed, together with 1s. a week for each child under age ten.[81]

Even where "smart money" was not involved, coalpit proprietors often stepped in to assist the widows and orphans of men killed in the pits. When the Carville mine near Wallsend exploded in 1821, its owners buried the dead bodies in the local churchyard, gave each affected family a little over £1 for present expenses, and promised them food and fuel for as long as needed.[82] After the Ferndale Colliery in Merthyr Tydvil exploded in 1867, its proprietors promised £1000 to an ad-hoc relief fund being set up and also offered to provide the necessities of life for the women and children until the relief fund was available.[83] The records of the Govan colliery show that, between January 1850 and December 1851, the company made disbursements to injured workers ranging from £2 17s. to £7 2s.[84] The colliery also had a funeral fund which, upon the death of a worker, paid a sum ranging from £2 to £6 to each widow and £1 to every minor child. This could work out to the payment of a substantial sum, since Govan miners who died often left multiple children and pregnant wives.[85]

Colliery masters created a flexible menu of benefits that might be available to individual workers. The surviving children of miners killed in the pits were sometimes hired as trapper boys.[86] Other options included the provision of free medical attention, pensions for widows, moving an injured worker to another grade of job, or allowing a family to remain in company housing.[87] In the coal mines of Maryland, boys over 12 years old were entitled to work underground, filling the container space allotted to an adult miner, if their fathers had died while employed by the coal company.[88] The combination of smart money, compensation, and the diversion of work tasks to family members was sufficiently attractive for employers to continue attracting an underground workforce.

Although deference and paternalism played a much smaller role in the culture of the antebellum United States than in Britain, the most detailed example of sustained and flexible employer paternalism in the face of workplace accidents is an American one. Eleuthere Irenee (E. I.) Du Pont's gunpowder-manufacturing concern, on the banks of the Delaware's Brandywine River, was home to a particularly far-reaching worker welfare system. In the wake of the first serious explosion at his factory, in 1815, the entrepreneur instituted a pension program that provided widows of workers killed in the line of duty with free rent and $100 a year for as long as they remained unmarried and living on the Du Pont grounds.[89] When a workman died, his widow was entered into the petit ledger in his stead, and his remaining pay credited to her, along with her widow's annuity. Petit ledgers indicate that after some explosions, widows also received a bonus amounting to the salary her husband would have earned had he lived another year. Over the period between 1815 and 1860, as many as twenty-two widows at a time benefited from this program, and at least one widow collected her annuity for forty years.[90]

The Du Pont pension system was part of a wider system of company benevolence. Few Du Pont workers died in debt, and many in fact accrued large savings, due to the company's maintenance of a saving system by which employees earned interest.[91] Some workers killed on the job were buried in the Du Pont family cemetery, located within easy walking distance of workers' homes.[92] Yard operations were suspended for employees' funerals, with workers even being paid for lost time.[93] Although today, whatever grave markers may have been erected to Du Pont's nineteenth-century workers have been consumed by creeping moss, the Du Ponts' willingness to be interred alongside their workmen was a grand gesture in the early nineteenth century.[94] Orphans and injured child workers sometimes received special treatment from the Du Pont Company. In 1818, Patrick Quig was injured in the explosion which killed thirty-four men; between 1820 and 1822, he was allocated $30 from a "widows and orphans account" raised by public subscription and an additional $32 for "schooling allowed him."[95] William Dougherty was "to be allowed $50 p/annum and $8 per month board," from May 24, 1848, until he reached the age of twenty-one.[96] The three young children of Michael Tonner, who were orphaned when both he and his wife were killed in 1818, were first boarded with another powder-making family at company expense and then sent to school in Philadelphia.[97]

These gestures would be hard to explain had not the management of the Du Pont company left behind a unique memorandum, illustrating their struggle to balance the demands of competitive capitalism against basic humanitarianism. In 1850, the company reevaluated the pension program; it was becoming costly, since widows were living a long time, longer than expected, without remarrying, and were therefore remaining a charge on the company. Alexis I. Du Pont defended the program his father had started, calling the payment a "just debt," and suggesting that if any changes were to be made, they should be announced before any future accidents happened.

Alexis Du Pont's memorandum shows that his vision of workers combined sentimental paternalism with an idea of equity based in the wage contract. He did mention the existence of the pension program as a sort of wage premium:

powdermen's wages could be relatively low because they knew that their families would be provided for in a time of need. The pension program was in fact paid for with foregone earnings (much like Social Security). On the other hand, the program was the result of more than just a cost-and-benefit analysis; Du Pont also felt morally responsible for the lives of workers who had died while working in the gunpowder plant. "Our mills, with only one well known exception, have destroyed more lives than any other set of mills in the world; this is of course comparing the number of hands killed to the amount of powder made." Du Pont's personal knowledge of his workforce led him to dismiss the compensation plan of a competitor, who presented each widow with a $500 payment and then "kicked her away; this appears to be a cheap plan, but the summary turning out of a poor woman, with perhaps many young children, may answer in New England, it would not do here."[98]

Employer paternalism eroded over time, even at the Du Pont manufactory. During the 1850s and 1860s, free house rent was eliminated, and the length of time that women could receive annuities was shortened to five years. Black powder widows were allotted $8 per month instead of a lump sum.[99] Even so, the company's generosity was notable enough to generate editorial comment in the wake of the July 1883 explosion; "Under the new rules it is said that the pensions only run for five years, but that the proprietors have never been known to turn their backs on the needy widow or orphan children of any of their deceased employes."[100]

In its other aspects besides the pension program, the Du Ponts' compensation regime was similar to that in other industries. Widows supplemented their income by taking in boarders for the company—an activity that might generate $17–21 dollars a month—and peeled bark from the willow limbs which were used to make charcoal, one of the three ingredients which composed black powder.[101] Widows and the wives of powdermen sewed canvas covers on powder kegs, scrubbed offices, pasted and tied canisters, and mended bags, all of which provided a little income. Further survival strategies included providing other items necessary to the functioning of Du Pont's compound—manure, for example—and sending older children or other relatives to work.[102]

The Du Pont companies on the Brandywine also retained doctors to look after their injured and ill workers and their families. Until 1834, Pierre Didier, a French emigrant, served as the company physician, followed by Thomas Mackie Smith, E. I. Du Pont's son-in-law, who served in the post until 1851.[103]

Didier and Smith provided medical services to Du Pont's workers in exchange for amounts debited from their wages.[104] The only exception was in the case of medical services after explosions, which were provided free of charge.[105] It was definitely to workers' advantage to have doctors close by. While writing a letter to his wife, Smith was interrupted by a man "running in out of breath to say that Mr. Carpenter had broke his leg at the refinery. I hastened up and sure enough I found him lying on the floor there, his left thigh being broken a short distance above the knee, by a bank of earth which they were excavating in the refinery having given way and fallen on his leg." Smith fashioned a makeshift stretcher from a door, moved the injured man to a nearby house belonging to members of the Du Pont family, and set his leg on the spot, providing instant relief."[106]

Pension plans and medical care, partial wages and "smart money," and free house rent and jobs for widows were among the many benefits that workers could claim with the right combination of work history, deferential attitude, and employer benevolence. But the shortcoming of this "system" of workplace compensation was that it was fragmentary, unpredictable, and entirely dependent on an employer's goodwill and moral compass. Without legislative or judicial compulsion, the situation would not improve; even at the beginning of the twentieth century, Progressive reformer Crystal Eastman found that in over 50 percent of the cases she studied in Pittsburgh, workers' families received no compensation for a death beyond reasonable funeral expenses.[107]

Working with larger American data sets, Fishback and Kantor agreed that accident compensation in the nineteenth century was meager. Almost no families were sufficiently compensated for the lost earnings of a lost worker; "the system looks something like a lottery where most people received nothing or relative small amounts that would cover burial expenses, while a few received large awards."[108] Deferring the social cost of accidents onto employees themselves had far-reaching, visible consequences: children were taken out of school early and sent to work, thus eliminating any opportunity for social mobility; women with large burdens, whether of debt or children, found the remarriage route shut off; and young widowed parents moved back in with their own parents, decreasing the standard of living of both parties.[109]

The Public Option

When employer charity failed, the social responsibility for workplace accidents sometimes devolved onto a compassionate public. The largest, and most consequential workplace accidents gave rise to subscription drives.[110] A characteristic of the Victorian period, subscription drives reflected the social norms of the time by relieving the poor without disturbing the social structure. One of the first such subscription drives of which we have good records occurred in the wake of an explosion at the Felling colliery, near Gateshead, England, in 1818. Ninety-two men and boys out of a workforce of 128 were killed, leaving numerous dependents. The day after the accident, a benevolent passer-by suggested starting a fund for the compensation of the widows and kin. Parish churches and dissenting meeting houses took up collections, amassing a total of £2806 15s.f 7d. Of the sum collected, £2200 was invested in exchequer bills to provide an ongoing source of income, and £436 5s. 5d. was paid to the widows.[111]

Public subscription in the wake of workplace accidents soon became a regular feature of nineteenth-century life, with participation and amounts collected growing all the time. After the Darley Main mine exploded in 1849, leaving thirty-one widows and fifty-five children without support, the mine's managers subscribed £200, and defrayed all funeral expenses, the owner of the coal field chipped in £100, and the Queen Dowager gave £25.[112] Even MP Richard Cobden, who noted that he usually turned down such solicitations, gave a donation, and the fund eventually reached £2000.[113] The amount collected was so large that the committee in charge of the distribution of the funds banked remaining funds in anticipation of future accidents.[114]

By the 1860s, the public subscription had become a species of national catharsis. The year 1862 saw one of England's worst and most well-known mining disasters, the cave-in at the Hartley colliery. The colliery had a single mineshaft, through which men descended, coal ascended, and a large beam-style engine pumped to provide power to the works. One day, the immensely heavy beam broke and fell into the shaft, immediately killing three of the five men who were on their way to work in the cage, and trapping the remainder of the workers on the shift underground. A rescue dig commenced immediately. It was hindered on the outside because civil engineering technology was just insufficient to the task, and it was hindered within the mine by the presence of suffocating gas that had built up in the absence of ventilation underground. By the time an entrance to the underground tomb was cleared, 199 corpses remained to be brought to the pitbank. The fact that the rescue dragged on allowed the pitbank to become a media event, with London newspapers featuring dispatches from reporters on the scene. Like all notable disasters of the nineteenth century, work related or otherwise, the Hartley tragedy attracted its fair share of tourists. Rubberneckers at Hartley were charged 6d. to see the devastation and could buy biscuits and gingerbread at the site of a mass grave.[115]

The sense of public ownership of the tragedy that resulted from this close media coverage of the Hartley disaster resulted in an unprecedented subscription of £81,000. Even the mine owners participated, despite their own financial hardship. So much money was collected, from everyone from Queen Victoria to miners and charladies, that the supervision committee had £20,000 left over to distribute to the other mining districts around England.[116] The Hartley disaster raised the bar for other charitable contributions in the wake of lesser mine disasters; the Blantyre fund of 1877 was £48,000; the Clifton Hall fund of 1885, £27,000.[117]

The distribution of these funds became a source of social conflict. As the extent of public subscriptions became common knowledge, working people and their families began openly to express resentment at the way in which they were at the mercy of fund administrators. Middle-class contributors resented workers who could afford more than the bare necessities. Fund administrators lost sight of the purpose for which funds had been collected, as happened after an 1844 explosion at the Haswell colliery. The charitable fund, once collected, amounted to between £4000 and £5000, but the committee invested £1800 in annuities for fourteen years and £1700 for seven years, making it impossible for workers to use most of it for present needs. Several widows reported that the committee was allowing them 3s. per week and 1s. per child, which was insufficient even to keep the families fed. One widow, who had three children under the age of seven, was asked to take in washing or do farm work to support her family.

The celebrity-headed committees that doled out accident funds exerted palpable social control in a way that was often objectionable to workers. They used donated funds to encourage thrift, education, and marrying wisely and going to work at an early age. They also set a value on human life that varied according to the social role of the wage earner. These trends were visible from the time of the Felling colliery accident in 1818. Younger widows were expected to supplement their incomes by working, or they might even remarry. Thus, widows above sixty years old were paid 5s. a week, those forty to sixty years old, 4s. per week, and under forty, 3s. per week. Boys older than seven and girls older than twelve should be contributing to the family income; thus, families received 2s. a week for boys under seven or girls under twelve, and 1s. 6d. for each additional young child. Pregnant widows could not work and therefore were to receive 5s. a week until a month after delivery (and in fact ten of the thirty widows were pregnant at the time of the accident).[118] Several families had lost young sons in the accident, but since they "suffered little abridgement of income by it, and were still able to support themselves; the claims of these were consequently not listened to."[119] The fact that lost children were worth nothing shows that workers' lives in the Felling case had no intrinsic value; rather, the monetary value they received was a social value, based on the importance of their earnings to their families.

The same assumptions prevailed after an explosion at the Burradon colliery on March 2, 1859. The committee empowered to collect and distribute funds included the Mayor and Sheriff of Newcastle and the Mayor of South Shields, all of whom were far estranged in class and custom from the objects of their charity. They divided the unfortunate residents of Burradon and Camperdown into three categories: widows and orphans, infirm and aged adults who had lost their supporting sons or other relatives, and families who still contained male heads of household but had lost valuable sons. From a total balance of over £5526, the committee created a weekly allowance that widows would receive for the next fifteen years or until their marriage, that sons would receive until age twelve, and daughters until age fifteen. The only widows who received lump sums were those who chose to open shops. A woman who remarried would get a £5 marriage portion (only if the committee approved of her choice), but the children's allowance would continue. The committee required that children over five be sent to school and the expense be defrayed out of the funds. The fund could also be used to provide proper clothing for children going into apprenticeship or service and for paying apprenticeship fees. Infirm adults, like widows, were entitled to a weekly allowance, but wage-earning families that had only lost sons would receive £10.[120]

The public subscription was not strictly a British phenomenon. Large public subscriptions in the wake of workplace accidents occurred in the United States as well. The 1818 explosion of the Du Pont gunpowder works elicited a public subscription from the citizens of Philadelphia. Handwritten forms informed the potentially charitable that,

> the late dreadful catastrophe which took place at the Manufactories of V. E. Du Pont Esq. on the Brandywine, has occasioned the extreme of distress to a number of families, leaving helpless men, women and children, some of whom are wounded, maimed, and destitute of support. We the subscribers desirous of aleviating [sic] those sufferings do promise to pay the sums affixed to our names . . . to the unhappy sufferers."[121]

Philanthropists signed their names and designated the amount paid; many of the contributions were both small and anonymous. In the Du Pont case, the newly minted widows and orphans, none of whom was literate enough to sign his or her name, reversed the usually hierarchical nature of charity by appointing their own committee to receive the sum and distribute it "among us according to our respective wants."[122]

In contrast with this democratic example, the falling of the Pemberton Mill in Massachusetts in 1862 illustrates an American case of charitable giving that functioned much more along the British model. Like the Hartley disaster, the Pemberton mill collapse was colossal in both its scope and the degree to which it captivated the attention of the public. Built in 1853, the Pemberton Mill encompassed a series of brick buildings in which cotton production was carried out. The main building was five stories tall, 280 feet long, and 84 feet wide—wider than most other mills built at that time. In addition, its stories were supported by hollow iron columns, which investigation would eventually show to have been badly forged. In the first story of this building, hundreds of Irishwomen watched over four hundred looms. The second story housed the carding apparatus; the third story the spinning and twisting; the fourth spinning, carding, and drawing in; and the fifth dressing warping, spooling, winding, quilling, and reeling. This veritable beehive of industry, second home to about six hundred operatives, collapsed without warning on January 10, 1860, just before 5 P.M., compressing all five floors into an undifferentiated mass of rubble.[123] As workers struggled to free themselves in the growing darkness, aided by bystanders with kerosene lamps, the wreckage caught fire. Despite the fact that the ruins were doused with water, the oil-saturated flooring and cotton waste at the bottom of the pile went up like a barbecue, roasting alive those still trapped. The air reverberated with the screams and moans of the dying and their heartsick relatives.[124]

The rescue effort began immediately. Bystanders climbed over the rubble in search of bodies, and official buildings were converted into a makeshift mortuary and hospital. Shortly afterward, a Relief Committee was set up, and a fund inaugurated, with the board of the Massachusetts Hospital Life Insurance Company donating the initial $2,000. The committee divided the city into wards for the purpose of distributing funds and arranged visits to ascertain need; these visits were necessary since the injured had initially been taken to their (ill-equipped) homes rather than being hospitalized. The Relief Committee reconstructed the workforce through use of the September 1859 payroll and pay vouchers carried by the workers.[125] They converted a room at the City Hall into a clearinghouse for medical supplies, food, and clothing sent from around the country to the sufferers. Despite the workers' native distrust of hospitals, the corporation created Pemberton Home, a temporary hospital, in one of their intact buildings. Here nursing care was provided, for the patients could not be well cared for at their homes by the fourteen doctors that the corporation hired.[126]

Subscriptions flooded in to aid the sufferers, and the sources of the subscriptions reflected a concern for the sufferers that cut across class. Donations came from the churches of Lawrence, and from operatives of other mills, including Amoskeag Mills, Manchester; the Lyman Mills of Holyoake; the Eagle Mills of Chelmsford; and the Manchester Corporation. Clarrisse Anne Poirier analyzed the sources of the contributions and found that 47 percent of individual donations were under $25; 9 percent of donations came from factory employees, 4 percent from clubs, and 17 percent from other individuals. An additional 1 percent came from benefit performances; the National Theater in Boston had a benefit performance of "Three Fast Men" on January 18, and the New Orleans and Metropolitan Troupe of minstrels in Louisville also donated the proceeds of a performance.[127] A total of $65,579.29 was collected, of which, amazingly, only 1.5 percent would go to administrative costs.[128]

Although the Pemberton Mill relief effort was a model of efficiency drawing widely on many sectors of American society, the distribution of aid was colored by assumptions about the class, immigration, and nature of the work. Of the 918 employees on the reconstructed payroll, 607 got aid in some form: an average of $92.45 per family or individual, most of which was distributed immediately following the disaster.[129] As in many English cases, the amount of compensation paid out varied with the importance of the dead worker to the support of his or her family. A head of household was worth $200–500; a worker on whom the family partially depended was worth $100–200; and in those cases in which a worker's wages did not significantly benefit the family, only $50–100 was given. The committee was also heavily involved in seeing how the money was used. Bank drafts were sent to people far away, but those living close by might have an account established for them. If a husband was habitually intemperate, his wife might be put in charge; if a whole family was thought to be intemperate, a local priest or a grocer might be put in charge.[130] The families of Irish workers—60 percent of the Pemberton workforce— received $20 less on average than native-born workers' families, a differential that might have reflected the stereotype that the Irish were used to a lower standard of living.[131]

Examination of public subscriptions given in the wake of workplace accidents shows the existence of social rules and norms that guided the distribution of charity.[132] The recipients of charitable funds had little say in the way
in which they were distributed; while the victims of workplace accidents were
classified as "the deserving poor," they remained so only as long as they made
no specific demands on the judicial or charitable systems. One Mrs. Oliver
had suffered almost unimaginable losses, losing her husband, four sons, and a
nephew in the Hartley incident. She traveled to London with another widow
and reportedly complained to the lord mayor of London that the distribution of the Hartley fund was unfair, since both widows were receiving less
per week than their husbands had earned while alive, and the disbursements
were small compared with the total amount of the fund. They were also angry
that anyone who had suffered similar mine disasters could have a claim on the
particular Hartley fund and complained that they were about to be turned out
of their homes. Having received no satisfaction from the lord mayor, the two
widows had the temerity to proceed to Buckingham Palace but were unable to
gain an audience with the queen, who was out. Even the *Newcastle Chronicle,*
usually a staunch friend of the worker, condemned Mrs. Oliver and her un-
named companion for seeking a larger share of the charitable pie.[133]

The desire to keep these public subscriptions classified as "charity" prevented them from becoming a social safety net for workers' families. It wasn't
that no one thought of the idea; the editors of the Newport *Reformer* suggested in the wake of the Hartley disaster that all of the pitmen of South Wales
should contribute to a widows' fund to be run by the miners of South Shields,
and pointed out that the toll from more mundane accidents (roof falls and the
like) was higher than that from major disasters but that these tended not to
capture the imagination of the public.

> Any future Act of Parliament ought to place a tax upon these fortunate gentle-
> men [mine owners], who, while they grasp at the property thus placed at their
> disposal, are base enough to shirk the responsibilities which its acquisition has
> entailed upon them. There is no doubt that Lord Campbell's Act would reach
> them in hundreds of cases, but who is to put it in force. A helpless widow, with
> half-a-dozen starving children clinging around her, cannot move in lawsuit,
> and hence the lucky colliery proprietor escapes scot free.[134]

But such calls went unheard.

The large public subscription appeared in time at the nexus of industrialization and mass print culture. But the burden of workplace accidents was

shouldered at the more modest and local level as well, through the "whip-round," a spur-of-the-moment collection that had fewer strings attached and might even function as a form of worker mutual aid. Richard Pilling, an Ashton-under-Lyne Chartist and advocate of the ten-hour workday, solicited the factory community on behalf of Margaret Ferguson, a young woman whose hand was torn off while she was cleaning a machine. When Pilling wrote a letter to the *Ten Hours' Advocate* to request help for the unfortunate woman, who had run out of both candles and meat, he was sure to add data suggesting that the accident was not her fault; "I asked her if she was compelled to clean the blowing machine while it was going, and she said if she stopped it she was afraid of being discharged. I asked her if she had ever cleaned the machine in the presence of the master or overlooker, and she said she had many times." Any contributions forthcoming from the *Ten Hours' Advocate* joined a contribution of 15s. 9d. from Ferguson's co-workers, which Ferguson's employer augmented to produce a round sum of £1.[135] A coroners' jury in Penzance, investigating an accident in which nine miners were killed, found a verdict of accidental death but then recommended that a subscription be opened on behalf of the widows and orphans, and it collected a total of £55 before the court was adjourned.[136]

It is apt that, in an age in which industrialization was widening consumer culture in both Britain and the United States, charitable givers might receive a commodified representation of thanks in return for their contributions. Sometimes in the wake of a work accident a poem was written, and printed on a nice piece of cloth with gold trim, and the charitable person would be presented with the result as a favor to commemorate the tragedy. These poems often ended with a subtle or obvious solicitation for funds based on the "there but for the grace of God go I" philosophy:

Shall we, who ere another sun
May meet a fate the same as theirs
Shall we, who selfsame hazards run
Turn coldly off, and slight their prayers?[137]

Sermons or lectures that were presented to commemorate tragic occasions were printed and the proceeds from the collection plate or from the sales of the printed sermons donated to the survivors or to the injured.[138] John Griffith gave a public speech in Merthyr Tydvil on colliery explosions, with the proceeds to benefit the widows and orphans of the Ferndale explosion. The speech, which blamed mine owners for negligence, was later printed as a pamphlet.[139] In the wake of one mine disaster, commemorative mugs were made and sold for the benefit of the workers.[140] Benefit performances were also held. When the Wheatsheaf pub in Upper-Street, Islington, collapsed, the local neighborhood had rallied to the cause of the families. Edward Giovanelli donated one entire night's receipts at his pub to the cause, and Sam Collins, an Irish singer and music hall proprietor, donated two evenings' take at the door to the same object.[141]

From the factory floor to the palace, no member of the public was immune to being solicited for donations to rectify the destruction caused by accidents. Public subscriptions were an essential element supporting the system of workers' compensation in Britain and the United States before the advent of employers' liability legislation. They served a dual purpose: not only did they alleviate the sufferings of some workers' families, they were also a forceful reminder of the human toll of workplace accidents for members of the public who escaped manual labor themselves. While it lasted, the tendency to meet workplace accidents with public subscriptions helped to reinforce existing beliefs about the importance of poverty as a spur to work and success, and about the worth of human lives as defined by wages.

The Benefits of Thrift

Charitable employers and public subscriptions supplemented whatever could be won through the courts, but for most workers these sources of payment were not guaranteed. Workers had to rely more often on their workmates, on their families, and on their own exertions to bear the burdens of workplace injury. Nineteenth-century workers who saw their workmates injured often took up collections, or "gatherings," for the sufferers. James Hayes, a Manchester factory boy of fourteen, was working as a piecer in a cotton factory when he attempted to oil a shaft. "I had the oil bottle in my hand; there was a string on to the oil bottle; this string catched in the wheel of the tumbling shaft; it drawed my hand into the wheel; my hand was torn; the fingers were all but off; I was sick, and taken to the dispensary." Over the course of six weeks, the doctors at the Ardwick and Ancoats dispensary cut off the thumb, then cut off two more fingers, and finally another. While Hayes received no pay or compensation from his employer, "the spinners gathered something for me; one went round and gathered pennies and two pence for me from the work people. Four shillings the first week, and two shillings a week for five weeks after I came out of the infirmary."[142] An eighteen-year-old worker at a nail and tip factory reported that when child workers there had their arms broken or lost their fingertips in the machinery, everyone, including the proprietor, would contribute a little something.[143]

Gathering was also a matter of course in the mines. According to one South Staffordshire collier, "When a man is injured and afterwards is able to come out, he comes on the reckoning-day, and sits near where the money is received, and every man of the pit cheerfully pays him 3d. a week out of his wages, and every boy 1 ½ d."[144] Similarly, experienced stone miner Robert Henderson reported that a circular was usually sent around among the workmen after an accident, and men would subscribe 6d. or 1s. according to their circumstances.[145] Even the railway navvies, considered by middle-class observers to be a degraded bunch, took up collections for their injured fellow workers.[146]

Gathering was so entrenched in workers' culture that it became a burden, and eventually helped to accelerate the call for a legislative solution to the compensation problem. "One Watching Events" wrote to the *Railway Gazette* to say that, considering the large number of accidents,

> it is quite certain that something should be done to find out the cause, and make railway companies liable in such matters, to support those left behind and not, after a man has been cut to pieces, oblige his mates to make a collection to pay for the company's neglect, as in the case of a poor truck carman on Saturday, the 15th January, at Nine Elms. This system is most objectionable to the men, and I fear the response was too small. Why did the company not bury the poor fellow, and grant to his widow and child a sufficient support, when he had been crushed up on their premises in performance of his most dangerous duties? Had his horses been killed, there would have been something done to prevent a recurrence, but being only a man, it did not matter.[147]

The "gathering" was the most informal aspect of worker mutual aid. Working people formalized the relationship between themselves and their colleagues on the job through friendly societies or mutual benefit organizations that served as life-insurance policies and funeral clubs (a funeral being a venerable institution for working people), but also to pay benefits when people were sick or injured. In most cases, these institutions were inadequate to the task, plagued by lack of actuarial skills, low and infrequently paid dues, and bad bookkeeping.[148] Furthermore, when large-scale accidents did occur, locally organized friendly societies went bankrupt. The friendly societies that were the most successful were those with many branches, since they pooled the risk and made it possible for people to move around without fear of losing their sick benefit. For both British and American workmen, the Odd Fellows, an example of a friendly society that was broad enough to pool risk, represented one possible source of money in times of sickness or death; membership was an important option for those workers whose dangerous trades rendered them poor insurance risks.[149] Even a tiny state like Delaware was home to Odd Fellows' lodges. In 1847, 81 of its 692 members were relieved during the year, at a cost of $799—almost $10 per family.[150]

Despite their many actuarial drawbacks, when they did remain solvent, friendly societies were important, especially in the case of illness, for which their benefits paid tended to be substantial, rather than death, for which their payments were often insufficient. For working people, unlike people occupying other social ranks, "illness" was defined by inability to work, thus encompassing the aftermath of accidents on the job as well as more lingering and organic illnesses.[151] James Riley has shown that by 1801 friendly societies enrolled about 30 percent of the eligible population, although only part of that group received sickness as well as burial benefits. The population covered by such benefits would have been skewed toward wealthier workers, since, especially up to the mid-nineteenth century, those earning less than 20s. a week would have had a hard time paying friendly society premiums, especially in locales like London.[152]

Friendly societies usually relieved their injured workers with a lump-sum payment followed by periodic payments for the length of the disability. Injured workers enrolled in the Amalgamated Union of Foundry Workers received a £50 lump-sum payment, followed by additional payments of £1 per week until a £150 payout had been reached.[153] Workers suffering from compound fractures, amputations, and paralysis qualified for receipt of these funds upon certification by a doctor. These amounts were paid for out of a levy that was imposed on all workers, including those already receiving accident benefits. The Friendly Society of Iron Moulders followed a similar tradition, and in fact secured for its members finer medical attention than most workers would have been able to obtain on their own.[154] Trade unions like these dealt in a large volume of injured workers. In Britain, the bricklayers' trade union dispensed over £17,451 in the wake of over 3,700 accidents between January 1868 and December 1880.[155] The Friendly Society of Iron Moulders dispensed £2258 in a single year.[156]

Friendly societies marked a transformation in the way in which working people sought medical treatment. Previously, they had depended on themselves, their relatives, and local wise men and women for medical advice, and tended not to send for the doctor until it was too late. As soon as friendly societies contracted—usually with surgeons—for the regular provision of medical services, workers began to have recourse to medical care more often and earlier.[157] The medical care available through friendly societies tended to be less expensive than medical care contracted on an individual basis, and thus, for the period until 1910, workingmen spent somewhere between .57 and 2 percent of their annual income on medical attendance.[158] While this figure seems small, it must be remembered that the sick benefit paid out to workers in lieu of their wages only compensated them for about 40 percent of their wages, meaning that workers absorbed a large share of the cost for their own illnesses and accidents through lost wages.[159]

Friendly societies were not the only repository for individual thrift. Labor aristocrats and those who did not work in dangerous trades might take out industrial insurance policies. The Mutual Insurance Benefit Institution, headquartered in London in the 1820s, provided weekly sums of money and medical attendance during sickness, endowments for children payable at age fourteen or twenty-one, annuities, and death benefits. In case of total disability, an injured worker received full pay in case of disability for one year, followed by half pay for one year and quarter pay for life.[160] Another underwriter, the Operatives Mutual Life Assurance Society, provided life insurance to workers. The premium for a thirty-year-old worker to ensure a payment of £20 was 9s. 10d. per year, which works out to slightly over 2d. per week.[161] Less solvent than these was the Friend-in-Need Life Assurance and Sick Fund Friendly Society, run by former Chartists Samuel Kydd and J. B. Leno.[162]

In the United States, ethnic mutual-benefit societies were another option. The National Croatian Society, operating in Pennsylvania, provided a sick or accident benefit of $5 a week for nine months, and a death benefit of $800 for a mere 56 cents a week dues payment.[163] Many Irish miners who immigrated to the United States belonged to the Ancient Order of Hibernians (AOH), a nationalist organization that had come to America in 1837. The AOH was open to those between sixteen and forty-five years of age, and paid death and sick benefits to members in good standing. In Butte, Montana, copper miners formed their own local branch of the Hibernians, since the national order explicitly barred hard-rock miners. Sick miners were paid $8 beginning in the second week after a workplace injury and were paid until they had received $104.[164]

Another option for American workers was cooperative insurance, which had grown from a nonentity in 1860 to an important form of insurance for workers by 1890, as John Witt has shown. Because commercial insurance policies for working people were almost nonexistent, due to their cost and the exclusion from them of workers in dangerous trades, a great number of local and national cooperative institutions were formed to provide benefits in case of illness, disability, or death. Drawing their membership disproportionately from urban workingmen in dangerous trades, these groups, whether based on locality, shared ethnicity, or shared trade, fostered traditions of mutuality through ritual and fraternal activity. They also policed their membership and used home visits to vet claimants for funds, keeping costs down. And, as Witt points out, the beauty of cooperative insurance was that it could be all things to all people. For those who believed in individual thrift and pulling oneself up by the bootstraps, it was proof of sober responsibility. For those who believed in transforming capitalism, it was proof of the power of mutuality against the crass capitalist.[165] Unfortunately, due to the structure of these schemes, which depended on a large pool of low-risk members and on a certain number of defaulters, many were financially unsound.[166] Despite the work of the National Fraternal Congress, an umbrella institution for some of the larger national associations, the workingmen's cooperatives did not pave the way for general social provision by the government, as happened in Britain; Americans were too obsessed with the problem of industrial accidents to see the larger social safety net that was missing.[167]

Unions or work-related accident funds might also provide benefits in case of sickness or death.[168] On the railroads, the Railway Benevolent Institution, founded in 1858, catered to officials and clerks. It gave small annuities and gratuities to widows and distressed members, and provided for orphans' educations. For men lower down on the prestige scale, a charity-based Casualty Fund was set up in 1864 to reduce the hardship of injured workers and of dependants of men killed. The fund took up an annual collection from workers and by 1876 was relieving over 1500 families per year.[169] Individual mills, like that at New Lanark, had similar systems—mandatory "sick clubs" that workers paid into, and had their contributions matched to some degree by employers.[170] Although benefit societies often excluded miners, who were thought to be too much of a risk, individual coalfields did run "field clubs" which were funded by compulsory deductions from the miner's pay packet. For the cost of perhaps 3 or 4d. a week the collier was protected by a surgeon who was retained to care for all the members of the club. The club also allowed to a man, during convalescence from work-related accidents only, a weekly payment of around 6–8s.[171]

To the extent possible with limited and intermittent unionization throughout the nineteenth century, the miners in particular struggled to create an
industry-wide provision for injury and occupational death. In 1814, Newcastle-
area viewer John Buddle, a member of an ad-hoc organization called the Society for Preventing Accidents in Coal Mines, proposed a relief fund that would
have required the men to pay a penny in the pound, and the coal masters one
farthing in the ton. Buddle reasoned "that as colliers are exposed to many accidents besides fire, it may not, perhaps, be deemed improper to combine with
the objects of this Society, the formation of a general Permanent Fund, for the
relief of the widows and orphans of such colliers and others, as may lose their
lives in the collieries of the Tyne and Wear, and for the support of such as are
maimed and disabled." Nothing appears to have come of his suggestion.[172]

Another attempt, this time at a Miner's Provident Association, was made
in Newcastle in 1858, led by John Baxter Langley, editor of the *Newcastle
Chronicle*. The masters contributed an amount to that fund, but it could only
be used for certain purposes and might be revoked in case the miners mis-
behaved.[173] A lack of national cohesiveness among the miners compromised
any efforts to move beyond a local scale. David Swallow, Corresponding Secretary of the Lancashire and Cheshire branch of the Miners' Association in
1853, said that his men would object to the formation of a national relief fund
because they preferred to assist men within their own country (by which they
meant Lancashire and Cheshire).[174]

The Hartley colliery disaster precipitated a round of talks between coal
mine owners and miners about the establishment of a permanent relief fund.
The talks served to illuminate the differences between masters and men on
the question of relief. As many employers did when approached with the idea
that they ought to shoulder the burden of workplace accidents, the coal owners
refused to be pressured into providing systematic relief rather than intermittently charity.[175] A letter writer to the *Newcastle Chronicle,* who called himself
"W. X. Y. Z," noted that the coal owners already gave widows a house and fuel,
regardless of whose fault the accident was that killed their workmen husbands,
and wondered whether that might discharge any moral obligation that the
coal owners had toward their workforce.[176] The secretary of the Coal Trade
Association asserted that the mine owners did not feel compelled to participate
in a permanent fund; due to the restrictions of the Truck Act, which guaranteed miners' wages in cash, the owners doubted that they could legally deduct
money from men's wages for this purpose.[177] Furthermore, the owners didn't

think Parliament would require of them a statutory contribution, since risk was inherent in mining and not due to carelessness on the mine owners' part.[178]

Although the coal owners refused to be drawn into participating, two separate permanent relief funds for miners were formed as a result of all this discussion. The first was national. John Towers, editor of the *British Miner and General Newsman,* helped to found the British Miners' Benefit Association, a friendly society for coal miners. As Towers explained at a public meeting,

> A collier's wife becomes a widow, on the average, fourteen years sooner than does the wife of an agricultural labourer; and she descends at once from 18s or 20s a week to 2s6d a week (the allowance of the parish) . . . Great catastrophes, I repeat, induce great and generous sympathy, and will, no doubt, always do so; but, however, to be admired, this is spasmodic, and the British miner should not be dependent upon it.

The rules of organization provided for local branches of at least 400 members, each of whom would pay 3.5 cents a week for the privilege of membership. In return, if a member were killed, the Association would pay £2 in funeral expenses, 4s. a week to the widow until death or remarriage, and 2s. a week to each male child under twelve or female child under fourteen. Dependants of an unmarried member received a lump sum of £15. In case of injury, members received 10d. per day for six months or until the person was able to earn 15s. a week on his own.[179]

Newcastle and Durham miners, who were suspicious of Towers's London background, formed their own two-county permanent relief fund, which by November had 8,000 paying members.[180] The existence of two miners' permanent relief funds reflected more than the provincial-metropolitan divide. Miners' letters to the editor show that the national fund attracted miners who sought systematic change and were more peremptory with their employers. In contrast, spokespeople for the local relief fund took a more fatalistic tone, acknowledging that mine accidents, like poverty, were endemic.

Friendly societies, sick clubs, and industrial insurance policies required of working people a degree of conscious thrift. This made sustaining contributions difficult even in the best of times and disqualified casual workers and those with incomes just sufficient to cover basic necessities from participation at all. The ability to keep up with payments could be a sign of working-class respectability, similar to being able to afford a decent funeral. Stonemason John Holly collected £100 in 1864, having been disabled by a fall from the top of a house two years earlier. He had fallen onto some iron used to support the scaffolding and injured his spine, such that he would never again be able to pursue his trade. At the ceremony at which Holly received his compensation, the president of the Stonemasons used his case as an example of how important it was for stonemasons to keep their payments to the society up to date. While Holly had been prudent, another member of the society had recently fallen sixty feet and died, leaving his family penniless because his payments were not up to date. Holly "assured them it was the only pleasure he had while lying in bed, to think that he belonged to that society which would provide for him in time of need."[181]

Workers who participated in the Stonemasons' society not only needed to be thrifty, they were also under the surveillance of their brothers, who policed the respectability of their members. The Stonemasons' society required not only that workers continue their payments to the accident fund, but also carefully vetted the claims of each member who tried to collect sick benefit. Because it was in the financial interest of the society to keep the number of successful claims to a minimum, workers faced strict scrutiny. Were there any witnesses to the accident? Was it clear that the injured party would never again resume his trade? The connection that workmen in the same trade supposedly had to each other should not be over romanticized. Just as workers collecting workmen's compensation are sometimes caught today having submitted false claims, so nineteenth-century workmen sometimes took advantage of the system. The Stonemasons' executive committee reported receiving such surgeons' notes as "This is to sertefie that John Murrouse of Keighley have a misfortune of crush on his foot, so that he is not able to work," and "This is to certify that Wedward Craven is unable to follow his employ on account of bad helth and as ben for som time."[182]

Friendly societies not only sought to inculcate the values that successful Victorians strove toward, they also helped situate their memberships within the sphere of the respectable through their investments. The Stonemasons debated where the funds of the society should be invested. The Carlisle lodge proposed that £500 of their funds should be sunk into the Land and Labour Bank associated with Feargus O'Connor's Chartist Land Company, because it paid interest at 4 percent per annum. The Manchester branch proposed to invest £2000. Not only was security in landed property superior to any other kind of security, but the bank also expressly catered to the working classes. "It is our interest and duty to assist in carrying out such a praiseworthy object by

every means in our power."[183] Many other branches objected to the Land and
Labour Bank's own investment in exchequer bills, or wondered whether fiscal
responsibility was giving way to Chartist enthusiasm.[184] Samuel Smiles would
have been proud.

This examination of the nineteenth-century compensation regime has illustrated the difficulties of suing an employer for compensation and looked at
a triumvirate of possibilities for sustaining life after a workplace accident: employer charity, public subscriptions, and mutual aid. But what if charity failed,
and mutual assistance was not forthcoming? Nineteenth-century workers who
were injured often continued working out of necessity. Such was the case with
Phineas Gage, with his jobs driving horses and working on farms. Such was
also the case with an English laborer named Oxenbridge, who was buried in
the debris of a falling quarry in 1844 and broke three ribs and several bones in
both arms. After four weeks in the hospital one arm was amputated, and after
eleven weeks he was released more or less well. According to his doctor, he was
working again a year after his release.[185] English miner William Morrow had
lost his leg at the age of eight, when he fell asleep minding a door and his leg
was run over by a full wagon of coal. Six years and several other mishaps later,
he was still working in the coal pit, aided by a wooden leg.[186] According to
J. R. Leifchild, a nineteenth-century anthropologist of the coal towns, disabled miners often made a living as schoolteachers; "should a vacancy occur
in the colliery where his misfortune happened, [the disabled miner] deems
himself, and is deemed by others, indisputably entitled to the suffrage of all
parties. This evinces sensibility to the claims of misfortune, and insensibility
to the claims of education."[187]

Workers who experienced catastrophic injuries were often forced into
less lucrative jobs, especially peddling. Having lost his arm in the machinery of a Brandywine, Delaware, cotton factory, young Robert McFarlan took
up selling religious books and also became a subscription agent for the *Blue
Hen's Chicken*. He used the proceeds of his sales career to put himself through
school in the hopes of becoming a schoolmaster—a popular career for factory amputees on both sides of the Atlantic.[188] Jennie Collins, a nineteenth-
century advocate for the National Labor Union, knew a young factory worker
who noticed that the cards in a wool-carding machine were about to crash and
cause property damage. When the workman tried to push the belt from the
pulley to stop the machine, he slipped and fell and his arm was crushed by the
machine. The arm was paralyzed for life, and the workman received nothing

from the company but thanks for saving the equipment. He was also given the opportunity to walk around the factory and sell candy to make a living.[189]

The great commodification of life that had injured these workers in the first place also assisted them to continue living and working. The creation of so many amputees by the American Civil War led to advances in prosthetics and to their marketing to injured workers. A trade catalogue for the Palmer leg featured a number of testimonials from amputees back in the workforce. James McEleney, who worked for the Philadelphia and Reading Railroad, lived some distance from his station and had to walk to it on a rough hilly road. Nonetheless, he was able to remain the breadwinner for a family of eleven children with the help of his Palmer leg.[190] For those unable to afford the Palmer leg (which at $150 was beyond the reach of most nonprofessional workers), a wooden peg leg for an amputation below the knee might be had for $10, with an above-the-knee version available for $20. An artificial arm without a hand sold for $25, and for another $25, a worker could purchase a wooden or rubber hand with a prehensile thumb, with a strong spring that made gripping possible.[191]

Sometimes the new right hand that an injured worker acquired was figurative rather than literal, with responsibilities for the family economy being redistributed to avoid recourse to meager government charity.[192] This was also often the case when occupational illness struck—as when colliers were forced to retire at an early age due to black lung, a condition which they referred to as "bad breath."[193] The wives of male workers, who were fairly uncommon otherwise in mills and factories, were often given preferential treatment in hiring by their husbands' employers. Before girls and women were barred from working underground in coal mines in 1842, the widows of injured Scottish colliers worked as "below basket women," hooking on tubs of coal, and their young daughters were sent underground to haul coal to the surface on their backs.[194]

Although the social responsibility for accidents was spread among more groups before 1880 than it is today, the regime for the compensation of workers was much less predictable and less equitable. Until the triumvirate of defenses against tort suits broke down in the late 1800s, most workers avoided suing their employers in the case of workplace accidents. With this route all but foreclosed, workers turned first to their employers for charity, to a compassionate public, and to their own devices and those of their friends and workmates. Workers who were especially thrifty or who worked for paternalistic employers, or who were injured in high-profile accidents, might find that, although they did suffer physical pain, the financial effects of an injury were limited. Other workers had to continue to work, shift work responsibilities to wives or children, beg on the streets, or enter workhouses or houses of refuge.

While the family financial implications of workplace accidents were usually hidden from the public, the accidents themselves were not. As the next chapter will show, the reading public in both Britain and the United States was informed again and again about the impact that machinery could have on the body. Workplace death and injury were the raw materials of stories of heroism and religious conversion, sin and abandonment, and melodrama and providence—stories that were told by newspaper reporters and by workers who had experienced job-related disasters firsthand. These stories helped to impart cultural meaning to the financial sacrifices that were made when a community contributed in the wake of a mine disaster, or a worker put a little something in his friend's upturned cap.

The Cultural Meanings of Workplace Accidents

Ding, dong the bell!
Not for the child, whose composure condones,
As it dies in a dream on its own mother's knee
By the light of a kindly hearth.
Ding, dong the bell!
But for children, whose anguish had melted the stones
As they cried, still in vain, for their mothers to see
In the chaotic bowels of the earth.

—J. Skipsey, the Pitman Poet (1862)[1]

THROUGHOUT THE NINETEENTH CENTURY, observers and participants alike struggled over the meaning of workplace accidents, and especially over the question of who was responsible for the growing industrial death toll. The outcome of the cultural struggle would help to determine which group—workers, employers, society at large, the government—should shoulder the increasing burden of supporting the injured and the families of those who lost their lives to machinery. Of course, as explained in Chapter 2, the fact that there was a compensation regime in place before 1880, as unpredictable and scattershot as it may have been, partially explains why legislatures in Britain and the United States were so slow to move on this question. But examining the cultural meanings of industrial accidents may also help to reveal why workers' compensation—in contrast with safety regulation or regulation of work hours—was so long in coming.

Was workers' relative apathy to blame for the failure of the state to act decisively on workers' compensation before 1880? Robert Asher has hypothesized that industrial safety was a subject about which workers were comparatively apathetic, at least in comparison with their feelings about speedups, low wages, and indiscriminate fines for poor-quality piecework or lateness. As Asher has noted, employers concerned to appease workers could only appease them on the issues that employees espoused as their own.[2] Yet as this chapter will show, using a wider array of popular sources than historians have looked at in detail before, industrial safety was indeed a concern, especially in the most dangerous industries. Workers' perceptions of workplace accidents were partially influenced by the presentation of these accidents in the press. These influences were, however, offset by the physical impact of these accidents on their own lives: pain, loss of family, and financial struggle.

As this chapter will show, the slow pace of reform certainly was not due to any failure by the press to cover workplace accidents. And as Thomas Haskell has suggested in reference to the abolitionist movement, it is this kind of plentiful information that is *capable* of changing the moral compass of an era and making even those who are not harmed or oppressed cry out for change.[3] Tom Lacqueur advanced a similar argument when he wrote that many of the common approaches to discussing the body in pain during this period constituted a "humanitarian narrative," a link between those who suffered and those who read about their suffering. The humanitarian narrative allowed an imaginative link to be made and thus impelled the moral imagination of the reader to go to work, exposing the possibility for reform.[4] But in order for humanitarianism to really result in reform, it is necessary for more than just a few people to feel as if there is something concrete that they can do to create change; in this case, legislatively or technologically. Moreover, it is necessary for them to feel guilty that they do not act—to see their failure to act as part of the causal chain that creates the problem.[5]

In fact, much press coverage of workplace accidents had the opposite effect. Accidents were by their nature accidental—seen as part and parcel of the workplace, a regrettable fact about which nothing could be done. Accidents were discussed in ways that underlined this fatalism by casting workers as hapless victims of circumstance or Providence, or even as hapless victims of their own attempted heroism! Furthermore, a chasm of understanding developed between workers, for whom the economic and social impact of accidents were primary concerns, and the classes that set the legislative agenda. For the latter group, sermons, public pronouncements, and newspapers alike concentrated on the emotional toll of workplace accidents, especially within the individual family. Sentimental tales of the havoc wreaked on individual families by accidents provided an emotional catharsis without amounting to a condemnation of a dangerous system or a cry for a different division of the social costs of workplace injuries. While humanitarian narratives may have promoted a moral imagination among their readers, the idea that they promoted specific reforms is not borne out in the majority of cases. Throughout most of the nineteenth century, neither the narrative of the victimization of workers' bodies, nor an alternative presentation of workplace accidents as opportunities for workers to demonstrate their heroism, would in themselves promote serious discussion of ways in which workplaces might be made safer or who should bear the cost of workplace accidents.

Maimed Workers, Voracious Machines, and Grieving Widows

At a time in which much popular fiction was melodramatic, newspapers intended for mass audiences often presented occupational accidents in melodramatic and pathetic terms. Reports of accidents were most often interspersed with news of murders, seductions, and other unusual occurrences. And like these other kinds of surprising and tragic events, workplace accidents were presented in familiar and similar ways. Again and again, reporters played on the sensibilities of readers by emphasizing such elements as the extreme youth, female gender, or inexperience of workers who were killed or wounded, the number and condition of dependents, and the workers' last words. Like the narratives of chattel slavery that emphasized the appalling impact of that institution on the family, these narratives invited the reader to empathize with families torn apart.[6]

The grief of surviving relatives was both omnipresent in the narrative and central to its interpretation. John Walker, for example, was killed at the Gloucester Point Mills when he stooped to pick up something and "he became entangled in the machinery, and his face and head were dreadfully crushed. He was carried home by his widowed mother, Mrs. Walker, wrapped up in a piece of bagging which they had hastily gathered up, covered with blood, just as she was getting his supper . . . The unrestrained piercing and agonized cries of the widow and her children made quite a harrowing spectacle."[7] Similarly, after the 1869, Avondale disaster, "the sobs and moans of mothers and wives broke at intervals into piercing shrieks and wails of agony as the bodies were recognized . . . Children too young to know their bereavement clung in mute astonishment to the sides of their weeping mothers, and shrank from the blackened corpses in which they were unable to recognize their fathers."[8] This was not the good death, the Christian death with the family members at the bedside, the death in which the dying person had time to come to terms with his chances for eternal life. It was, instead, nasty, brutish, and sudden.

Accident narratives both drew from and contributed to a mass of contemporary clichés about gender-appropriate behavior. Newspaper reports described widows throwing themselves upon coffins, weeping, shrieking, and rending their hair and garments.[9] The *Harrisburg Republican* described the aftermath of a gunpowder explosion:

> Here was a wretched mother distractedly carrying and dragging her orphan children while she was searching for the shattered corpse of their father. There sat another weeping; one who having found the blackened remains of a man was gazing upon it with wild anxiety uncertain whether indeed it was the beloved being who but a few hours before had pillowed his head upon her now aching bosom. A little further with clasped hands and streaming eyes was seen a young woman who had just found the body of her father and with loud cries was lamenting his untimely death.[10]

A Pennsylvania newspaper reported a similar reaction after a man was killed while placing some props under the roof of the local Methodist Meeting House. "His corpse was carried to his place of residence, and the scene exhibited on its arrival was heart-rending in the extreme. His wife went frantic with grief, and would have torn the coffin to pieces, had not she been restricted by friendly hands."[11] Widows were so notorious for their excesses of grief that at the Hartley disaster, only male relatives of the dead miners were allowed on the pitbank. The issue, according to the *Newcastle Chronicle,* was the inability of widows and mothers to restrain their grief.[12] Men were normally described as containing their grief within the stoic norms of working-class masculinity, but the bonds of brotherhood could bring a man to tears as he watched a dying comrade. Writing about the Avondale, Pennsylvania, mine fire and cave-in, Thomas Knox recalled "many of the men were overcome with grief as they saw the remains of their comrades, and tears trickled down their cheeks from eyes unused to tears."[13]

The imposition of middle-class ideals of family and of gender roles extended to descriptions of the social impact of workplace accidents. When men were killed, newspapers often reported whether they left behind widows and children, and if children, their number and their ages.[14] Reporters commented on families having been left entirely destitute, with the word connoting a hole in the family as much as a hole in the finances.[15] As one early report in the London *Times* noted, "A melancholy accident happened on Saturday last to Thomas Barefoot, one of the persons employed in the mill near Mill Pond Bridge, Rotherhithe, occasioned by the entangling of his clothes in the cogs of the mill, by which he was mangled in a shocking manner, his left thigh being torn off, and his body crushed to pieces.—He has left a wife and one child to deplore his loss; and, what is still more shocking, she is now far advanced in pregnancy."[16] While male workers injured and killed in accidents were lamented in newspapers as lost breadwinners, women who were injured or killed were lamented as lost mothers, whether actual or potential. An English newspaper reported that at the Coalport China Works,

> A poor woman, engaged in feeding a bone mill, had unfortunately approached so near the machinery as to get her clothes entangled in the wheels. The result was that she was drawn in between the teeth of a pair of rapidly-revolving wheels, and the flesh was literally pinched in large pieces by the remorseless machine from the thick part of her thighs. An additional shade of melancholy is given to the circumstance by the fact that she was *enceinte* at the time.[17]

Similarly, testimony that women who worked as coal movers ("hurriers") in mines often miscarried was among the evidence that moved legislators to bar women and girls from underground mine work in 1842.[18]

In story after story, Victorian newspapers painted an emotional picture of the destructive impact of workplace accidents on workers' families. But what lesson were readers to draw from this? Robert Asher has argued that newspapers of the period emphasized the impact of industrial accidents on widows and children in order to explain the social cost of such accidents.[19] It is true that injured workers fell into the Victorian taxonomy of morals under the heading "worthy poor," and newspapers recognized this designation by calling the injured party "unfortunate"—a sign of empathy.[20] Nonetheless, because they were rendered as individual stories of bad luck, these narratives of families destroyed usually failed to make the connection between repeated accidents and the need for increased safety or more certain monetary compensation for the worker and his family. Each family was an object of pity and perhaps of charity; but individual worker deaths normally did not result in editorials calling for systematic changes in the workplace.

Rather, the narratives of workplace accidents and their social devastation which littered nineteenth-century newspapers enabled readers to exercise their Christian feeling toward the less fortunate without really thinking about inequalities of wealth distribution or unsafe work practices.[21] After describing the impact of a gunpowder explosion, the *Harrisburg Republican* editorialized, "These were scenes which were calculated to make man feel for man and make in his agony of soul exclaim—'to what better, to what nobler, use can gold be applied than to bind up the broken heart, be a father to the fatherless and a friend to him who has none to help him?'"[22] As has been noted, the families of workers injured or killed on the job relied heavily on public subscriptions to meet daily needs. Appeals such as these allowed a simple donation to the cause to serve as a catharsis, without raising larger questions of social responsibility.[23] And attract donations they certainly did, as the public money collected in the wake of coal mine disasters shows.[24]

If popular accounts of workplace accidents distracted readers from issues of long-term change by channeling readers' thoughts onto a religious plane, sermons generated in the wake of serious workplace disasters reinforced this process. Clerics impressed upon accident victims the need to accept a subservient position in the face of divine forces beyond their control. In the wake of the collapse of the Felling colliery in 1812, in which ninety-two miners were killed, the clergyman presiding over a mass funeral warned all to remember that "Christian resignation should guard us against all expressions of impatience and unthankfulness at the plans of Providence."[25] In the wake of particularly bad disasters, days of prayer and fasting were proclaimed, the community joining together to answer an angry Providence by expressing communal awe.[26] A Delaware newspaper informed its readers of the loss of life following the 1847 gunpowder explosion at DuPont; almost all of the dead were from Ireland, and fourteen had left behind widows or families. "The ways of Providence are inscrutable . . . the wives and children of the deceased claim our warmest sympathy," the editor mused.[27] If the strange ways of God were responsible for mine cave-ins and gunpowder explosions, then the possibility that man could make inroads against such disasters was circumscribed. Workplace accidents called into question man's ability to control and to progress, contravening the spirit of Victorian positivism.

In their suddenness, workplace accidents were the worst kind of death for the Victorians, depriving their sufferers of the opportunity for spiritual preparation. Nor were families able to gather and witness the last moments of the dying person looking for signs of salvation.[28] Nonetheless, writers tried to find signs of the "good death" in these disasters, or to derive from them a more optimistic message than the idea that God had condemned sinners to a horrible death. The Religious Tract Society issued an account of the Hartley disaster which paid special attention to the fact that several of the dying men had held a prayer meeting underground and another had inscribed "Mercy, O God!" on his tin lunchbox before being asphyxiated.

> The occurrence is one which speaks in the most solemn and forcible terms to all of us. It is a loud call upon us to consider the mysteriousness of God's

providence. God's ways are not our ways, neither are his thoughts our thoughts . . . It should be ours therefore not to question or cavil in such a case as that before us; not hastily and rashly to infer that the catastrophe is a judgement of Divine wrath against the wisdom and Goodness of God.[29]

Alexander Reid agreed in his own tract about the Hartley catastrophe. He emphasized that while pitmen had their sinful practices, including drinking, theatergoing, racing, wrestling, boxing, and betting, observers should not conclude that it was the pitmen's sins that were being expiated at Hartley. Rather, the sudden deaths of the men were meant as an object lesson for all. "Your sins, dear reader, may be of a very different order from these; they may be carefully concealed from the view of those around you, and you may yourself be only partially aware of their enormity . . . but God knows them all, hates them all, and will judge you for them all."[30] Commenting on an explosion at the Oaks Pit at Arsdley Main in 1847, preacher Benjamin Beddow saw in the accident analogies to the judgment day. Just as men had been judged by fire underground, so all who sinned would be judged by fire after their deaths.[31] The author of an evangelical children's book called *Fuel for our Fires* reflected on the horror that those trapped in the Hartley mine must have felt while underground. "Who shall say how these men had suffered? How dreadful must it be to be buried alive! To feel that no human help was possible! Let us hope that in that awful hour some light from the Sun of Righteousness came to the souls of those poor men in their dreary dungeon, and that they remembered the gracious promise of the Savior."[32] Rather than an example of God's wrath, workplace accidents might be construed as object lessons for all good Christians to ponder their relationships with God.

Workplace accidents were also interpreted as opportunities not to question God's will, but rather to lead a life of Christian resignation. Thomas Hodgkin, an observer at the scene of the Hartley disaster, was moved to think about religion by observing the men's widows: "Everywhere, as far as I have heard, there seems to be that meek resignation to God's will, the bowed head and lips dumb before the Lord by which the poor, or at any rate the women of the poor, so often shame us."[33] Like so many press writers, Hodgkin was an outsider to the Hartley community, so it is an open question about how much Christian resignation and silence he would have encountered had he been invited inside a miner's cottage—but at least for Hodgkin and his readers, that was the lesson.

In addition to underlining the folly of attempting to predict life and death, sermons following accidents sometimes pointed to accidents as a reprisal for sin. After Samuel Hammond's mill collapsed in 1853, Leeds Reverend Charles Gutch daringly blamed Hammond; his failure to remove a tyrannical overseer who had impregnated two of his women workers had brought the wrath of God upon him.[34] Similarly, when the Pemberton mill collapsed and caught fire in 1860, killing hundreds of immigrant Irish workers, every clergyman in the town of Lawrence, Massachusetts, tried to find a higher moral, rather than a scientific, explanation. The Congregationalist opined that the collapse was a demonstration of men's vanity and God's power. The local Baptist minister pointed his finger at the love of money. Others noted that the Irish workers had been licentious and violated the Sabbath. All the clergymen took the collapse as a lesson that men were required to place God above worldly things.[35]

The attempt to find a salutary religious moral in a workplace accident could sometime be taken to offensive extremes, as it was in the case of the 1835 explosion in the Wallsend colliery. At the inquest, the coroner not only charged the jury with the conviction that no blame could be apportioned anywhere, but also rejoiced that relatively sinless children rather than sinful, bread-winning adults had died in the mine. "Perhaps this awful visitation could never have happened at a time when the consequences attending so great a waste of life, could have been less serious and distressing to the surviving friends. A small portion of men who had families depending upon them were down the pit; nor could there have been a class of sufferers, so suddenly removed, better fitted for being called into another state of being, than those who have suffered, the most of them being children, having little to answer for."[36] To his credit, he followed this callous remark with a wish that some good might come from the accident, by provoking government investigations into mine safety.

The linkage between workplace accidents and family destruction, and between workplace accidents and religious salvation, allowed working people to use the middle-class sympathy industry to their own advantage. As objects of pity, they were ready recipients of charity. The poems and ballads printed in memory of the dead and sold for their benefit emphasized the themes of pity and compassion.[37] One such poem, printed after the Crystal Palace collapsed, invoked God and the public on behalf of the deceased construction workers and their families:

Oh God! Dry up the widow's tears
And ease the orphan's grief
Look with compassion down on them
And send to them relief;

Be a father to the orphan child
A husband to the wife
And be a kind protector
Unto them during life.[38]

This poem contained all of the ingredients for catharsis: a charitable donation, a prayer, and the idea that God was capable of repairing the damage that the workplace accident had caused to working families, by performing the roles of father and husband.

Irony, Judgment and Providence

Not all accident narratives reflected the dominant nineteenth-century pre-occupation with pity and piety. While the majority of accident narratives were written to elicit pity, others were meant to amuse, employing irony and coincidence revolving around men's misguided attempts to outguess Providence. A Quaker who owned a steam-grinding mill had for a long time maintained a partition in a certain part of his mill in order to prevent accidents. Shortly after ordering it to be removed, he fell into his own machinery at that exact spot and was killed.[39] An extremely persistent mother managed to secure employment in a coal mine for her three young sons (despite their recent dismissal from another coal mine) just in time to see them all killed in the 1819 explosion at the Sherriff-Hill colliery.[40] Another coal mine exploded when two workmen carrying naked candles went through the works to make a collection among the colliers for a workmate of theirs who had recently been injured.[41] Two sand-pit workers were killed in a cave-in; ironically, one of the workers had quit his job at the Du Pont gunpowder works expressly because he wanted to avoid danger. The *Blue Hen's Chicken* found it "singular" that:

Two men have recently moved from the powder mills, in the neighborhood of Wilmington, on account of the danger, and both have met their death from other causes, viz; poor McCoy, who moved from Gareschee's and was almost immediately afterwards killed by the blowing up of the boiler of the paper mill; and James Green, who lately moved from Dupont's . . . The ways of Providence are strange.[42]

The pamphleteers who described the Pemberton Mill collapse recounted several incidents of irony in their narrative. One man, trapped in rubble, attempted to commit suicide in the face of a fiery death, only to be rescued before being consumed by flames. Another man recognized his wife's dead body by the ring she wore on her finger, and gave out a whoop of joy, only moments later realizing his discovery was no grounds for celebration. In a third case, a girl who was otherwise unharmed by the collapse was trapped in the rubble by her two fingers which were caught in the machinery. In despair, she tore them off, only to have them returned to her by the disaster cleanup crew two days later.[43]

Occasionally, workplace accidents were narrated in such a way that one wonders whether the editors were trying to elicit a chuckle from their readers through gallows humor. The *Times* reprinted a report from the Oxford Journal, telling of twenty-four-year-old John Collier, who was oiling the works when one of the pins caught part of his clothing. His arm, thigh, and body were successively dragged into the machine, "and the head crushed and completely severed from the body, from which it was found at a distance of two or three feet." When Collier found he could not extricate himself he shouted "take care of my wife and children," and then died. Mrs. Collier, having heard what happened, ran in and yelled, "Do speak to me again!" The editor commented, wryly, that "it would appear that she was not aware that he was at that moment a corpse."[44]

Of course, Providence could spare workers as well as condemning them, and tales of close scrapes were also popular. One man escaped from a gunpowder mill—his third such escape—only moments before it exploded.[45] In another case, the proprietor of a gunpowder mill walked away from it just before it exploded, but another man who had just entered the mill was killed instantly.[46] Although it is never explicitly said, these stories suggest that fate, or even more strongly, the hand of God was behind these miraculous survivals and condemnations. During this pre-Darwinian period, when categorization, statistics, and certainty were emerging to challenge evangelicalism and faith, the newspaper narratives expressed a populist, nonscientific way of looking at and thinking about the world.

While melodrama, pathos, religious sensibility, and a certain amount of irony can all be related back to Victorian religious beliefs, it is less easy to attempt to explain the goriness of Victorian accident narratives. Throughout the nineteenth century, but particularly before the American Civil War, newspaper accounts of workplace accidents—as well as other kinds of disasters—described depredations on the body in almost loving detail.[47] Steam-driven machinery and other technological advancements were, after all, new, and the impact that they had on humans was unprecedented.[48] While in many cases the impact of workplace accidents on men and women was different, workers were described similarly when they were injured or killed by machinery; the machines didn't discriminate on the basis of sex.[49] Rather, these machines seemed to have voracious appetites for limbs, as unguarded drive belts caught workers and dragged them into the whirling gears: "On Friday last, a boy about 14 or 15 years of age, named Moses Lowther, was working in the woollen factory of Charles I. Dupont Esq, by some means got his arm caught in the machinery, and before it could be stopped, it was terribly crushed and lacerated. His arm was being ground up in that horrible manner three or four minutes, before the machinery could be stopped." Lowther's arm was not just crushed and lacerated, but terribly and horribly so; the image "ground up" further suggests meat being fed through a grinder, here a youthful human body through a voracious machine.[50]

Self-acting mule spinners, machines to spin yarn, closed with a bang and trapped and crushed children's heads. Gearing tore off errant fingers. Most spectacularly, unfenced vertical or horizontal shafts running from the motive power to the machinery sucked in hair or loose clothing and, once the belts running from these shafts had a victim in their grasp, beat him or her mercilessly against ceilings or crushed them between drums.[51] Nor were machine-related accidents limited to factories. A Reading newspaper reported that a nameless "12-year-old daughter of William Saltzer" was killed when she was caught in a threshing machine. She stepped over a connecting rod, her dress was caught on a nail, and her body was wound around the rod, crushing her to death instantly. "Her neck was fractured and the whole body dreadfully lacerated and mangled."[52]

Some accidents produced results verging on the fantastic or the gothic. A Pennsylvania newspaper noted that during an explosion, one of two men killed was literally blown out of his slippers, which were afterwards found in the place where the man had been standing.[53] After a train derailment in New York's Union Square, the engine crew was absorbed in the train wreck and forgot to monitor the steam on the boiler. When it burst, according to one bystander, "The chief engineer was blown to pieces. His legs went into Union Park, his arms to a pile of lumber on the other side of the avenue, and his head was split in two parts. His abdomen also burst, and his intestines scattered over the road."[54] When an exploding boiler in a carpet factory in England flew through several buildings and across the River Wear, rescuers carried away three women. Their "clothes were torn and wet, their hair dishevelled, the scalded and blackened skin lay rough on their arms, necks and shoulders, and their features were scarcely distinguishable among bruises and blood."[55] In the wake of a gunpowder explosion in Northern New Jersey, searchers with sharp sticks walked about in the woods looking for human remains, spearing "a morsel of flesh here and a bone there." According to the newspaper, they collected enough bits of human bones and strips of scorched and tattered flesh to fill two bushel baskets.[56] L. Simonin, the author of a text that in its minute description of mining life recalled the voyeuristic descriptions of city life typical of later in the century, described three miners trapped underground who seemed to have arranged their own funerals before suffocating.[57] Even working-class newspapers were not immune to this trend. The reformist *Beehive* newspaper reported that a boiler exploded on the Great Western Railway near Paddington, England, killing two cleaners. "Wilson was not much disfigured, but poor Elridge was so mutilated that his remains had to be collected in a bag. His head was found in one place and his limbs scattered about in other directions."[58]

By providing minute descriptions of the state of workers' bodies after accidents, newspapers may have been striving to imitate the "scientific" and exacting language of the autopsy, which tended to be both graphic and literary. For example, Dr. A. Davison of Seaton Delaval, England, categorized workers killed at Hartley into three categories based on the degree of mottling of their skin. While twenty of the dead "did not present any unusual appearance" the majority "were slightly swollen and relaxed, the arms and fingers bent and rigid, the skin of the palm of the hand sodden as if immersed in water, and the eyes sunk and dim. In various parts of the body the skin presented patches of a bright appearance, occasionally intermingled with streaks of a paler colour. In some instances a bloody fluid, of a bright red colour, oozed from the mouth and nostrils . . . many of the bodies were recognized with difficulty." The men found near the furnace had been transformed the farthest from men into monsters: "The head and face were greatly swollen, the features distorted, &c., fluid from the mouth dark and red; eyes prominent and somewhat reddened; abdomen much distended with gas, &c., strong odours from the bodies; patches of a red colour observed on various parts . . . the skin of two of the bodies was charred in several places."[59]

But gory descriptions also reflected surprise about the very variety of ways in which workers' bodies could interact with machines. Workers were scalped and lost eyes or ears.[60] Whirling belts caused compound fractures of the legs.[61] In one very early case of a worker falling into a machine and being killed, the London *Times* noted, "A few days ago a young man working at the iron foundry at Rotherhithe, fell into the slatting mill, when in an instant he was cut into seven pieces. His head and bones at length stopped the mill, which was thought a very extraordinary thing, which set the men to seek into the cause of it, when they found this shocking spectacle."[62]

Most of the time the view of violent death and mutilation to which newspaper readers were privy was even more graphic than what spectators on the scene saw. After the Pemberton Mill in Massachusetts collapsed, and a corner of City Hall was converted into a makeshift morgue, the more gruesome corpses were covered for the sake of "humanity." Newspaper readers, however, learned that "Twenty-seven bodies had been carried there, and nearly all presented a spectacle of frightful wounds and bruises and showed signs of painful death . . . They lay as they had been recovered from the ruins, some nearly naked and covered with blood, or blackened with dirt and smoke."[63]

Accident descriptions were generally gorier before the Civil War; war, combined with photography, familiarized people on both sides of the Atlantic with the appearance of mutilated corpses. Nonetheless, the fascination with mutilation on the job did not completely cease. A late-nineteenth-century Wilmington, Delaware, newspaper described one explosion as carrying its victims clear across the Brandywine River, reducing their flesh to pieces so small that it had to be collected in buckets. In addition, Thomas Knox, badly burned by inhaling fire, "was a pitiable sight, with his hair burned from his head and face and his lips swollen to several times their usual size. His face was literally baked and he could not be told from a negro."[64] The force of technology gone awry was powerful enough to turn a white man into a black man.

The logical end of gothic and gory newspaper description was the sublime— a level of destruction that filled the observer with wonder and emotion and literally beggared description. Taking a page from the Romantic poets, Victorian journalists described workplace disasters as indescribably horrific, while simultaneously attempting to describe them: "The loud wailing of widows and the shrill cry of orphans so suddenly made; the passionate grief of mothers and the lamentations of brothers and sisters so unexpectedly bereaved; together with the deep and heart-sickening emotion of the spectators . . . combined to produce an impression which few can adequately conceive and which none, who did not witness it, can fully understand."[65]

T. Wemyss Reid, the correspondent for the *Newcastle Daily Chronicle,* commented on a long funeral procession after the Hartley colliery cave-in, "It is impossible to describe the effect produced by this strange procession of death."[66] An editorial in the same newspaper showed the editors were searching in vain for a literary genre that would do justice to everyone's overwrought emotions. "We cannot more appropriately characterize the Hartley catastrophe than as an all-absorbing drama—a combination of life and death, of hope and despair, or horror, suspense, and dismay, of moral heroism and physical endurance, such as never [a] poet imagined in his most inspired moments."[67] In this case, the truth made a more absorbing narrative than fiction.

The level of gory detail present in the Victorian newspaper is missing from modern disaster coverage, but we cannot assume that the Victorians found it as offensive as modern readers might. This was a society much more familiar with death than our own. Workers who were fatally injured on the job were brought to their homes, where they expired in full sight of their families, and were laid out on the only beds in the house. Who, after all, had an extra room in which the injured party could expire in peace?[68] As the *Times* noted after the Wallsend colliery explosion of 1835, "In one instance two brothers were laid on the same bed, and in another house lay, stretched side by side, the father and son. In almost every case the body was strewed with evergreen and flowers; with the parents, sisters, or brothers, weeping around the bed of death.[69]

In an era without newspaper photographs, the exacting description of dead bodies was titillating and sold newspapers—a pornography of death. The editor of the *American Watchman* acknowledged as much when describing the 1818 gunpowder explosion at DuPont: "endeavouring to avoid the Editorial sin of spinning out horrible descriptions and wracking the nerves of others for the sake of selfish profit or amusement of the idle."[70] But gory descriptions also conveyed other lessons. They reinforced the notion that, even in the face of the great inventions and enormous optimism of the nineteenth century, humans were fragile, and life was easily extinguished. To a few, as to the editor of the *British Miner and General Newsman,* these gory descriptions conveyed a lesson of personal responsibility as well:

What if some of the horrifying remnants of the many explosions were placed before the next meeting of the coal trade, stern in all their ghastly hideousness— some without limbs, some with faces which were once as joyous as their own, but upon which a smile could never show itself again, because that every feature had been blown or battered into one; some with sockets where the eyes had been, but with no eyes remaining. Such an array of horrors would surely induce the mine owners of this country to consider more anxiously the safety of those by whom their wealth is produced.[71]

In most cases, however, editors printed accident reports without further commentary or calls for specific change. Like murders most foul, cases of rape and incest, or the results of natural disasters, workplace accidents were regrettable but impossible to eliminate.

The Heroism of the Worker

Although the nineteenth-century workplace was clearly the site of much death and destruction, comparisons between industrialization and wartime, and emphasis on the heroism of the worker, helped to reposition this carnage as necessary sacrifice.[72] Thomas Tancred, author of the first Parliamentary report by the Midland Mining Commission, noted in passing that "there is a regular system of relief for men wounded or killed *in the service* (for no other than military terms are appropriate to the subject)."[73] *The Lancet*, England's premier medical journal, commented on the casualties wreaked by the Hartley colliery cave-in, "Such a loss of life, from any sudden accident in Great Britain, has not taken place since the rebellion of 1745. We can only compare it to a battle-field after an engagement."[74] Similarly, Edwin Chadwick and others reporting on the toll of dead and injured in railway construction noted that the number of casualties on this one project was nearly equal to the casualties of a campaign or severe battle—3 percent killed, and 14 percent wounded.[75]

The American writer Jennie Collins described the fall of the Pemberton mill in a style that recalled the chaos of the battlefield. "Headless, armless, crushed, torn, and dissevered bodies, soaking in blood, were drawn out to get at the living, whose cries could be heard far, far down beneath the rubbish. Fainting ones, slashed and mangled ones, living and dying ones, came swiftly by on the shoulders of stout men, while the wild and frenzied assembly of relatives shouldered, crowded, and fought for a glimpse of each bleeding mass, to know if it were the body of their beloved."[76] In this description it is the "shoulders of stout men," clearly workers, which break through the chaos and move the rescue along.

Anthony Bale interprets the language of worker heroism and the workplace as wartime through a Marxist framework, claiming that limping workers or industrial amputees came to symbolize oppressive capitalist labor relations, and to embody the abuse of power.[77] Occasionally, workers did deploy language in that way, as when the *Warehousemen and Drapers Trade Journal* likened service on the British railways to service against the Ashanti, but without the pensions and the good war stories.[78] It must be remembered, however, that despite the carnage of the civil war, in both England and the United States wartime images were contested. War deaths were considered heroic as much as tragic by many at least until the First World War, when the glory of war finally gave way to cynicism.[79] In the midst of the heroic narrative of industrialization in the nineteenth century, injured workers might be perceived as participants in, rather than strictly innocent victims of, battle. The similarity between heroic wartime and industrial production was enhanced, for example, by the proposals of the Order of St. John of Jerusalem in England that all collieries and other large employers train ambulance crews. As in wartime, they were advised to keep on hand such wartime medical supplies as "Moffit's Battlefield Splints," an "army hospital attendants' dressing case," and the two-wheeled Neuss hand-litter, which was then in use by the Prussian army.[80]

Like the battlefield in wartime, the workplace in time of danger provided working-class men with the opportunity to act out their deep attachments to each other. Collins wrote of two male friends, Mortley and Wesley, who worked in a factory in Chicopee, Massachusetts, in 1854. One day, Mortley got his hand caught in a pulley, and Wesley, seeing that his friend's hand was in danger, used his foot to throw off the belt that was about to draw his friend's hand in. Wesley injured his ankle by doing this, and Mortley had the forefinger of his right hand crushed. Although the injuries were permanent, the two remained inseparable, and the following year, took as their wives a pair of sisters. When Wesley died young, Mortley anonymously donated money to his widow. Monthly deposits into her bank account continued until Mortley was finally killed in a boiler explosion seven years later.[81]

Workers themselves celebrated acts of heroism in the wake of mine disasters in both patriotic and nationalistic terms. Fred Albert wrote a song that was sold as a keepsake to benefit the national Colliery Fund and later won a prize at the Welsh National Eisteddfodd in 1867:

> I'll sing a song of suffering and bravery combined
> The like of which no parallel in history we find.
> Of the men who were imprisoned in the pit at Pontypridd
> And their truly gallant comrades who their work so nobly did.

Albert described the miners working underground in dreadful darkness, minding their own business, when all of a sudden water rushed in and they were trapped. All was not lost, however: "Though it was thought that death was nigh—pluck and skill prevails; Bravely they were rescued by their comrades down in Wales." Five men were trapped underground, with nothing to eat but candle grease. If ever men stood upon the brink of death, it was these five; but just when the water was up to their waists, they were saved by the courage of the Welsh: "All honor to the Welshmen, the saviors and the saved; another mark of honor on our banner they have graved . . . and children yet unborn shall live to hear the glorious tales, of the rescuers and the rescued from the colliery in Wales."[82]

The heroism shown by rescuers in these situations was described as transcending class, although occasionally the rhetoric used to congratulate workers on their heroism ended up emphasizing class distinctions. The South Shields Committee report on safety in mines retold the account of a heroic rescue; "The men who were exerting themselves for the recovery of their unfortunate friends, acted with a solemn, high-wrought, steady courage, without bustle, scarcely with a remark," thus reflecting human nature "in its most vigorous, perfect, and ennobling moments."[83] The *Newcastle Chronicle* painted a portrait of the Hartley rescuers resting in their cabin. "While the ruddy glare of the fire was cast over their broad, manly features and well-moulded forms, they seemed to be the living embodiment of all those attributes of courage and strength which . . . [distinguish] the inhabitants of the British Isles."[84] Philadelphia lawyer William P. Brobson, having recently witnessed a gunpowder explosion at the Du Pont factory, mused about the workers who continued to work there, "They are fortunate who can fix themselves in this kind of insensibility, which probably constitutes, in the great mass of mankind what is called courage or bravery."[85] In a similar vein, after the Hartley disaster, the *Illustrated London News* praised "manifestations of self-sacrificing courage, of magnanimous oblivion of self, of cool presence of mind in view of appalling dangers, of readiness to do and to dare anything for the sake of saving life," which had been observed around the blocked coal shaft. At the same time, its correspondent noted that "these efforts . . . have disclosed to us a rich vein of character imbedded beneath the uncomely exterior of a rude and uncultivated class which ought to raise them in the estimation of the public and bespeak for them its warmest sympathy."[86]

Rude and uncultivated as they might have been, industrial rescuers were rewarded like wartime heroes. In the wake of the Hartley colliery disaster, a Presentation Committee funded and oversaw the production of handsome gold medals to reward the rescuers.[87] The reverse side of each medal details, in a style approaching socialist realism, the barechested rescuers shoveling debris from the sprawled bodies of the dead as Mercury looks on. The Order of

St. John publicly awarded its own Order of Merit, along with other incentives, to Frederick Vickers and Elijah Hallam, who rescued survivors at the Albert Colliery in 1875. As he presented the two men with their medals, Sir Edmund Lechmere, secretary of the order, noted that, as in wartime, heroism in the aftermath of workplace accidents transcended class: "True chivalry may exist in every class and condition of men; its impulses may beat in every breast, whether that breast be covered by the broadcloth of the gentleman or by the working dress of the collier."[88]

The reconfiguration of workplace sacrifice as wartime sacrifice helped to gloss over the real burdens that accidents caused. John Chiddy, a platelayer on the Bristol and Exeter railroad, was killed while trying to prevent an accident. A block of stone fell on the line when the express train was only a few hundred yards off. Chiddy ran and removed the stone—thus potentially saving not only lives but property—but was caught by the train, and the railroad refused to pay his survivors any compensation. Lord Elcho had gotten up in the Commons to present the case, remarking "that for an equivalent deed of bravery on the field Chiddy would have been decorated with the Victoria Cross, or at sea with the Albert Medal." Although only £3 17s. had been raised for the family, the government offered Chiddy's family a posthumous medal rather than a pension.[89]

The many analogies between wartime and the workplace do not end here. Sadly, just as in wartime, industrial accidents might leave in their wake unknown and unmarked dead. After the Pembroke Mill collapse, nine bodies and parts of the remains of others were buried in two boxes in the Lawrence cemetery—the unknown soldiers of the technology war, a war that knew no rules of just combat.[90] Similarly, just as every English town would eventually sport its own Great War memorial to testify to unprecedented carnage, so the churchyard at Earsdon even today features an obelisk dedicated to the men and boys who died in the nearby Hartley colliery cave-in in 1862.[91]

Nineteenth-century newspaper readers were presented with news of workplace accidents that was couched in a number of different popular forms. Accidents were presented as incursions on the family, helping to convert working-class families into suffering members of the deserving poor; they were presented as judgments by God, or as man's doomed and foolish attempts to avoid the judgments of providence; or they were expressions of a sacrifice akin to that shouldered by soldiers in wartime. Readers were particularly well-saturated with descriptions of the amazing and new ways in which trains, mine collapses, industrial machinery, and exploding boilers could reshape the human body.

As a result of all this coverage, many outsiders felt drawn to the scenes of accidents; the increased ease of transportation gave rise to a set of "accidental tourists." By the hundreds, they rushed to the scene of major workplace disasters to take in the ambience. In contrast with present practice, visitors did not come to share sadness or to create "instant shrines" to the deceased, but rather to be entertained by novelty or moved by human suffering. Thus Thomas Knox reported that in the wake of the Avondale, Pennsylvania, mine-shaft fire and cave-in, thousands of people converged on the town, some to help and others as sightseers.[92] After an 1865 mine explosion in Steubensville, Ohio, miners were drawn up burnt and insensible, only to be confronted with observers at the surface who joked, "Oh, go for a dram, that's what they want."[93] The tourists who flocked to the collapsed Pemberton mill site took away souvenirs of the disaster. A person from St. Louis got a large bundle, including burned fragments of the victims' clothing, spindles and yarn from the mill, and part of the fallen building. Finally, orders had to be given against people getting close enough to the accident scene to walk away with the evidence.[94] These were not people who had come to the scene in order to help; they were seemingly unconvinced by the humanitarian narrative.

Finding the Worker's Voice: The Labor Press

Given the background noise represented by newspaper reports with their formulaic presentations, it is easy to lose sight of the way in which nineteenth-century workers perceived and categorized the accidents that befell them on the job. Workers' views can, however, be partially teased out, by looking at a number of sources that historians have not mined comprehensively, including broadsides, personal narratives, testimony before government commissions, and popular poetry and song. These sources suggest that working people were influenced by the dominant discourse surrounding workplace accidents, but that workers were also deeply concerned about the financial impact of the accidents—something that the newspapers' presentation tended to ignore.

Broadsides intended for the consumption of working people shared many narrative strategies with newspapers mainly consumed by middle-class readers but, more often than the newspapers, drew larger conclusions about reform instead of serving as a cleansing device for the individual conscience. In the area around Newcastle, England, coal mine accidents were so frequent that printers made a cottage industry of printing broadsides to announce accidents. Broadsides alerted readers to the "dreadful" nature of the explosion and outcome and provided basic information about the causes of accidents, the number of casualties, the number and condition of the survivors left behind, and the location and disposition of inquests.[95] Like newspaper articles, they drew heavily on the traditional forms to relate the tension and grief suffered by workers' families. One described how "as usual, the relatives and friends of those in the mine were first at the shaft, followed by numerous parties, giving vent to their feelings in loud lamentations, while others more firm, waited in deep suspense and keen anxiety to know the result of the disaster."[96] Another noted that "the cries of women and children was most awful, all hastening to the scene of death, eagerly looking for, and inquiring after, those who were so dear unto them, and who, such a short time before, had left them happy and healthy."[97] A broadside from Jarrow went a step further by quoting the miners' widows in their grief:

> Here was the mother crying "O my child, my poor Tommy, he's lost, he's lost! for ever! my God! that I should live to see this day." Another might be seen crying for her husband, one of this number had been married only three weeks. She screamed "O John Wilson, John Wilson, are you for ever gone, are you lost to my sight for ever. No more shall I see you, no more, no more. His face blackened in death? Perhaps he's torn limb from limb, he may be crushed, and I unable to recognize him."[98]

Another broadside contained a prayer for the souls of those killed, in the form of a poem.[99]

Broadsides also shared the newspapers' concern with the physical condition of the killed and wounded, seemingly with little concern for the feelings of family members. In one case, "Mr. Hunter, the Overman, had met the fire and was so severely mutilated that he was unfit to be seen, there were several other men and boys about the place which shared the same fate, even so much, that some of their heads have not yet been found."[100] In another case, "many of the persons brought to bank with life were much burnt; one man's arm was so severely scorched that the Flesh dropped from it while enduring the operation of dressing."[101] Occasionally, these broadsides attempted to invoke a mental or physical picture of the devastation. One broadside commemorating a pit explosion at Jarrow in 1845 showed the top of a pit with an enormous explosion coming out of the area in front of the headstock and coals flying into the air.[102] Another likened the sound of an explosion to the report of an artillery gun; an immense volume of smoke then rose out from the pit like a cloud. As it traveled north, the cloud covered everything with soot.[103]

But while broadsides intended for working people often adopted the same format and some of the same language as that printed in newspapers, the ephemera could and did serve a political purpose. The author of one broadside was so impressed by the state of the casualties after one mine explosion that he recommended higher pay for all miners.[104] Another broadside balladeer wrote about the contrast between the financial rewards of mining and its earthly punishments:

This is thy work, fell tyrant! This the miner's common lot!
In danger's darkling den he toils, and dies lamented not!
Ah! who regards the mining slave, that for his country's wealth
Resigns his sleep, his pleasures, home, his freedom and his health?
From the glad skies and fragrant fields he cheerfully descends
And eats his bread in stenchy caves, where his existence ends.
Aye! this is he the masters grind and level with the dust
The SLAVE that barters life to gain the pittance of a crust![105]

An 1850 broadside in the wake of an explosion at the Usworth colliery informed readers that "you have been appealed to by placard and half-bill, and through the public press, to assist the miners in obtaining a preventative measure for these awful calamities. It is painful to state that such appeals have met with but indifferent attention." Even public meetings had failed to attract much of an audience. The broadside's author warned that the Usworth calamity was just a shadow of things to come. "The miners are quite sure that more explosions are in embryo. There are more collieries than this which are about to blow up; and it was but the other week that a workman at the above colliery refused to work, because of the danger, but was compelled to return to work by ORDER OF THE MAGISTRATE!"[106] Another broadside printed inquest testimony pointing to the fact that workers had worried that a mine was unsafe well in advance of the actual explosion.[107] For unionists and other coalfield activists, broadsides could be weapons in a war against apathy.

Newspapers published by working people or aimed primarily at a labor audience shared and reflected the political orientation toward accidents and safety that was reflected in the broadsides. The *British Miner and General Newsman* is a case in point. Founded in 1862, the newspaper sought to improve the condition of working miners and to acquaint the public with the "fearful and fatal risks by which the miner is surrounded."[108] The newspaper's editor, having noted that approximately 1,109 British miners had died in mine accidents in 1861, often leaving widows and children without any visible means of support, determined to record in the newspaper every mining accident about which he could gain any information. In addition to the statistics, The *British Miner and General Newsman* printed about two pages' worth of letters in every issue, many of which tied safety in and around the mines to unionization. These letters firmly illustrate that safety and compensation were concerns of the nineteenth-century worker. Richard Mitchell of Barnsley encouraged miners to combine lest they "go on and suffer, and die at twenty-seven, be slaughtered at the rate of 1000 a year, endure the pauperism resulting from 10,000 permanent disablements, coupled with 40,000 to 50,000 accidents of a less serious nature, all of which cause an appalling amount of physical suffering and monetary loss to the family of the miner." A Northumberland miner called for the establishment of a Permanent Relief Fund, since "no man knows when he leaves his happy fireside in the morning but ere night he may be carried home a mangled corpse."[109]

The concerns about safety reflected in these letters mirrored a concern expressed on a more everyday level in the localities. In Wigan, miners interested in enlarging the Miners' Sick and Provident Benefit Society heard the annual figures on deaths in the mines read aloud, and responded with "hear, hear," when one of their number suggested that "if 1000 persons were killed in a year on the railway, the railway company would have to pay thousands of pounds as compensation, while nothing was paid to the poor colliers . . . Some provision ought to be made for them."[110] The editor of the miners' newspaper denied that the annual carnage was inevitable, noting " it would be very much diminished if the inspectors of coal mines could succeed in enforcing obedience to their regulations and that obedience would be far better enforced if it were made the direct and palpable interest of owners and managers of coal mines to observe and enforce them."[111]

Labor newspapers like the *British Miner,* the Chartist *Northern Star,* or the *Ten Hours' Advocate* chronicled workplace accidents with a particular focus on the number of deaths and injuries and on the results of coroners' inquests. Often, they had a particular political goal; the *Ten Hours' Advocate* reported industrial accidents in the context of violations against the 1846 Factory Act, which required some dangerous machinery to be fenced in.[112] Despite the magnitude of their coverage of accidents and the political context into which they were set, these newspapers had little impact outside the community of workers themselves. They could help unify workers in their own quest for legislative reform, but could do nothing to convince the majority of Members of Parliament of the immediacy of their cause.

The Individual Worker

If the middle-class press focused on religion and emotion, and the labor press focused on revealing the number of workplace accidents and calling for political rectification of safety issues, how did this congeries of ideas percolating around in nineteenth-century society trickle down to the individual worker? What of this did workers accept, and what did they reject? Some evidence can be found that suggests that individual workers integrated many different explanations for, and ideas about, workplace accidents into their understandings of the world—from religious ideas to fatalism, from emotion to stoicism. What links most workers' musings on workplace accidents, however, is a focus on the economic impact.

Many workers were touched by the evangelical religion of their time, and for Christians of any social class, an accident was an opportunity to rethink one's relationship with God and to prepare for the inevitable.[113] Some mine accidents in particular encouraged such thought, resembling as they did the "rapture" of Christian premillennial evangelicalism, taking one workman and sparing the one right next to him. John Buddle, a mine "viewer," testified with wonder about how a miner had brought his son to work one day, for his first day of work as a trapper boy. The boy was visiting him when an explosion occurred. The man had the boy by the hand, but as the man was standing in a little niche, the force of the explosion grabbed his son's body and propelled it up the shaft and out, while sparing the father.[114]

Particularly religious workers who were killed in workplace accidents were celebrated as exemplary lives, sometimes in ways that were financially productive. William Thew, a seventeen-year-old collier, was killed along with his father, an older brother, and seventy-two others in an 1815 inundation at the Heaton Main colliery near Newcastle. A Methodist who regularly attended Sunday school, William managed to scratch an inspirational message into his tin lunch pail before he died. The box said on one side, "Fret not, dear mother, for we were singing while we had time, and praising God. Mother, follow God more than ever I did." The other side contained a message dictated by William Thew's father: "If Johnny [the youngest brother in the family] is saved, be a good lad to God, and thy mother." After the inundation, this amazing memento of working-class piety and familial love was loaned to a local minister, who charged the curious to see it and was able to raise more than £130 for the support of Thew's widowed mother. When that money ran out, in the 1840s, a pamphlet was printed describing Thew's life and death, again with the express purpose of raising funds.[115]

John Thompson, killed in the Felling disaster, was another deceased worker celebrated for his piety. Thompson and another man killed had been Methodist class leaders, men of "sterling piety, uniform practice, and burning zeal for the salvation of souls and the prosperity of the Church of God."[116] Thompson had, in fact, been unpopular among his workmates due to his propensity to preach to them. Shortly after Thompson's untimely death, a friend published his diary, which showed him to have been a great Bible reader who attended chapel and love feasts. Thompson's last diary entry expressed his satisfaction with God and his lot: "The Lord is good to me and my family; there are many in these trying times who know what it is to want bread; and we do not. O! That we may be thankful, and love in return with all our hearts."[117] For the author, Thompson's life was a lesson to other workmen "to keep the true believer always upon his watch."[118] "An Undergraduate" who wrote a poem about the Hartley disaster drew a similar conclusion. He asserted that God had some reason for allowing the disaster to happen and included in his poem an improbable scene of last-minute, underground conversions, led by a workman whose companions had previously scoffed at his piety.[119]

For workers as well as their observers and social betters, concern for the Christian "good death" created social pressure to reinterpret workplace accidents, to find last-minute conversions and speeches of repentance that would make up in some way for the absence of family at the bedside. One late-nineteenth-century story about miners, published in a working-class newspaper, ends not with the expected rescue, but rather with last-minute conversion and supplication to God. Hartley survivor Thomas Watson became a popular speaker in the Newcastle area after the disaster precipitated his religious conversion.[120] In a similar vein, former collier Richard Weaver appealed to fellow miners with the story of a fatally injured co-worker who died the nineteenth-century equivalent of a good Christian death, with his wife giving his grimy face a farewell kiss and his daughter coming from the factory to witness his last moments.[121]

An American, Patrick Vance, wrote to his son's employer in the hopes that his son had died a good death; "The only grief that strikes us at present is to think he was either blown up, or taken away in a moment, perhaps without time to pray to God for to have mercy on his soul . . . let me know everything respecting his death."[122] Similarly, the widows of the men killed in the Hartley colliery cave-in might have taken some comfort from the inscription that one of their husbands inscribed in a little notebook found on his body. It indicated that as the air ran out among them, the men sang hymns and one of them repeatedly exhorted the rest to Christian belief.[123] For Victorian readers, rescue from imminent death might not constitute the only possible happy ending.[124]

Even in cases in which the circumstances of death seemed to offer little instruction, workers could find consolation in religion. Peter Dennison, who in 1816 wrote a poem commemorating the inundation of the Hetton Colliery and the subsequent deaths of its workers, turned to the Old Testament for consolation. By combining nonconsecutive verses from Psalm 88, Dennison was able to craft a new psalm, whose opening line addressed the coal miners in particular:

> I am counted with them that go down into the pit; I am as man that hath no strength.
> Free among the dead, like the slain that lie in the grave, whom thou rememberest no more; and they are cut off from thy hand.
> Thou hast put away mine acquaintance far from me: thou hast made me an abomination unto them; I am shut up, and I cannot come forth.
> Mine eye mourneth by reason of affliction; Lord, I have called daily upon thee; I have stretched out my hands unto thee.
> Lover and friend hast thou put far from me, and mine acquaintance into darkness.[125]

Working people involved in accidents were not just the objects of sermons; they also requested sermons. Twenty two of thirty-four men were killed in an explosion at the Hetton colliery in 1860; the survivors called upon a local minister to preach a sermon "to return thanks to God for a merciful as well as a miraculous escape from death, and of affording then an opportunity of adding their quota to the fund being raised for the relief of those who have to mourn the loss of a father, a husband, a brother, a son."[126] Sermons were also preached in the wake of the Hartley disaster, and the crowds of mine widows and orphans were said to have taken particular comfort from the words of the Old Hundredth Psalm: "He can create, and he can destroy."[127] John Roberton told of one railway worker who, after a devastating workplace accident, was more concerned by his failure to get anyone to read the Scriptures to him than he was about his bodily discomfort.[128]

The death of a loved one in a mine could also test religious convictions, as workers bargained with God to save their imperiled loved ones or attempted to bear sacrifice with Christian resignation. Jim Bullock's older brother was killed in a mine early in the twentieth century. "When my father was told that John Willie was trapped, we heard him breathing heavily, and then a kind of half-stifled sobbing, and him saying, 'Oh Lord, it is hard, help us now. If we ever needed Thy help we need it this mornin, but if it is Thy will, if it is Thy will, Thy will be done." Bullock's miner father knelt by the side of his bed and prayed; "Oh God, help us to bear this heavy cross thou hast given us. Oh give me help to keep my faith in thee."[129] Bullock described his mother's actions as she kept vigil at the pithead as those of a mining Pietá:

> She just stood there, immovable, like a statue; a living symbol of real tragic heartbroken grief. Friendly neighbors kept bringing her cups of tea but there was no conversation, just sympathy of silence that somehow one could feel passing from them to her. Then my brother's body was brought out and she followed the stretcher to his house and bathed his broken body. She cradled it to her breast and kept murmuring, "Oh Lord help us, help me to bear it, help me to bear it."[130]

At least one group of mining wives dispensed with Christian methods entirely. When an explosion rocked the Felling Colliery in 1812, the grieving widows turned to a "conjurer," who "had set his spells and charms to work, and penetrated the whole secrets of the mine. It was reported that he discovered one famishing group receiving drops of water from the roof of the mine; another eating their shoes and clothes; and other such tales of misery."[131] Religious interpretations of workplace accidents clearly cut across class, as some workers embraced religion in their house of suffering,

While religious interpretations of workplace accidents and their aftermath did cut across class, financial interpretations did not. Workers emphasized the financial impact of workplace accidents to a much greater degree than did others higher up the social scale. Most nineteenth-century workers who left any record of their feelings about workplace accidents expressed concern about their financial impact, since the idea of being rendered destitute was not to them a cliché that brought to mind Dickens's Tiny Tim, but rather a palpable experience. Workers commented on whether or not their employers paid for their medical expenses.[132] One anonymous miner who began working underground at age 8, in 1853, remembered an accident in which his younger brother had broken a leg. He did recall trauma and discomfort:

I got him out of the pit and they put him into a coal cart, and we set off on a journey of six or seven miles on a road some places being very good, but mostly very bad. You can imagine the plight of my poor brother, as he was being jostled about for such a long distance and with a broken leg, being the 11th day of March and the pitiless rain beating down on us all the way.[133]

His memory of the discomfort, however, was inextricable from the accident's financial consequences. After traveling a distance of four or five miles they were intercepted by a doctor.

It would be deemed inhuman today to allow anyone to travel such a distance with a broken leg without being attended to. But such was the case of my brother even though the colliery proprietor was extremely wealthy . . . the doctor set the leg and he was off work about 20 weeks. This was a serious loss to us as my father had to pay another lad to hurry for him."[134]

The same miner noted that after another accident, a roof fall, the miners' tools were all buried under the rubble and they were told they would have to pay for new ones.[135]

The financial toll of workplace accidents for American families is illustrated in the letters that the Du Ponts received from the relatives of workmen killed in their gunpowder mills. Jane Reed wrote to Alfred Du Pont from Richmond, Indiana, complaining that the little money she was able to reap from W. Gegan's estate was a poor recompense for what she had already spent. Among the outstanding expenses were a $50 doctor's bill, $30 in store debt, $74 for two nurses, and $37 in boarding and ale. In addition, Reed was responsible for caring for and boarding out Gegan's two children.[136] Elizabeth MacFarlane, whose father Robert had died on the job, wrote to Du Pont with a plaintive plea:

Sir: I take my pen to ask a favour of you and that is to let me know if our money is entirely lost I would like to know I think it is hard that us poor children has to be ronged out of what little My Father left to help is a long through this unfriendly world I have been working and trying since I was ten years old to get a home for my Mother but all in vain but young am I but I have had a grate deal of trouble since my father died I have been draged about from place to place My poor mother is almost harte broken with trouble. Wil you be so kind as to write to me and let me know if you think we wil ever get any of that money.[137]

Two Irish sisters wrote to Du Pont thanking him for giving their brother a Christian burial and inquired about the £8 remaining on the books in his name.[138] For Irish families accustomed to receiving remittances, and by the end of the 1840s facing the ravages of famine, the loss of a worker to an American accident had to be a terrible tragedy.

Actions as well as words conveyed the primacy of the financial struggle among workers, as in the ritual of "killing a dead man." Knocking out a pit prop and allowing a piece of roof to fall on the head of a man who had died underground of some organic cause (like a heart attack) might bring some employer compensation to a needy family.[139] Even for the twentieth-century miner, the struggle to wrest compensation from sometimes unscrupulous employers, and the contrasting willingness of the community of miners to pitch in after an accident, were central to the experience and interpretation of workplace accidents.[140]

Financial considerations linked to workplace safety impelled workers to take political action. English miners on strike in 1844 cited lack of compensation for workplace accidents as a major grievance and lobbied for the institution of "smart money" that made wages for injury a matter of right rather than privilege.[141] At one meeting in the Tyneside area, Thomas Cleugh, of Thornley, described being overcome by gas in the mine where he worked.

> On his recovering, however, he had to go back again, and the consequence was, that he was laid up for fifteen weeks. He then applied for smart money but could obtain none, because it was not in the bond [collective labor contract]; and he therefore thought it hard, that while a man received smart money when his arm or leg was broken, he could not be remunerated when his constitution was impaired by poisonous air.[142]

The striking workers also sought a guarantee of sufficient medical attendance and medicine, and that in the event of a miner's death, free house rent, fuel, and £2 for funeral expenses would be granted to the widow.[143]

Financial hardship hurt more than just the wallet. It undermined a workingman's confidence in his masculinity, his role as provider for the family. Of course, working-class wives provided valuable services to their families by taking in boarders, being thrifty, and scavenging materials, but all of these services went largely unacknowledged—the male was supposed to be the winner of the household's "family wage."[144] "Jane B," a working-class wife, acknowledged as much when she wrote to the British Miner and General Newsman in 1862, "My man will either have to join your fund, or I will take my tea without sugar and enter him. Better take tea without sugar than have to take tea without either bread or a man to work for any."[145] Workers who had been injured or seen friends injured on the job often spoke or wrote of the length of time they were unable to work. Many workers relied on mutual benefit clubs for their subsistence when injured, and the inability to work was the definition of injury or sickness in many of the clubs' rules. But the ability or inability to work was also the inability to perform the male role. Permanent inability to perform the male role due to a spinal injury sustained on the job was seen as a fate worse than death. As Jim Bullock explained, nineteenth-century workers paralyzed by accidents spent their remaining years on a waterbed,

> helpless, completely dependent on relatives and subject to awful bedsores . . . Besides the pain involved, the loss of independence affected them mentally . . . Usually they were incontinent, and under the sparse, primitive conditions in which they normally lived, this was an addition which made life virtually impossible for both himself and his relatives. It was all right when it first happened, when all his friends and relatives were helpful and sympathetic; but as he lay there, a physical wreck, and he knew he was becoming a burden, he began to grumble and curse about the cruel blow struck him in the prime of life. His complete manhood had been taken away from him.[146]

The importance of manfully remaining at work after an injury led B. L. Coombes, injured by a roof fall, to pretend not to be injured until he had finished loading some coal. "When finishing time came I could not put my foot to the ground, and had to be carried out after a few vain attempts to walk."[147] For Coombes, the difficulty of collecting compensation for his injury not only made his rehabilitation harder, but also encouraged him to return to work before the original injury was healed, causing a re-injury within a week.[148] Alexander Boyle of Manchester was working on the Stockport Railway when a rail fell on his foot and crushed it. His comment, "Oh my God, Martin, I am lamed; I shall be forced to go home; I can't stand," suggests that the reality of being "forced to go home" was just as painful as the injury itself.[149]

Adult male workers who had been permanently disabled on the job were objects of pity but also objects of scorn. A union newspaper, the *Railway Service Gazette,* described the armies of workers who had been disabled by railroad work: "If ever railway reform reaches such a pitch of perfection as to set directors pondering on the advisability of atoning for past neglect toward their old servants, what a spectacle might be provided by gathering together for review the great army of cripples who, during the past few years, have lost legs, arms, and sustained spinal injuries, dooming them throughout the remainder of their wretched, lingering existence, to crutches."[150] According to the union, part of what made the lives of the disabled so "wretched" and "lingering" was the decision of railway owners to relegate amputees to employment only out of the sight of the public, at jobs that tended to pay less, in order to avoid offending public sensibilities.[151] Far worse off than one shunted from the public eye was a formerly able workman now completely unable to work: "A man whose frame is shattered to such an extent as to render him a cripple for the remainder of his existence, is practically dead so far as active work is concerned."[152]

Behind workers' concern for workplace safety was the fear not only of losing one's personal identity and role, but also of losing one's friends, relatives, and physical space. After the New Poor Law of 1834, England's destitute poor were taunted by the specter of the workhouse, presided over by what Victorians invariably called the "cold hand of charity." Bad luck could send even a thrifty man to the workhouse; one collier who had been employed at the same place for twenty-two years, paying fourpence every two weeks for medical care, had been burned so badly at work that his arm was tucked and could not be lifted as high as his shoulder, making him unfit for pit work. After two years, the company stopped paying him field pay and said that now it was the parish's job to provide for him.[153] An injured stonemason, who by dint of constant complaining was able to wrest a settlement from his benefit society, thanked his union brothers "for this munificent gift, and I trust, by economy and frugality, that it will be the means of preserving myself and family from the dreadful horrors of a union workhouse, which must inevitably have been our fate had it not been for the noble gift of my brethren in union."[154] Nothing was worse than being cast off from friends and relatives. After the Felling Colliery explosion, some widows said that they could have borne their loss better had all their neighbors been rendered as miserable and destitute as themselves; communal poverty and grief was bearable; individual poverty and grief was not.[155]

Financial need and social expectations about manliness contributed to a certain stoicism or fatalism about workplace accidents.[156] Colliery viewer Nicholas Wood testified before a Parliamentary Select Committee that there was no difficulty engaging workmen to fill the place of others who had died in an exploded mine.[157] B. L. Coombes, elaborating on this point, described a cycle: in the immediate aftermath of an accident, colliers would be filled with fear, and some might even stay away from work. After a while, however, they would forget about the danger, only to be reminded forcefully by the next accident.[158] Colliers sometimes found themselves pressured to choose between avoiding danger and being dismissed.[159] The statutes governing collieries prevented workers from leaving their places underground when they sensed danger. And even pit widows were often only able to survive by putting their young children to pit work, and thus the cycle of work, death, forgetting, and returning to work repeated itself.[160] As the United Pitmen stated in 1825, "To no set of men do the beautiful words of our burial service apply with more force and propriety than to the pitmen; 'in the midst of life we are in death.'"[161]

The agency that miners were able to exert was circumscribed by law and by lack of occupational mobility. They therefore reconciled themselves to the dangers of their workplace by being prepared. In South Staffordshire, miners themselves kept on hand supplies for the surgeon who might treat them.[162] They developed their own local forms of expertise about avoiding accidents— expertise which might have no basis in reality, but which was reassuring. Bolton miner David Swallow reported that because many miners didn't understand the mechanism of gas explosions, their own ability to duck the odds day after day bulked larger in their own minds than any scientific advice about safety that might be given to them by mine viewers. "Where one man happens to meet with an accident, it is considered a sort of misfortune or bad luck; the man says 'I have carried it on so long,' or 'I have worked with a lamp red hot.'"[163]

They also called in supernatural assistance. According to one mine owner, the men in his pit considered that God had rewarded them with a good safety record because they met and prayed every day during their lunch break.[164] Just as prayer could avert tragedy, so sin could bring it on. One collier had been caught removing a co-worker's metal tag from a full cart of coal and replacing it with his own (thus getting credit for another's work). One of the man's sons got his arm caught between tubs and broken; another was killed a year later by a runaway tub; a cousin who worked with the latter son had his leg broken. As Jim Bullock noted, "so terribly did bad luck pursue that family that four sons were out of the pit injured, without compensation, all at the same time. Whether this all had anything to do with the father's misdeed, anyone can judge, but there is no doubt that everyone down the pit thought that it was the hand of fate working."[165] Miner Robert Redding was able to avoid being killed in an explosion in the Jarrow colliery because he had heeded a supernatural warning. He had been out of work for nine days with an injured finger, and would have gone back to work, but "just as I was going to the pit, a woman came to me and said, 'Don't you go to the pit!' and as sure as God is in heaven, some accident will happen to-day, for I dreamt last night the same dream that I did the night I lost my father by the accident fifteen years since."[166]

Workers at the Du Pont gunpowder manufactory were influenced to stay and work there through a combination of high wages, employer reassurances, and a moral pressure that appealed to their pride as men.[167] After an 1847 explosion, Du Pont noted to one of his business contacts that "very few of our hands have left, for out of so many it was out of the question that all should be possessed of the moral courage required to bear up against the sight of friends torn to pieces without a moment's warning; but taken as a whole our people are behaving nobly." DuPont noted that he was able to short-circuit workers' fear of gunpowder work by making sure that he or another member of the family was present "at each and every spot where danger can be anticipated."[168] After another explosion, DuPont estimated that he only needed about a day to restore confidence in his worried workforce.[169]

Clearly, workers had to balance financial impact of accidents against the need for work, however dangerous. But the immediacy of the material aspect of workplace accidents was not the only way in which workers' interpretations diverged from the middle-class versions. The Victorian narrative of workplace accidents was deeply rooted in the emotions, intended as it was to wrench an emotional reaction from the reader. In contrast with the prevailing public style, workers who recounted their workplace injuries to parliamentary investigators very rarely gave any account of the pain they had suffered, even when the temporal distance between any two accidents was an individual's way of marking the passage of time![170] The world of shredded skin and weeping widows seems very distant from the testimony of a worker like Jane Vinay. Although her hand was squeezed in paper mill machinery and she was forced to stay out of work for six weeks, her only comment was that her hand "hurt very much."[171] Similarly an American woman weaver noted of her workplace that "Accidents occur very often. It seems to be of no account to have a finger taken off."[172]

What might account for the failure of injured workpeople to leave accounts of their pain with the bureaucrats who documented their work lives? Pain is a physical sensation, but social norms regulate the degree to which people acknowledge and give vent to their own pain. It is possible that, for working people who lived with higher levels of physical discomfort in their daily lives, the "social definition" of pain was different than it was for physically comfortable middle-class observers.[173] Many workers suffered cold and hunger on a daily basis. Children might experience physical discomfort at home, work, and school. Everyday work practices inflicted pain, whether the acute pain of undermining coal while kneeling or lying down, or the nagging pain of standing for twelve hours a day in a deafening cotton factory, or the chronic pain of having a condition like brown lung or black lung and having no access to a doctor. Furthermore, many workers lacked the florid and colorful vocabularies deployed with such melodramatic effect by Victorian journalists.[174]

A report in the working-class *Beehive* about injuries to a miner named Pickering suggests that the stoicism expected of working-class men might have enhanced their reluctance to talk about pain:

> There he lay on a temporary bed in the house-place in an agony of pain, carefully tended by his wife and daughters, who were administering such remedies as they were able. Around the bed stood a group of grimy colliers, some of whom had been in the pit when the accident happened, and others who had come to assist their afflicted neighbour. As the poor fellow groaned and moved uneasily on his couch, a ready hand was near him to assist and give a cheerful word of encouragement. "I can't lie; I can't sit; I can't stand; what shall I do?" exclaimed the sufferer. "Pray to God to help you through," said his daughter. "Thou'll weather it yet, George," said one of his fellow-workmen; but the moaning of Pickering mingled with the sighs and tears of the women as he feebly urged his friends, if they wanted to see him, to come at once.[175]

While Pickering struggles to find the right words to express the depth of his discomfort, his friends and relatives encourage him to "weather it" or pray to God for relief rather than to lie there moaning. Sighs and tears are reserved for the women present. In a similar incident, miner Thomas Burt, later a member of Parliament (MP), was injured when he stepped into a reservoir of boiling water. "Though he was severely scalded, he decided to make light of it, and limped home on his scalded foot, with the result that when his stocking was pulled off part of the skin came along with it. There was neither working nor walking for some weeks after that."[176] As Burt was pressured by the norms of working-class manhood into a stoicism that exacerbated his original injury, so a Welsh miner later nicknamed "Dai Peg" was moved to make light of his injury. After a sharp stone amputated his foot at the ankle, his one complaint was that he had just purchased a new pair of shoes the previous week.[177]

Trauma surely also encouraged workers to downplay pain in their own narratives. Some workplace accidents were unimaginably wrenching. John Atkinson, a coal hewer, had lost an eleven-year-old son in a mine explosion, and noted: "He was torn limb from limb by the explosion, and different parts of the body were sent to me at different times. I buried him with his body and one leg; another was sent to me next day, and some parts of him were buried that I never saw. The masters treated me with much kindness, and endeavoured to spare my feelings as much as possible."[178] George Pickering, another coal miner, described running from the report of an explosion with his young son running behind him, hanging on to the waistband of his trousers. Succumbing to choke damp, Pickering stumbled over a horse and fell down, and his son lost his grip. George kept running, and managed to save himself, but his boy Thomas was dead.[179] Workers wishing to support their families had to return to workplaces where such scenes had taken place, putting a premium on resilience and giving them good reason to reject narratives of pain.[180]

Parliamentary subcommissioners who interviewed working people collected terse evidence which might suggest emotional detachment from workplace deaths.[181] But it is not clear that the interviewees perceived parliamentary interviews as the proper forum for expressing emotion or volunteering opinions. Workers were asked factual questions and seem to have provided factual answers accordingly (although this could also have been an artifact of the way in which the interviewers recorded the answers). Working people knew their interlocutors as outsiders both to their community and their class—the workers' emotional lives were thus none of their business. Finally, workers, not knowing the uses to which their testimonies might be put may have feared reprisals from their employers if they gave full vent to their feelings.[182] The inability or unwillingness of working people to fully elaborate the impact of workplace accidents for those studying the issue meant that the cultural meanings of such accidents for workers remained less visible than the meanings for onlookers.

Instead of using their stories of workplace hardship to lobby the government for change, workers throughout most of the nineteenth century commemorated their workplace hardships within their own communities, using popular culture. Almost every traditional song that discusses the miner's life advertises the risks that the miner faced. Some of these songs are almost protest songs, attempting to assign blame directly or obliquely for the miner's condition.[183] In one mine song ostensibly written before women were banished from working underground in 1842, the narrator, "Polly Parker," enumerates all the dangers that wait for her underground. In her case, it is her family's poverty, with seven children to support, that has condemned her to her fate.[184] The 1828 dialect song "The Pitman's Pay" takes a more fatalistic tone, describing the miner's life as literally the work of the devil: "A scheme o'senseless pain and strife/Hatchd by wor deadly foe, Awd Harry."[185] "Down in the Coalmine," a music-hall song, adopts a more systemic view of the problem, pointing out that the very fires that made the lives of rich men comfortable are lit at the cost of miners' lives.[186] Another song, "Five in the Morning," presents the listener to a catalogue of causes of death, including broken ropes, gas explosions, and roof falls, and cautions the listener to "look to the danger the miner is in / as he hangs in the air night and morning."[187] The instruction to "look to the danger" is a call to action, or at least to consciousness. While miner's songs are the most numerous, colliers were not the only nineteenth-century occupation whose hazards were commemorated in song; cutlery grinders and textile workers' songs also contained allusions to the occupational dangers they faced.[188]

Elegiac poetry was another socially acceptable outlet for feelings of loss, as expressed by a Tredegar working man after a mine accident at Bedwelty in 1864:

Down in the valley green
With mountains on each side
Twenty five still forms were seen
Brave pit-lads who died.
Mothers there in sorrow groaned
And fathers cried, 'My son, my son.' . . .

They left their homes that morn
The aged and the young
Regardless of the harm
Or dangers that may come.
But ah! that day, it closed in gloom
And bitter tears in the pitman's home.[189]

The poem ends with its author beseeching the Christian reader to pray for the families of the dead, thus combining the emotional impact with families torn asunder and the Christian message. In a work called "The Collier's Appeal to the Country," a pitman poet named R. Holder compares the miner's lot with that of the Israelites in Egypt and calls for a Moses to lead them out of bondage.[190]

Expression through poetry allowed miners to combine sentimentality and emotion with politics. One poem described the dead in sentimental terms but then abruptly shifted feeling and ended with a demand for protection and inspection:

Now to conclude and make an end
Let masters their men defend
See that the laws are carried out

And true protection will come about . . .
Inspectors all your duty do
Have the mines inspected through and through.[191]

Another poem, produced during a period of negotiation between masters
and men in 1844, set the men's grievances and demands to verse:

And the Ten Shillings Smart [money], we will have it is true
And then let them keep the place safe where we hew.
No longer we'll work in the mines without air
Ventilation we'll have and we'll make it our care.
Two shafts they may sink for the down and up-cast
To prevent the strong hydrogen making a blast . . .
Five shillings per week, we all think it too small
For the widow and children when losing their all
A coffin for those who are killed we now crave
With five pounds to lay them with mence in the grave.[192]

A third poem used several stanzas to document the coroner's inquest following one mine explosion and invited the reader to judge whether the verdict
of "accidental death" was fair.[193] Like the singing of songs, the reading of such
poetry was not necessarily a solitary activity; it could be used to stir feelings
at large gatherings.[194]

Workers shared stories, within their own communities, of heroic actions
that testified to deep emotional bonds. Father and son colliers killed in a mine
explosion were found with their arms around each other.[195] Colliers made
strenuous efforts, often risking their own lives, to aid their workmates.[196] One
father, who worked in a lead mine, described how his twelve-year-old son, "a
very fine and strong boy of his age," who had only been in the mine five weeks,
sustained a leg and collarbone fracture. Although the man worked in a distant
part of the mine, when he heard of the accident, he dropped everything and
ran. "When I was told what had happened, I travelled as fast as I could to the
place; and I seemed to see, every few fathoms as I went, the body of my poor
boy all crushed together; it was so clear that I stopped and rubbed my eyes,
and asked myself whether I was in my right mind or no." When he got there,
he was relieved to find his son sitting up and only crying a little.[197] Another
father had to be put under a doctor's care, not just because he had lost three
sons in an explosion, but because one dead son had pulled the hair right out of
another dead son's scalp in a futile attempt to save him.[198] Miner Jim Bullock's

grandfather was rescued by his own father after being pinned under a large piece of fallen roof; the roof then fell on the rescuing father, killing him:

> The miners tried to cheer him, saying "Ne-er mind, lad, he didn't suffer." But my grandfather knew different. As he had lain under that stone which fastened his legs, he had watched his father's face, seen the muscular legs dithering and trembling with the sheer weight of that huge stone. He had seen the sweat gush from every pore of his naked body and the agony in his father's eyes. What is more, he knew that his father had given his own life so that he might live.[199]

Workers remembered the details of accidents that had occurred years before, suggesting that they were haunted by the strong images:

> About four years ago at the Elvet pit, when two men were going down, a hook of another rope caught him by the thigh, and ripped off the skin like a stocking. He got down to the foot of the shaft and then they drew him back up again, in the same condition as when he went down, and then they sent for the surgeon. The surgeon came to his house and sewed up the leg, but it all became dead flesh, and the man died five or six months after.[200]

Similarly, some seventy years after it happened, Jim Bullock's grandfather recounted the story of forty-four children killed in a mine inundation in 1840.[201]

Finally, the families of injured workers showed their attachment to their family members through the refusal to give up hope after workplace disasters, often carrying out exhausting vigils over coal pits.[202] A man who became ill standing outside the recently exploded St. Hilda Pit in Newcastle was revived by a doctor and asked where it hurt. He replied simply, "I am not well, Sir. I have two sons in there."[203] Joe Kenyon described the agony of waiting for news: "One of the unbearable things about a pit disaster is the intensity of the waiting; more dread than patience—lest the question asked should bring an answer that snuffs out that last flicker of hope."[204] The individual human cost of workplace accidents, and the highly individual emotional responses, were largely swept away on a newsprint wave of grieving widows tearing their hair.

The evidence shows that the image of workplace accidents in the middle-class press in nineteenth-century Britain and the United States was strongly shaped by familiar narratives casting the worker as innocent victim of circumstances, of Providence, or of the industrial battle zone. A regular feature of almost every issue of any urban newspaper, workplace accidents became opportunities to celebrate heroism or exercise Christian kindness rather than appearing to be lasting tragedies. These narratives were shaped by the religious beliefs and expectations of the newsreading public more than they reflected workers' lives on the job.

In contrast, workers' behavior and their memoirs both suggest that, while there were religious ramifications of accidents, and while workers did display emotions through their songs, memories, and actions, the economic consequences bulked just as large in their memories. For workers, an injury lasted as long as it kept one from returning to the same or a similar job at the same pay rate. When one returned to the job, the trauma surely remained but the potentially deadly economic aspect of the episode ended. The loss of a finger did not create a permanent sense of outrage; an intact body in the long run was of no use, if in the short run one starved to death. As long as you could still work, having a work-related handicap was simply a badge of the times: English coal pits were full of the limping wounded; factories were filled with workers missing parts of their fingers. Most railway companies had watchmen who had lost limbs while working as brakemen, and the British railway union's newspaper carried advertisements aimed specifically at maimed railroad workers.[205] Workers were also more likely than was the mainstream press to use their newspapers, poems, songs and memoirs to call for systemic change.

The tendency of Victorian newspapers to ignore the voices of the workers themselves was not the only factor that held workers back from aggressive pursuit of safety reform or workers' compensation before 1880. As this chapter has suggested, particularly among male workers, a culture of masculine stoicism and of fatalism may also have been influential. As the next chapter shows in detail, for workers themselves as well as the wider society, the identification of the injured worker as male and a free agent (despite the fact that sometimes neither of these conditions were true) made it much more difficult for injured workers to claim the protection of the law, or to call for an alteration in the law.

The Paradox of Free Labor

THROUGHOUT THE FIRST HALF OF THE NINETEENTH CENTURY in the Anglo-American juridical world, respect for the laws of the market and of supply and demand, and unwillingness to effectively regulate industry, created a real resistance to government regulation or protection and something like worship of free trade.[1] To attempt to intervene in any way in a contract between employer and employee might somehow pervert the economic system, harming business and thus the economic health of the nation. Within this system, workers had certain clearly delineated rights, including the right to sign their own contracts.[2] The assumption that workers were free agents helped to grease the wheels of untrammeled commercial activity; but this was complicated by the fact that although under the ideology of free labor workers were construed as white, adult, and male, the actual workforce in both countries was much more diverse.

The diversity of the workforce in both Britain and the United States meant that workers experienced workplace accidents and their consequences differently, depending on their age, gender, and condition of servitude.[3] Even as the discourse of "freedom of contract" began to claim complete victory over white, male workers, the worst excesses of industrialization were buffered for women and children by the notion that their irrationality made them incompetent judges of workplace dangers. At the same time, racist assumptions influenced the consequences of workplace accidents for many of the United States' millions of slaves. But while it protected these workers in a somewhat scattershot way, this disaggregation of the workforce into components based on age, gender, and condition of servitude finally slowed progress toward universal safety and compensation legislation. White male workers, seeking to uphold their own identities as men and as breadwinners, resisted being lumped into the same categories of protection and helplessness as women and children. Employers used this to their advantage. They referred to their male workers in ways which showed that they believed male workers to be just as irrational as women or children, and employers simultaneously used the language of free agency to discourage political action.

Women, Children, and Slaves

Like adult male workers, women, children, and "young persons" aged thirteen to twenty-one were subject to workplace death and injury. In fact, due to their large presence in mechanized industries, women and teenagers were injured in factories in large numbers. As a result, to some extent in the realm of law, and to an even greater extent when it came to the more intangible cultural perceptions of workplace injuries and accidents, women and young workers were regarded differently from men.[4] The differential treatment afforded to women and child workers gave male workers a potential opportunity. They could have used women and children as the "thin edge of the wedge," to call for compensation legislation for all workers. This had been the exact proce-dure followed when workers campaigned for factory reform in Britain in the 1830s. Amid a welter of heartrending stories of pregnant women working at looms and young children being dashed with water in the face to wake them up to finish a twelve-hour shift, the hours worked by women and children were reduced. Later, with much less sentimentality, the Ten Hours movement called for a reduction of male workers' hours.[5] However, the ideology of free agency helped to fragment the workforce and prevent male workers from campaigning hard for legislative change.

The question of free agency arose for the first time in the context of fac-tory working hours. With canny self-interest, mill owners argued that it was fundamentally unjust for the government to interfere in the work relationship between master and man. An adult male was a free agent. If he perceived that, due to a large family or for other financial reasons, that he needed to work more than ten hours, then who was the government to say that he should not do so?[6]

When it came to the question of dangerous workplaces, male workers were unwilling to use the same strategies that had been used to such good effect during the Ten Hour movement. The cotton factories, largely the province of women and child workers, were subject to safety regulation beginning in the 1840s. As this chapter will show, although the cultural reaction to young and female workers injured on the job was uneven, in many cases they did receive greater protection and compensation than did male workers, particularly when accidents were due to employers ignoring safety legislation. In contrast, mines, railroads, and construction sites were masculine places in which workers demonstrated their free agency and their masculinity by putting their bodies on the line and received higher pay for their strength and "skill." Although workers intermittently criticized differences in power within the workplace that made it possible for employers to ignore safety issues, not until the 1870s did male workers in dangerous trades begin seriously to undermine the idea of free agency in their quest for compensation for workplace injuries.

The idea that child workers were not "free agents" underlay British factory legislation from its very inception. As the members of the 1833 Royal Commission on children's work in factories noted, "At the age when children suffer these injuries from the labour they undergo, they are not free agents, but are let out to hire, the wages they earn being received and appropriated by their parents and guardians."[7] The Commissioners proposed that, around age fourteen, workers became free agents as a result of changes in the relationships of power within the household. Adolescents were not usually punished corporally in the home. They ceased to be under the complete control of their parents. They began to retain a portion of their wages for themselves. Most importantly, they began to make their own labor contracts. All of these factors together designated the leap to free agency.[8] Mill owners recognized that their youngest workers were not free agents through differential treatment in the workplace; instead of being fined for poor workmanship, the youngest children were beaten. Given that they gave their wages to their parents, a fine would mean nothing to them, while a beating was a direct and easily interpreted message.[9]

Workers who were to be considered free agents on the job not only kept their own wages and controlled their own bodies, but also were assumed to have a level of rationality that allowed them to see and avoid danger. The 1833 Royal Commission held that child workers could not be capable of culpable neglect, since their lack of rationality held them to a lower standard to begin with. As the Royal Commissioners noted,

The refusal [by mill owners] to contribute to the expence of the cure of those who have been maimed, is usually founded on the assertion that the accident was caused by culpable heedlessness or temerity. In the cases of the children of tender years we do not consider this a valid defence against the claim for contribution by the employer. We cannot suppose an obligation to perpetual caution and discretion imposed on children at an age when those qualities do not usually exist.[10]

Could workers who were not free agents under the law be held responsible for workplace accidents? Opinions on this key issue varied. Employers and managers liked to assert that young workers chose to be heedless and that they could have chosen to be otherwise. Thomas Leeming, the superintendent of carding rooms at a Salford mill, saw his eldest child, a boy of eleven, killed in 1819. When asked how his son was killed he said, "It was an accident, arising from negligence . . . he was carelessly cleaning the machine, and was seized by the straps and taken round the drum, and he lived about six hours."[11] In testimony before a House of Lords Select Committee on Mine Accidents, Geology Professor David Thomas Ansted, of Kings College London, blamed a little boy with a naked candle for igniting gas that caused a mine to explode. Because other workers carried Davy lamps, Ansted said the accident "was entirely from the carelessness of that boy," even though he described him as a "little boy."[12] Similarly, in the mills, even workers admitted that the carelessness or heedlessness of child workers was as much to blame for accidents as was the failure by employers to box the moving parts of dangerous machinery. James Carpenter, testified before a Royal Commission on child labor in factories: "I have seen the children put their fingers into the arms of the wheel out of bravado like, and run it round with the wheel till it came to the bite nearly, and sometimes it has been too sharp for them, and taken hold and bitten them. They'd call to each other to see how far they durst carry it."[13] William Hebden, a twenty-two-year-old with seventeen years of experience in the mills who had himself been seriously injured three times, agreed. "I have seen several get their fingers taken off. I have seen them play with the wheels a good deal, and let their finger run round with the wheel; they generally get catched."[14] The repeated references to carelessness suggest that these onlookers believed the injured children had known what they were doing was wrong.

Despite this, there was a fair amount of ambiguity concerning children's degree of rationality, even in cases in which a child did not collect compensation, as much as in cases in which children did. Both kinds of cases are linked by the expectation that child workers need to be well-directed and to follow directions, rather than to follow their own lines of rational thought. The question of whether child employees were "doing anything which [they] had no business to do" was a serious one.[15] It played out in the case of Thomas Francis, a twelve-year-old boy employed along with several hundred other workers in a silk mill in London. Francis was killed when he came in from a break and went to hide from his co-workers in a different room in the factory. He got caught around the upright shaft under the drum of the throwing mill, and died almost immediately. The jury found accidental death "and concurred with the Coroner that not the slightest blame could be attributed to any one—the boy having had no occasion to go near the machine which was the cause of his death."[16]

In another case in which young persons were killed but did not collect compensation, it was the bad judgment of their father, rather than their own judgment, that was to blame. When the Coppull Mine near Bolton exploded, among those killed were Jane Halliwell, thirteen, whose father died in the blast; and two drawers, Mary Booth, eleven, and Jane Booth, twenty-one. Both the *Times* and the coroner attached responsibility for their deaths not to the mine owners, but rather to Halliwell's father, who had evidently snuck them into the mine dressed as boys in order to work for him. Three weeks before the accident, the mine surveyor had told the manager that he thought Halliwell's assistants were girls, due to their high voices. "When the manager told Halliwell that he would have his drawer examined to ascertain whether it was his daughter or not, he said he would stick his pick into any one who would attempt to examine a drawer of his." Halliwell having asserted his workplace privilege, nothing more was done about the matter. Thus, when the mine exploded, Halliwell had the responsibility for his assistants in death just as he had in life.[17] The three girls were clearly where they had no business to be, but, as both young and female, were assumed to have been under the direction of someone else rather than acting on their own accord.

A similar decision was reached in the case of *Lumsden v. Russell*. William Russel, aged nine, carried gunpowder into the works where he was not employed, to his father, who was a miner there.[18] His father told him to take water to another miner. To get the water, the boy had to cross a gap that was spanned only by a plank. To avoid losing his balance, William caught hold of the winding chain that was just hanging there, unprotected, and was killed by being drawn into the machinery, which started the moment he grabbed the chain. The judge in this case held that the father had no claim of damages against the master because the boy was in a place where he had no lawful occasion to be. While masters had a general responsibility to maintain safe workplaces, in this case the judge held the father responsible "in his rendering it necessary for the boy to go near the work with the gunpowder. Had the father neglected to take it himself? Then it was his fault. Had he exhausted all the supply that he had down below? Or was a boy of nine the proper person to get to bring him more, with all the risks a boy must necessarily run in such a place? The whole blame rests with the father, for the boy was not employed by the masters, nor engaged in doing anything the masters were bound to provide for."

The fact that children were not considered free agents becomes even more obvious when one looks at examples of successful compensation. Child workers were often able to claim compensation in scenarios in which adult male workers would have been barred. An injured thirteen-year-old named Nancy Coe was treated kindly by the judicial system in 1851, because she was hurt doing exactly what she had been instructed to do, and her employers had also disregarded safety rules designed to protect young workers. Coe, employed in Sutcliffe's mill at Lostock near Bolton, England, lost her arm when it was caught in an upright shaft that had been left uncased. Her employers were prosecuted under the Factory Acts, convicted of leaving dangerous machinery unfenced, and assessed with a £10 fine and court costs. The fine was deposited in the Manchester Savings Bank and saved for Nancy Coe, and it and the interest would be given to her when she reached 21 or was married. Although it is unclear whether they did so out of a sense of duty or whether they were forced to do so by the court, the mill proprietors also employed a surgeon to attend to her and paid the bill. They continued to pay her 4s. 6d. in wages for several weeks, and when the Surgeon said that she was recovered (as much as one can be with the loss of an arm), offered to hire her as an errand girl. Even after all this generosity on the part of the company, when her father was unable to support her, he was advised to sue for damages, which he did, winning £120 plus costs.[19]

Because women and child workers were assumed to need more guidance and protection, courts and legislatures raised the bar for their employers. In Scotland, whose courts had for a long time disregarded the fellow-servant rule, judges found that employers should fence any mill gearing that was accessible to women, children, and young persons, whether or not such categories of workers were likely to come into contact with it in the course of their regular duties.[20] One plaintiff, Miss O'Byrne, had been employed in a clay mill for only nine days when her supervisor ordered her to remove clay from between some rollers while the rollers were running. Of course, her clothing became entangled in the machinery and she was horribly mangled. O'Byrne sued her employer, and the Scottish judge in the girl's case ruled in her favor. He did so not on the grounds that a worker had some abstract right to a safe workplace, but rather because she was a child, and a female child at that. "She was an inexperienced girl employed in a hazardous manufactory, placed under the control, and, it may be added, the protection, of an overseer, who was appointed by the defendant, and intrusted with the duty; and it might well be considered that by employing such a helpless and ignorant child, the master contracted to keep her out of harm's way in assigning her to any work to be performed."[21] A similar verdict was forthcoming in the case of James Whitelaw, a collier lad whose leg amputation owed, in the estimation of the judges, to his employer's failure to inspect a chain link by link. One of the judges went so far as to note that "the safety both of the workmen and of the public requires that in a case of this kind any doubt which may exist should be given against the master in whose hands such insufficient chains may have created damages."[22]

Similarly, in the case of *Grizzle v. Frost,* a young carder had been working for only a few days changing cans of roving by the carding machine when her foreman instructed her to pick up pieces of hemp that fell out of the machine and put them back between the rollers. After she did this for two or three days she caught her fingers between the rollers and injured her arm so badly that it was later amputated. Chief Justice Cockburn instructed the jury

> that the foreman was put by the defendants in their place to employ this young person in and about dangerous machinery of which she was quite ignorant, and I think any negligence of his in the matter would be negligence for which they [the master] would be responsible. There is evidence both of negative and positive negligence on his part—negative in not giving the girl proper instructions as to the use of the machine—positive in expressly directing her to do the very thing she had done and which it is admitted was dangerous—so dangerous, indeed, that the case for the defense was that she had been told not to do it.[23]

Cockburn held that when young persons were involved and foremen failed to give proper directions or take reasonable care to avert the danger, the masters were responsible.

Although the decisions in these court cases varied depending on whether or not a child or young female worker was following employer instructions, all of them are similar in that judges in these cases held that the employer was responsible for their injuries. Contributory negligence by a parent could bar a claim, but these workers were not derailed by "assumption of risk," because children and young people lacked the rationality and experience to assume risk on their own behalf.[24] This is illustrated in *Hayden v. Smithville Manufacturing Co.,* the case of a ten-year-old worker in Connecticut who had lost his hand in the gearing of an unguarded piece of textile machinery. As presented in the lower court, the case hinged on whether or not the Smithville Manufacuring Company had been negligent by failing to install bonnets around dangerous machinery. Also at issue was the extent to which a child of the plaintiff's age was able to understand the dangers of his employment. The lower court suggested that Emory Hayden be held only to a standard of prudence usual for those of his age, throwing out the notion that a worker accepted all the risks of his employment and was thus foreclosed from collecting any damages. The lower-court jury sympathized with Hayden and awarded him $1,875, a substantial sum at the time.[25] On appeal, the decision was reversed and sent back for a new trial, on the grounds that the lower-court judge had erred in rejecting English common law on accidents as not pertinent to the state of Connecticut. Nonetheless, the justices refused to completely buy into the argument of the company's lawyers, that any person old enough to work was rational enough to understand the dangers of that work—rather, they specified that the issue of what Hayden was able to comprehend was central to the case.[26] James Schmidt has shown how the case of thirteen-year-old Elias Coombs, injured while working at a New Bedford, Massachusetts, ropewalk, revolved around the same issues; Coombs's lawyers even invoked the English factory acts that mandated safer workplaces for children as evidence that Coombs was entitled to be held to a different standard than an adult male would have been.[27]

The cases outlined above hinged on the tender ages and incomplete self-mastery of the child workers in question, helping to establish exceptions to the doctrines of free agency and personal responsibility that had been established by such cases as *Priestley* and *Farwell.* But women and children were not the only nineteenth-century workers who did not meet the standards of rationality or intentionality needed to classify them as "free agents." In the thinking of most Southern jurists before the Civil War, slaves met none of the tests of the independent worker that Shaw had specified in the *Farwell* case. Racist thought suggested that slaves, although able to act on instinct, were unable to reason. Furthermore, the implicit and explicit rules of Southern society rendered slaves unable to reprimand white workers for dangerous work practices. Although slaves sometimes did walk off the job when they considered their lives to be in danger, at least in the legal realm such behavior was unimaginable.[28]

Due to the rising price of slaves, which made purchase of slaves for large industries impractical, slave hiring was becoming a more and more popular practice before the Civil War. Frederick Wertheim suggests that about 40,000 of the 200,000 slaves used in Southern industry at that time were hired out.[29] These slaves were heir to all the potential injuries sustained by industrial workers. Legal decisions about compensation to owners for injured slaves varied from state to state, and legal reasoning was somewhat inconsistent in most of the early cases. By the 1850s, however, as slave hiring became more common, a general pattern developed. Slave hires were considered to be part of bailment law. Thus, a hired slave was rented property that had to be returned to the ultimate owner in the same condition as he or she was in when turned over to the hirer. Hirers thus became responsible for providing medical care to injured slaves and to pay compensation to owners if they put a slave's life in danger by using that slave for an unintended or dangerous purpose.[30] The net effect of this was that slaves' owners were able to collect damages for injured slaves in the courts with much greater regularity than white workers were able to collect damages for their own injuries. This ironic situation could have been avoided had Southern jurists been willing to reject the fellow-servant rule, but as Wertheim notes, many of them were slavish followers of English precedent.[31]

Judges in many of these legal decisions noted that slaves were human, and therefore had some degree of independent thought and action, but, like women and children, slaves were held to a lesser standard of rationality than adult white males, and their hirers were held to a more strict standard of supervision.[32] Injured slaves were not generally restricted by the fellow-servant rule, since they could not walk away from a dangerous job; and, in fact, Southern jurists almost waxed poetic about the fact that slaves had to stand dumbly in the face of danger and obey their masters' orders.[33] If a white worker were injured by the actions of his fellow servant who happened to be a slave, he had even less recourse than he would have had had his fellow servant been white; there was no way to sue a piece of property.[34] The logical respondent in the case of a slave injured after being hired out, or a white worker injured by the actions of a slave, would have been the owner of the injuring slave (slaves could not be sued), yet almost all Southern jurists were dedicated to the preservation of the slave-owning class, to the point of illogically minimizing a slaveholder's liability for the actions of his slaves.[35] The result was a compromise between what was legally logical and what was socially permissible.

While white workers were rarely able to contract with their employers for danger pay, slave owners could and did limit by contract the nature of work their slaves were expected to do. Even though this meant that literal rather than implied contracts existed between slave masters and hirers, only in one Southern state—North Carolina—did a jurist find this enough to enforce the fellow-servant rule against the master, with the slave as his proxy.[36] In the other Southern states where fellow-servant type cases arose before the Civil War, hirers and their employees, who were considered "agents of the hirers," were held to a stringent duty of care when it came to black employees. As Finkelman argues, the South departed in legal culture from the North on the question of fellow servants precisely because protecting the interests of slave-holders was such a cultural priority. While the impact of these decisions on in-dustrialization in the South was small, they were part of a much larger scheme by which slavery deformed the South from the pattern in the North.[37]

Female, child, and enslaved workers within the Anglo-American workforce often found that the common-law defenses used to block male workers from collecting compensation were not used to their fullest extent against them, because they were held to a lower standard of rationality and independent judgment. But work accidents and injured workers were judged differently within the larger culture as well as within the boundaries of the law. Work-ers themselves considered gender as a factor in workplace safety. Coal miners considered that there were certain jobs that could only safely be occupied by adult males. The *British Miner and General Newsman*'s editor complained that overseers were foolhardy when they "allowed a child of eight years of age to be in sole charge of the 'gin' or drawing apparatus; that child lowered a man to, and raised a man from the bottom of the shaft; or take the case of Belcher, also a chartermaster; he permitted a man to be lowered down a shaft by a young woman, by her own sheer strength of arm."[38]

Newspapers also conveyed differences between work accidents that hap-pened to men and those that happened to women. A reader of nineteenth-century newspapers would have concluded that women were more rarely in-jured, when, in fact, the difference in coverage stemmed in part from the defi-nition of the workplace as the area outside the home.[39] The greater frequency with which accidents to men were discussed helped to create the idea of the worker within the real, dangerous, workplace as a man.[40]

Newspaper articles also suggested that it was possible for men but not women to be killed on the job in the midst of acts of heroism. A man didn't have to rescue his fellow workers in a mine to be described as heroic; in 1818, three Englishmen were digging a hole to receive the contents of a sewer. One man, having nearly completed the hole, came up the ladder but accidentally dropped his shovel. He went down to get it and the whole contents of the adjoining privy burst onto him. He was overcome by fumes and fainted. When a workman tried to come down and help him, he also was overcome by the fumes and fell in, unconscious. Two more men tried to help and suffered the same fate. Finally, a heroic plumber went down and rescued three of them, after which he himself was overcome, and lay on his deathbed. The *Times* framed the tale as an example of selfless sacrifice in the cause of humanity.[41] Women had few such opportunities to acquit themselves as heroes and many more opportunities to be portrayed as grieving widows.

Machinery was responsible for some of the most appalling deaths in the early industrial period, and it claimed "helpless" male and female workers alike.[42] But while women were hardly ever killed by anything other than machinery, men on the job died in many other ways, some of which could be chalked up to lapses in professional judgment of the kind that women were not thought to exercise. For example, the editor of a newspaper in a region hard struck by both railroad and mining accidents in the early nineteenth century condemned what he saw as the carelessness that characterized local workmen; "Not a week passes but we are called upon to record an accident of some kind—and indeed sometimes several of them some of which frequently result in death. Most of these accidents occur on the railroads and in mines, and in the majority of cases are the result of carelessness. Men who care not for their lives as to risk them for the most trifling thing, should not be retained."[43]

Motivated by the notion that workers who were not free agents were incapable of calculating risks, assessing danger, and otherwise protecting themselves on the job, Parliament created legislative tools that could be used to compensate female and child workers—anticipating steps that the United States would take much later. At the same time that thousands of Massachusetts women failed to secure a fair hearing for a bill to secure a ten-hour day, in Britain a series of legislative acts passed between 1819 and 1847 regulated the hours and ages of child and women factory workers and banned women and children from work in underground mines.[44] These acts also designated that machinery which could be dangerous to these categories of workers had to be made safe.

Although it can hardly be argued that anyone injured under the English factory system was actively encouraged to seek redress, factory commissioners took a special interest in, and were willing to prosecute employers on behalf of, injured women and young persons.[45] At the discretion of the secretary of state, any fines levied in these cases could be granted to the family of a worker or to the worker him- or herself, making this route to compensation more secure than a tort claim.[46] R. H. Howells cites the example of *Cotterell v. Stocks,* a case which came before the Lancashire assizes in 1840. The injured party, a girl who had her arm torn off by unfenced mill machinery, received £100. While this may not have been enough to pay her court costs of £600, the hefty fine made enough of an example of her employer to strike fear into the hearts of other factory owners.[47] Eight years later, Factory Inspector R. J. Saunders oversaw the case of twenty-five-year-old Hannah Brook, an engine feeder, who got her clothes caught in an upright shaft and was whirled around several times and broke her arm in two places. Saunders reported the mill owners for not having fenced the upright shaft. Although the magistrates found that Brook was partly responsible for her own injuries, a concept that often completely barred male workers from any redress, they levied a fine of £10, which was appropriated to the woman's benefit. With it, she and her husband were able to move to larger living quarters and begin a small business.[48]

In the same year, Factory Inspector Leonard Horner avidly pursued the case of Emmanuel Gill, a fourteen-year-old boy who was squeezed to death while working as a scavenger under a self-acting cotton spinning mule. Horner was outraged because technological innovation had made the use of child scavengers unnecessary, and only indifference and stinginess prevented safer methods from being adopted. Furthermore, this was the third death caused by scavenging in Blackburn alone in a short time. Horner went out of his way to give the case publicity, to make sure that legal charges were lodged against the mill owners, and to alert *the Manchester Guardian,* which sent a special reporter to Blackburn for the trial. Unfortunately, despite the evidence before their own eyes, the magistrates there refused to entertain the notion that Gill's employer could possibly have allowed machinery to be cleaned while in motion and levied only a token fine.[49]

Factory inspectors like Leonard Horner could be energetic advocates for the viewpoint that children could not possibly be free agents. Testifying before the Children's Employment Commission, Horner was scathing in his assessment of working conditions at one nail factory where a boy had been killed by falling through a floor:

The rooms are all crowded with dangerous machinery, so close that you can scarcely pass; indeed some operations have to be stopped in order that you may pass at all . . . Not any of this machinery is boxed off, or guarded in any way. It is a frightful place, turn which way you will. There is a constant hammering roar of wheels, so that you could not possibly hear any warning voice . . . Little boys and girls are here seen at work at the tip-punching machine (all acting by steam power) with their fingers in constant danger of being punched off once in every second, while at the same time they have their heads between two whirling wheels a few inches distant from each ear. "They seldom lose the hand," said one of the proprietors to me, in explanation; "it only takes off a finger at the first or second joint. Sheer carelessness—looking about them— entirely through carelessness!"[50]

Although the employer here alleged that children were careless when they lost fingers to machinery, it is clear from Horner's tone that he not only found such a statement ludicrous, but also expected his audience to agree with him. Children and young persons were also the subjects of particular inquiries into the causes of work accidents.[51]

The prosecution of an employer required the support—and in some cases the active advocacy—of working people against their employers, in ways that deviated from the expectations of deference elsewhere in the compensation regime. The case of Martha Appleton affords an interesting and detailed look into one of these factory prosecutions. On August 8, 1859, thirteen-year-old Martha Appleton of Scholes, near Wigan, England, was at work in the spinning room of Messrs. Woods and Co. While removing spindles from the spinning machine, she suddenly felt faint and reached out one hand to steady herself, grabbing the unfenced and moving spinning mule. The mule proceeded to amputate all of the fingers on her hand.[52] Afterwards, Martha's father, Samuel, sprang into action. His first inclination after the accident was to approach William Prowting Roberts, the attorney who had long been an advocate for Chartists, coal miners, and other working people. Roberts advised him to set his case before the local factory inspector, as neatly as possible, and without exaggeration.[53] Appleton wrote to his local Factory Inspector, Robert Baker, to let him know that his daughter Martha "met with a sad misfortune on the 8 instant. She being at work, tenting the self-actors—or mules—the[y] not being boxed off as the[y] aught to have been, and something being a miss with the Machinery and the over looker not being present at the time which caused my Childs hand to be taken off through the negligence of the over looker."[54]

Appleton reported that Martha was prevented from seeing the subinspector and was not given any recompense for her pain, suffering, or lost wages. He mentioned that he had talked to an attorney and suggested £200 as an appropriate settlement. On August 29, Appleton met with Baker and presented his case in person. Baker seems to have suggested a settlement of £150 might be more reasonable than £200, but in a note sent two days after the meeting Appleton was obstinate, arguing that he had attorney's fees to take care of and that a dressmaking apprenticeship would make his daughter a charge on him for five to six years before she was able to earn her keep.[55]

Although Appleton was doing what he was entitled to under the law, Robert Baker became infuriated at him, both for having consulted an attorney and for failing to go cap in hand to Messrs. Wood and Co., Martha's former employer:

> I do not think under all the circumstances . . . I should be justified in recommending the Sec'y of State to being an action against Messrs. Woods on behalf of your daughter . . . you had yourself applied to Messrs. Wood for compensation through an Attorney, which is not the way I think you ought to have applied. A spirit of good feeling (and as far as I could discover from your own statements, you had had no reason to the contrary) should have led you, I think in the first instance, to Messrs. Woods themselves, to have made your case known to them—Had you done so, I am sure from what the Firm has said to me, you would have been met, with kindness and sympathy.[56]

Despite what seemed like a dismissal, Baker did do his job. He wrote to Woods the same day, mentioning that Appleton seemed inclined to settle out of court and acknowledging that putting Martha out to be a dressmaker would indeed cost something in maintenance. Baker further noted that the wheels in question could be boxed off without detriment to the action of the machinery, and so they should have been. "And if they had, even though the child was faint, the accident could not have happened, and therefore you are morally bound to do something for her by way of compensation."[57]

William Woods informed Baker that while they were happy to negotiate with Appleton, they objected to paying him a lump sum for his daughter's injuries since to do so seemed like an admission of liability.[58] Appleton also wrote to Baker, mentioning that Messrs. Woods had offered to pay Martha 3s. 6d. per week for three years. Appleton was happy with the amount but insisted that it would do more good to both him and the child if it were paid in a lump sum. He promised to sign a letter waiving any further rights if he could get this lump sum—a little over £27, nowhere near the £200 he had originally asked for.[59] Woods corroborated this story, with one change—Woods and Co. were willing to continue weekly payments until the girl could support herself by her own wages, even if this took longer than three years.[60]

At this point, Robert Baker's attitude shifted. His attempt to prevail on Woods and Co. as one gentleman to another had failed, and he began to take a tougher line with the company:

> There is one thing more which you seem to have overlooked and that is compensation for the loss of that which is part of her sole property and maintenance through life. Had she not lost her hand by your neglect to fence these wheels, which by the law it was your duty to do without any notice from me, she would have been independent of any help of yours for her future maintenance; but having so lost it, she is fairly entitled to compensation, as well as maintenance till she can earn for herself a new livelihood.[61]

Baker admitted that Woods might not like the precedent that the case would set, but that was not the child's fault—and Woods and Co.'s remedy of course was to fence off the machinery in question. But William Woods responded as employers in this period traditionally did when backed to the wall with the threat of legal action; he became obstinate. Woods noted that his company did not feel itself legally liable; anything the company proposed to do for the girl was strictly on charitable grounds. They also refused to guarantee the payment for any particular time period. The letter presented Baker with a choice: consider it charity and let the company decide how much to give or take his chances pursuing the company through the legal system.[62]

Only after exhausting all of these avenues did Baker present the case to the secretary of state, describing Martha's injuries and asking whether there were any impediments to legal action. Baker described the whole past history of the affair, including his initial worry that Appleton wanted to use the incident to extend his own business rather than look to the girl's welfare. Under rebuffs from the company, Baker now felt it was a matter of abstract right. He was convinced that Woods and Co. planned to sweep it under the rug once his back was turned; he wanted to pursue the legal channels.[63]

Seemingly faced with a dead end in the factory inspector, Samuel Appleton had turned to the secretary of state long before Robert Baker had. His petition explained that he was hardworking and industrious and had raised a family of fifteen children. He also explained the hardship inherent in Woods's failure to pay a lump sum. Because the company would pay the money only to Martha, not her father, she would have to walk to and from to the mill every week. The lump sum signified more to Appleton than convenience; it signified justice. As he explained, with a lump sum, "If I had even that small but I could put my girl to some respectable trial in business, and for want of it I cannot, so that your honour may see how the poor man is humbug'd even out of his lawful rights."[64]

Unfortunately, the paper trail in the case of Martha Appleton stops there; the rest of the record is tantalizing but incomplete. What is certain is that Woods and Co. subsequently fenced in their dangerous machinery, including the mule that had claimed Martha's fingers. It is also true that Samuel Appleton closed his beer shop and became a coal miner, which suggests that the family had never received its lump sum payment; on the other hand, two younger sons were in school, which was unusual for a working family. In the 1861 census, two years after the accident, young Martha was listed in the census as a dressmaker, the object of her ambition; and yet the loss of Martha's hand was not enough to drive her older sister from the cotton mill.[65]

Despite the unsatisfactory lack of an ending one way or the other, the Appleton incident does illustrate certain relevant points. First, pursuing a prosecution under the Factory Acts required a family member to summon up great nerve and to leave deference behind in the pursuit of justice. Second, it illustrates the prevalent notion that employees should go cap-in-hand to employers despite the existence of a parallel system of settling these disputes through the Factory Acts. Barriers of class made Factory Inspector Robert Baker willing to assume the worst about Appleton and the best about William Woods, and only experience changed his mind. Finally, the case illustrates a point made in Chapter 2; that nineteenth-century employers' charity stopped at the point where legal liabilty began. Finally, the case shows that Appleton, as a female child who had been disabled for life by a workplace accident, could gain a hearing and sympathy, because she was not a free agent.

Although clearly Factory Act prosecutions did not bear fruit in every case, by 1848, Factory Inspector T. Jones Howell was able to report that the ability to prosecute employers for safety violations had materially improved conditions in the factories. Furthermore, "in those instances where proceedings have been taken under Sec. 60, the most seasonable assistance has been afforded to sufferers, some of whom, disabled for Factory employment, have by these means, been placed in a position to secure a livelihood."[66] The one major drawback, according to Howell, was that serious factory accidents often resulted in death, and the law had been interpreted in such a way as to foreclose the families of workers killed on the job from prosecuting employers under the Factory Act. While they still had the right to prosecute under Lord Campbell's Act (1846), it was a much slower and more expensive process.[67]

Factory inspection prosecutions were not the only arena in which workplace injustices to women and children might be recognized. While, as Chapter 5 will show, coroners' juries almost always classified workplace deaths as accidental, in the case of a child laborer a jury might be willing to go out on a limb. Twelve-year-old Michael Murphy was killed in the explosion of a match manufactory at Stratford. He was one of fifteen children employed in the factory, only four of whom were older than ten. The children worked with flammable material with which they coated the matches, and when the explosion occurred Murphy was burnt and his larynx injured so that he was unable to breathe. Even an emergency tracheotomy failed to save him. The jury found "That the deceased died from asphyxia, through an accidental explosion, while he was engaged in stirring a composition for the manufacture of Vesuvian lights, and the jury consider that the manufacturer is open to censure for entrusting such combustible materials to children of so young an age."[68] In a similar case in Lancashire, twelve-year-old Ellen Hampson was fatally injured in her first hour on the job at a coal mine. Instead of picking the dirt and shale out of the coal she tried to move a wagon to the coal screen. When she let the brake out the wagon started to move downhill, and when she tried to stop it she got run over. Mr. Higson, the mine inspector for that district, referred to her in his report to the government as "the poor little thing." He had attended the inquest on her body, and "took the opportunity of expressing my opinion on the transaction in very plain language . . . but many of the jurymen would not say that the manager had acted unwisely, to say the least of it, in employing one so young."[69]

The desire to protect women and young workers who were not thought of as free agents from risky workplaces had been one of the motivations for excluding women and children from underground mine work in 1842. As a result, the public was scandalized to learn that some miners killed in a mine explosion near Wigan in 1846 were women dressed in men's clothing. "The Coroner said, he observed that the attention of the London newspapers had been directed to this melancholy accident, on account of women being in the mine, which was contrary to law. Now, he wished to know whether something could not be done to prevent them going down in disguise in this manner?"

One of the jurymen present testified that women were in fact assuming the risks of the employment in exchange for higher pay. "The women are fonder of working in the pits than anywhere else, and you cannot keep them out because they get good wages."[70] But the reality of the situation did not militate against the extremely durable cultural norm that women lacked free agency and did not make these kinds of calculations.

In the press and in the legal system, women and child workers, and slaves who had been hired out by their owners, sometimes benefited from the assumption that they were not free agents on the job. Judicial decisions favored women, slaves, and child workers on the grounds that they were young, inexperienced, objects of pity, or less rational than free white men. Legislation had been passed to enable the families of injured child or female workers to pursue compensation for workplace accidents and punishment of refractory factory owners; this type of legislation foreshadowed a host of other acts that would seek to protect women and children, as weaker vessels, on the job.[71] But the fact that newspapers and judges, legislators and factory inspectors, were sometimes willing to bend the rules for these protected classes, or to create new ones, helped to split the workforce, investing even more significance in free agency as a characteristic of white male workers and making it even harder for white males to create positive change.

Were White Male Workers Free Agents?

Unlike women and young people, who could be described as unfree agents and therefore entitled to some kinds of protection in the workplace, adult men were the category by which free agency was defined. It must be noted, however, that from the employer's perspective, the idea of free agency could be deployed when it was convenient. For example, the common claim that worker carelessness caused most workplace accidents muddied the waters of free agency. If a worker was habitually careless, was he rational enough to avoid danger? Was he educated enough to understand instructions or insightful enough to see what the consequences of his actions might be? Many of those who observed and wrote about industrial accidents in the nineteenth century conveyed the idea that those who owned mines and mills were naturally more rational than their ill-educated workpeople.

As early as 1821, the *Times* editorialized that while coal-owning "gentlemen" might be lightly chastised for their preference for old working methods over safety, any fault that they might have for recent mine accidents was far outweighed by the incredible carelessness of the labor force. "The carelessness, the fearlessness, the fool-hardiness of those who are constantly employed in dangerous operations, would exceed the belief of any but a eye-witness; frequent escapes soon produce a feeling of absolute security; and the most dreadful accident is looked upon rather as a piece of ill-luck than as an incident necessarily connected with their business, or the result of culpable inattention."[72] The idea that workers were responsible, through carelessness, for their own injuries was a constant refrain in the *Times*'s pages.[73]

J. T. Arlidge, author of one of the two central treatises on industrial safety published in nineteenth-century England, also characterized the workforce in a way that called into question their rationality. In chemical plants,

> the labour followed is almost wholly unskilled, demanding little but brute strength, endurance and indifference to annoyances, hardships, and perils. It therefore attracts an inferior class of men, upon whom, in its turn, it can exercise no humanising influence . . . Workmen of this class bring numerous ills upon themselves by their ignorance, indifference to cleanliness and rules of health, as well as by utter carelessness in their way of work, and of needless exposure to danger.[74]

Miners were similarly situated. Arlidge noted that,

> work in mines is of a rough character, and its surroundings also are not calculated to quicken the sentiment of self-respect, or even that of self-preservation. Miners, as a class, exhibit a strange amount of recklessness in the face of danger. So in the case of men engaged in the lowest callings—e.g. scavengers and sewerage labourers, there is a parallel indifference to their own well-being. Their sensibilities are blunted, and require strong impressions to arouse them.[75]

Dull-witted workers not only failed to perceive danger, but also shunned safety measures taken for their benefit, as in the case of the white-lead workers who refused to wear unflattering special protective uniforms[76] Within the working class there were gradations of fitness and skill: "The Irish supply the staple for unskilled labour; the Italians display facility for delicate occupations."[77] Nonetheless, the big picture was one of workpeople who were clearly inferior in learning and rationality to their bosses and social superiors.

American commentators also claimed worker carelessness was the primary cause of workplace accidents. As Anthony Wallace has noted, alleging that workers were habitually careless was a way for American mine owners to minimize both their legal and any perceived moral responsibility.[78] While native-born white men had the vote—a strong marker of free agency—the hordes of immigrants who poured into the country from southern and eastern Europe in the last decades of the nineteenth century did not. Their presence in the workforce helped to erode the discourse of free agency as it applied to the white male workforce. Even as sympathetic a critic of the industrial order as Crystal Eastman, whose *Work Accidents and the Law* paved the way for modern workers' compensation, blamed accidents on immigrant ignorance. She suggested that steel workers improve safety by ensuring that "ignorant non-English-speaking foreigners employed on or about tracks and cars might be under direction of a foreman who speaks their tongue."[79] She also recounted the tale of a foolhardy ditchdigger who blew up his workmates with dynamite, reasoning that "it takes a vigilant foreman to prevent accidents from dynamite among the ignorant Italians who usually handle it."[80] Eastman's running critique of uneducated foreigners who brought danger to the American workplace was evident even in the book's photographs; one miner, captioned "An English-speaking miner," is juxtaposed against a later picture in the book, of "Immigrant Laborer—A Slav." The latter wears pants held up with one suspender, and the heavy brow-ridge over his dark eyes gives him the appearance of an evolutionary throwback. Another steel worker is labelled "Steel Worker—A Genuine American."[81]

While it was common to allege that workers were habitually careless, "free agency" was a very durable legal fiction. If, at least under the law, white male workers were rational and well equipped to avoid sources of danger, workplace accidents became a moral issue, and the failure to avoid accidents became a moral failure. The idea that male workers were free agents absolved employers from thinking about structural dangers in the workplace. Francis Gurney Du Pont kept a notebook in which he recorded all the gunpowder accidents that had occurred at the company since its inception. Most of the time, Du Pont recorded no cause for a particular accident, but when a cause was given, it was invariably related to worker error rather than (for example) workplace structure. In one case, it was alleged that an employee purposely torched his gunpowder mills in order to get back at his employer for some perceived insult, and ended up killing two of his co-workers. In another, the explosion in downtown Wilmington in 1854, which killed six people and leveled many homes, Du Pont wrote "Cause unknown, but thought to have been caused by an evil person who was seen to mount the rear wagon a short time before the explosion." The next accident was blamed on improper use of hammer and nails by workmen and another on the possible suicidal tendencies of one of the workers. Sometimes Du Pont hinted that men had been grossly negligent, as in the case of James Donohoe, who struck fire by using a copper scraper around the black powder even though he was cautioned to be careful.[82]

English mine owners sought to distance themselves from any allegations of negligence by claiming that workers' carelessness had caused their own deaths. Richard Wood, general manager of the British Iron Company's coal and iron works in North Wales, testified before a Royal Commission that young colliers who were killed had only themselves to blame when they failed to check whether the ropes and chains by which they were going to descend were in good condition. The Marchioness of Londonderry was likewise expressing popular sentiment among the mine owners when she addressed her workforce after a mine accident at a neighboring mine. In a celebration that recalled feudal England, she had gathered the men and boys on the grounds of her country house to partake of a dinner of beef and beer. Her message was:

Thank God, we have had no serious or fatal calamity since I saw you last, but the details of the accident at Lundhill Colliery must be fresh in all your minds, where above 189 human beings were, without any preparation, launched into eternity, leaving mothers and sisters, widows and orphans, to mourn their loss. Think on these horrors my friends, and may your reflections induce you at least to do your duty, and be less callous and more careful, and never for an instant forget yourselves to unscrew your lamps to light your pipe or fire your shot. It makes my blood run cold, and I think any great calamity among you would break my heart ... if you are sensible of my anxiety, you will show it by your care of yourselves and your fellow-labourers.

This speech was not Lady Londonderry's only philanthropic gesture. On the occasion of a fatal colliery accident at Houghton-le-Spring (not one of her properties), she purchased for her workmen 1,000 copies of *The Miner, John Brown*, and of *The Pit-Boy and His Candle-box*, all inspirational publications of the London Tract Society.[83]

The willingness of employers to invoke the doctrine of free agency, while simultaneously portraying their workers as habitually careless, was not the only ambiguity that surrounded the doctrine of free agency. Some employers wondered whether employees wanted to protect themselves at all, invoking the moral hazard doctrine just as Justice Spalding had done in *Little Miami v. Stevens*. One factory owner reacted to legislation during a Select Committee hearing: "By this clause the master is to be convicted on the evidence of the plaintiff or party interested, and a child of nine years old, as to his culpable neglect. What a temptation to a person of poor and low circumstances to commit perjury! Besides, the magnitude of the compensation is sufficient to induce persons to put themselves in the way of meeting with an accident."[84] In 1844, a committee of pitmen approached a committee of coal owners to ask for the institutionalization of 10s. per week "smart money." Said the coal owners; "The demand of so large a sum as 10s per week, smart money, would, the committee are confident, if complied with, operate prejudicially on the workmen themselves, and their families, by holding out a direct premium to idleness, and by inducing a degree of carelessness, the consequences of which might be highly mischievous."[85] There was no appreciation of the inverse fact; that the absence of a sanction against coal owners for dangerous workplaces removed any motivation that the coal owners might have to maintain safe workplaces.[86]

The free agency doctrine proposed a fictive equality between the worker and the employer in the employment relationship; but employers undermined doctrine by demanding special privileges. For example, manufacturers claimed that they should be immune from any safety legislation because the legislation was an insulting attempt to question their moral commitment to safety.

> To subject master manufacturers to be committed as felons by the warrant of a coroner on the verdict of a jury (generally selected from the dregs of the people) for an accident that none can deplore more than the masters themselves, is so monstrous a proposition that no person of common feeling, who could by any means get rid of his establishment, would think of remaining one hour longer a manufacturer subject to the operation of such an enactment."[87]

Employers were somewhat opportunistic, portraying their white male workers as rational and able to avoid danger when to do so suited them (as in courts of law). In other arenas, where liability and fault were not under discussion, they described their workers as habitually careless to the point at which safety modifications were useless and a steady toll of accidents simply a fact of life.

Of course, workers *could* sometimes be both rational and careless. In trades in which they considered themselves skilled or experienced, workers might prefer older methods of doing things, rejecting new technologies and risking their lives in the process. Mine viewer John Buddle reported that one explosion had been caused by a man taking the top of his safety lamp off because he could not see well enough. The naked light caused the gassy air to ignite. His workmate tried to remonstrate with him, but since the man would not comply, he came quickly to the surface and avoided being exploded.[88] In other cases, even adult male workers seem to have been doing stupid things to pass the time, as in the case of the foundry workers who poured small bits of molten metal into a pot of water just to see what would happen, until too much metal fell into the water, causing the pot to shatter and become shrapnel.[89] Nonetheless, the point must be made that employers presumptively assumed that worker carelessness caused workplace accidents in almost every instance. This assumption conflicts with the notion that male workers were capable of or interested in keeping the workforce safe. At the same time, employers never admitted to carelessness or even to taking calculated risks.

Were employers careless? Although of course it is rare for evidence directly indicating employer negligence to survive, it is remarkable that some surviving evidence does implicate employers. Letterbooks generated by the Govan colliery in Scotland indicate that the management there knowingly used wire ropes that broke without any warning, endangering the lives of their miners. After one such rope broke, the colliery manager, instead of taking it out of commission, had it repaired and stationed men to watch it at all times to see if it was beginning to slip.[90] The following year, a letter from the mine manager to the rope makers complained that a rope that they had recently bought had broken with a load of coal in the cage, and that "it was a fortunate circumstance that no man was on the cage at the time, [since] the run preceding the one which gave way had men upon it."[91] In June 1845, the mine manager finally wrote to the mine owner that he could no longer "continue to expose so many lives to apparent danger, putting property out of the question."[92] Only after three years' worth of knowingly exposing workmen to danger did the mine owner replace the faulty wire ropes with hemp ropes. Of course this is only one example, but given the infrequency with which nineteenth-century business records survive at all, it is safe to say that the Govan colliery was not alone in taking calculated risks with workers' lives.

This chapter has so far suggested that while women, children, and slaves reaped some benefits, in judicial decisions and protective legislation, by being seen as unfree agents, white men were hamstrung by the pervasive association of protection and dependency. Before the rise of large and effective unions representing men in dangerous trades, few workers were willing to claim that they were entitled to safety legislation or provisions in the workplace on the grounds that they were not free agents; but colliers were the one great exception. Colliers—hemmed in by rules and regulations in one of the most dangerous workplaces—were more likely to present their workplace power relationships as dangerously unequal. Both colliers and observers of the industry emphasized the importance of allowing the sons of colliers to follow their fathers into the mines at a young age. The very purpose of early entry into the coalfields was to indoctrinate young workers into acceptance of a dangerous workplace before they were capable of independent decision making. As the South Shields committee investigating worker safety underground noted,

> After the age of 12, habits are beginning to be formed and tastes acquired much more in accordance with the ordinary employments on the surface, and it is probable that then even a pitman's son may have grown into a repugnance to exchange the light of day and the companionship of his fellows, which most other trades afford, for the solitary darkness of the mine, and its confined and severe labor.[93]

It was common knowledge that adults old enough to understand the dirt, danger, and discomfort of the coal mine, would never make good miners.[94]

Colliers were constricted in their choices and freedom of action not only by their early socialization to the mine, but also by their yearly "bond" or contract to work a certain number of days in every fortnight. To fail to do so was punishable by imprisonment. Thus, a coal miner who sensed danger in the mine was ordinarily not allowed to leave his "place" in the coal workings. He might alert his immediate supervisors, the mine's fireman or underviewer, but was forced to defer to their decisions about danger.[95] Furthermore, as mines became increasingly extensive, workers were unable to monitor the behavior of colleagues in distant parts of the mine and to act accordingly in furtherance of their own safety.

Miners themselves understood that they were not really free agents, and in one case they devised a really ingenious way to work around the prevailing system. Lancashire and Cheshire miners established a "Victims Fund," upon which a man was entitled to draw (after paying in for eight weeks) if he discovered that his life was in danger from explosions, black damp, lack of roof timbering, sudden flooding, or bad ropes. A man presented with such evidence of a dangerous workplace was allowed then to cease work immediately. Other less immediate dangers, including being assigned a "bad place" or an alteration in the system of working, could be justification for leaving work if all of a man's workmates agreed. Victims could only be victims for thirteen weeks and had to meet every other day to ascertain whether there was any work the union had for them to do.[96] Their collection also had to end whenever they found work or a brother miner found work for them. In addition to their Victim's Fund, Lancashire and Cheshire miners institutionalized their own status as the sole acceptable breadwinners in their families by lobbying for "smart money," a fixed sum to be paid by coalowners to workers who were injured in the mines.[97] Northumberland and Durham miners had also instituted a widespread system of smart money by the mid-1850s.[98]

Accepting that structural features of their workplace put them into a relationship with their employers that cried out for legislative protection, colliers were more likely than were other workers to exploit a language of dependency throughout the Victorian period. The editors of the Newport *Reformer,* a Welsh newspaper with a strong procollier slant, compared the working collier to the African slave, noting that there had never been any expose on the order of an *Uncle Tom's Cabin* to draw the attention of the public to the horrors of life underground.[99] The pitmen of Durham and Northumberland explicitly compared their lot to that of the black slave. While the claim of "wage slavery" or "white slavery" was not uncommon in this period, the 130-degree temperatures in the coal mines made a more satisfactory analogy between the conditions of the mines and the Southern cotton fields in the United States.[100] J. Robson, author of a poem to commemorate the Hartley tragedy, also compared the working miner to a slave, in a bitter stanza meant to blame greed for the absence of a second shaft at Hartley.

> Say, why was not a "rising shaft" in this dread dungeon seen?
> Hath harsh neglect or avarice the ruthless murd'rer been?
> Shall love of gold or niggardness prove still the miner's bane?
> Shall man's immortal soul be staked for owner's greed and gain?
> Give to the slaving serfs below the means from death to fly
> And then no blame shall blot the name of wealth when poor men die.[101]

Robinson extended his metaphor of colliers as trapped in coercive workplace relationships by presenting colliers not only as "slaving serfs" but also as "seamen cast on islands drear, amid the treach'rous main" and corpses "rising from the grave to liberty and light."[102] But in contrast with African slaves, thought to be incapable of rational self-preservation, mine workers were portrayed as "extremely watchful against danger."[103]

The *Labour Press and Miner's and Workmen's Examiner* trod the line between free agency and finding employers to blame for accidents. Its editors noted that workmen were to blame for many of the accidents. "But although this is so in fact, still from other considerations we should rather lay the blame on the shoulders of the employers. Often colliers are put to a great deal of annoyance and trouble to obtain even the most necessary appliances for their safety. Often when danger is complained of they are either pooh-poohed or threatened from making a complaint at the proper quarters, and so the danger is allowed to go on until the public is startled by some awful explosion and loss of life."[104]

William Prowting Roberts, the attorney who had represented both Chartists and striking miners in court in the 1840s, also accused both workers and employers, finding the former to be too fatalistic to force the latter to care about anything but profit:

> I say—do not let us deceive ourselves. This horrible contempt of life—your life; this quiet, *good tempered* consignment of you all to a periodical series of "Accidental deaths, and no blame attached to any one," is the natural and necessary result of your own criminal indifference. In tens—and fifties—and hundreds you have seen your brothers fall around you; widows and orphans, and old grandfathers, have been drafted in dozens to the Poorhouse, and in unuttered sorrow, died there; and you—pale for a moment, and stupefied—have looked calmly and submissively on—with a sort of child-like confiding humility—as if God ALMIGHTY had made the fire-damp and choke-damp on purpose for you—especially to kill you! Do I not say truly—and is this always to be so?

Roberts encouraged the men to become indignant and politicized, to distinguish between "Providence and profit."[105] Despite Roberts's urgings, working men remained for the most part unwilling to press the issue with their few parliamentary friends; they contributed to their friendly societies and sent their children to work when they themselves were injured.

This chapter has shown that the doctrine of free agency, which carried much of the weight for explaining the compensation regime in the nineteenth century, was based on untenable assumptions about the gender, age, and condition of servitude of workers. While women, children, and slaves were able to use their difference from the stereotypical white male worker to claim additional levels of protection, white male workers were by definition less able to make those claims. The free agency doctrine was clearly an ambiguous one: working men's levels of rationality and agency were constantly called into question by employers who blamed them for causing most workplace accidents or warned about moral hazard. Nonetheless, when it came to suing an employer for an accidental injury or seeking safety legislation, free agency was such an overpowering (and potentially empowering) doctrine that it was hard to throw over.[106] Working men who had viewed the rise and fall of the Chartist movement had seen that it was possible for men to be written off as political children if they rejected free agency. The mid-Victorian era celebrated the somber, bootstrapping mentality of the Samuel Smiles hero, not the work of a crusading state.[107]

Why would white male workers be attracted to the idea of free agency even at such great cost? American and British workingmen alike couched their quest for political equality and social respect in terms of equal rights.[108] "Citizen workers," or British workers seeking voting rights and full citizenship, were loath to accept protection and compensation if presented to them as part of a dependent master-servant relationship.

The trade-off between workplace compensation and being perceived as a dependent noncitizen was indeed at stake in a courtroom in Pennsylvania in 1854. A railway workman was injured when a gravel-filled railroad car on which he was riding tipped, not having been rightly secured. The plaintiff blamed the engineer and conductor, his fellow servants. The judge ruled against the plaintiff on the grounds that, in the absence of a written contract providing for employer liability in the case of personal injury, an employer had no common-law duty of care toward his employee. He went on to note that the kind of protection implied by such a duty of care would also imply a relationship of dependence from the servant to the master, similar to that existing between mother and child or between a weak-minded person and his benefactor, but "there is no relation of protection and dependence between master and servant, or of confidence in the institution of the relation . . . The servant is no Roman client or feudal villein, with a lord to protect him. Both are equal before the laws, and considered equally competent to take care of themselves, and very often the servant is the more intelligent of the two."[109] When compensation was couched in such negative terms, and self-sufficiency in such glowing ones, it is not surprising that workmen would accept the theory that they were free agents under the law, no matter what level of risk this entailed.

With the important exception of the coal miners, whose long-term contracts and illegal truck payments contradicted the idea of free agency, most male workers accepted the burden of that ideology by not agitating for special protective legislation. Fatalism may have been an element here, as William Prowting Roberts suggested, but there were surely other explanations, as workmen sought the right to vote and the achievement of a family wage that would make them the sole breadwinners. By the 1870s, the franchise had been broadened, the lack of compensation for workplace accidents was finally being challenged on a yearly basis in Parliament, and workingmen's organizations were at long last ridiculing the argument for free agency. As the editors of the *Railway Service Gazette* noted,

> Should [the human machine] break down, or be utterly smashed by accident, the company may, for convenience of unimpeded traffic, pick up the pieces; but beyond this it has no concern; another human machine can be procured, at a moment's notice, on the same terms as the one that has failed, therefore why should the company care a straw about the disabled lumber? . . . The human machine called Bob or Bill was a free agent. He was well aware of the terms of the contract; he has failed in his part—never mind from what cause—and there is an end of it.[110]

By the 1870s, working men realized that free agency could only take them so far; at a certain point, an appeal to morality had to be made based on the inequality of power that existed between working people and their employees.

5 Industrial Accidents and State Power

AS THE PREVIOUS CHAPTER HAS SHOWN THAT, although the Anglo-American common-law defenses that generally barred workers from collecting compensation through torts for their accidents on the job constructed workers as free-agent white males, women, child workers, and slaves sometimes found that their dependent status buffered their experiences of the compensation regime. Despite the fact that white male workers in practice faced inequalities that made it difficult or inadvisable for them to assert their free agency, they did not have the same opportunity to be protected under the law. Male workers were caught between a rock and a hard place—to band together with child workers and female workers and demand safety measures and help from the factory inspectorate was to compromise their masculinity, of which free agency was a central tenet. On the other hand, to band together with other free, white males and rely only on the doctrines of self-help to deal with workplace accidents, was to miss an opportunity to deploy the occasional paternalism of Parliament to their own ends for once.

In the end, male workers chose the latter strategy—to put off calls for workplace safety in favor of a quest for citizenship. This explains in part why it was not until the 1870s—after changes wrought to the electorate by the 1867 Reform Act—that workers' compensation was placed in earnest on the table. Before that date, suggestions for revisions of the compensation regime along the lines of those in other European countries were put forward, but without much support from the workers themselves. A second factor that made the achievement of the first Employers' Liability Act possible was the entry into politics of representatives of strong unions representing dangerous industries. By the 1870s, these unions were shifting the discourse, from one that presented workplace protections as unmanly to one which presented them as essentially just and necessary.[1]

Although Britain and the United States shared a common legal framework and presented workers with similar obstacles to compensation, reform on this issue came to Britain decades before it came to the United States. British centralization was a key factor—as this chapter will show, legislation had to be achieved in just one forum rather than in a multiplicity of states, and a few newspapers concentrated in urban areas could keep up the pressure for reform.[2] Equally important, however, was the existence, in Britain, of a more thoroughly developed theory of worker exploitation, derived in part from continental models of no-fault compensation that had been proposed since the 1830s. American policymakers would not seriously consider European examples until the twentieth century.[3] One of the most important influences on the earlier development of a predictable workplace accident amelioration regime in Britain was the milieu in which various problems related to poverty were being reconfigured. In the first half of the nineteenth century, as James Vernon has described, individual failure to cope with the exigencies of the market was portrayed by economic liberals as a moral failure and want as a spur to harder work. By the 1860s and the 1870s, poverty, hunger, and the inability to save effectively for a rainy day were becoming to be seen—amidst a profusion of voluntary societies and the development of the field of sociology—as intractable social problems that merited governmental solutions.[4]

Revolutions in government are not like revolutions in the hard sciences; the development of concern for worker safety as a social problem was uneven. While the *Times* occasionally expressed concerns about workers' safety, particularly in gunpowder mills, as early as the 1790s, organized attempts to legislate safer workplaces did not begin until the 1830s.[5] During that decade, as workers protested long factory hours and the New Poor Law, they occasionally voiced a call for legislation to monitor factory safety conditions. One correspondent to the *London Mercury* asked,

> Does not the law affect, in yet other matters, a tender concern for the preservation of human life? Is not the speed of steam-boats for some miles below London-bridge regulated by law? And is not the pretext for this interference with the freedom of trade, the paramount necessity of preventing accidents to life and limb? The labourers throughout England now demand that the same

spirit of superintendence which watches over the movements of steam-boats, should also watch over the movements of factories.[6]

And indeed, the same forces in government that regulated steamboats were beginning to consider the regulation of factories. The Royal Commissioners who proposed regulation of factories employing child workers in 1833 issued an interesting dictum on the cause of accidents:

> The accidents which occur to the adults are of themselves evidence (unless they were willfully incurred in a state of delirium) that the individual used all the caution of which he is capable; as it may be presumed that the loss of life or limb, or the infliction of severe pain, would rarely be wantonly incurred . . . Unless we are to impose on the workman the obligation of perpetual care and apprehension of danger, the nature of the injuries inflicted are of themselves evidence that all the care which can be taken by individuals attending to their work is taken by then; it is only the proprietor of the machinery who has the most effectual means of guarding against the dangers attendant upon its use.[7]

The insistence that workplace accidents were beyond the control of the worker belied the assertion, commonly made by employers, that employees were free agents who were to blame for their own accidents and should therefore bear the social costs.

Thinking along these lines, Thomas Tooke, Southwood Smith, and Edwin Chadwick proposed a system of no-fault workers' compensation legislation. According to their proposal, in the case of accidents to children under fourteen, mill owners would be compelled by magistrates to pay for medical attendance, the expenses of the cure, and half the child's wages during the period of convalescence. When accidents occurred to workers over fourteen, "in all cases where the injury was received from accidents in the ordinary course of business, where there was no culpable temerity," the worker should also receive full medical expenses paid and half wages (to pay full wages was to invite fraud, and of course to contravene the principle of less eligibility).[8] Their proposals went nowhere; employers opposed no-fault compensation for obvious reasons, given their insistence that they bore no monetary liability for workers' accidents. But it is instructive to see that at least for some reformers, justice required that society assume some of the cost for accidents.

Into the 1840s, these analysts continued to note that the prevailing system of compensation was unfair to workers. Robert Rawlinson, author of

"Descriptive Remarks Relative to Railway Contracts and Railway Workmen," noted that no matter what the source of the injury to railway workmen, coroners' juries usually noted that it was the men's own fault. "Many of the men are reckless, but what is the cause? No man cares for them; they labour like degraded brutes; they feed and lodge like savages; they are enveloped in vice as with an atmosphere; the sensual only is present. The 'naveys,' from the nature of their employment, and their hitherto utterly neglected state, form as it were, a distinct race."[9]

Edwin Chadwick noted that coroners' juries were full of people who didn't know any better than to return accidental death verdicts. Engineers had told Chadwick privately that cost cutting and neglect of due precautions, especially on the part of contractors, had made workplaces accidents waiting to happen. The construction workers themselves knew what was going on. "The older and more experienced navigators are aware of the dangers of the practice, and prevail upon the younger and less experienced of the labourers to go in front whilst such work is carried on." Chadwick noted bitterly that if the directors and shareholders, rather than the taxpayers or individual families, had to bear the expenses of the maintenance and education of orphan children and the maintenance of widows, it would amount to £300–400 per man. Faced with these burdens, railway directors would find some way to make the contractors liable.[10] In Chadwick's opinion, even worker recklessness did not excuse railway companies for shifting the burden for worker injuries onto the wider society. After all, why should the nation at large have to assume the burden for the company's decision to hire reckless workers? Rather than assume that any accident involving a worker was willful on the part of the worker, the company should automatically be held responsible.[11]

Despite the existence of a fully articulated, alternative ideology about collective social responsibility for workplace accidents, little was achieved in the way of legislation to promote workplace safety, except in mills largely staffed by women and children. For those classes of workers, enveloped by ideas about dependency, the existing legislation could be meaningful and was the next step taken chronologically. The Factory Act of 1844 set certain minimum standards of industrial safety, especially regarding guards on equipment. Inspectors could notice and classify this machinery as dangerous, but this did not oblige occupiers to fence it off. Still, if someone got hurt on it they would then be liable to fines. The Factory Act also barred children from cleaning mill gearing or in working between moving and stationary parts of self-acting mules. From 1844 to 1871, British factory law made mandatory the reporting of any accidents that prevented worker return by 9 A.M. the following day. Reportable accidents had to be caused by machinery, explosion, or a vat of boiling liquid. Worker injury due to falling objects, although a common enough happening in the factory, was excluded.[12] As noted in Chapter 4, under the Factory Acts, employers could be prosecuted and compensation could be paid under the terms of Section 60. The compensation would be raised from a fine imposed as a result of injury or death caused by machinery on which notice of danger had been served.[13] The *Ten Hours' Advocate* noted that the factory inspectors had reported 2,548 injury accidents in the half year ending in April 1846 and estimated that the number had been five times that before rudimentary safety laws were passed.[14]

Yet even where precedents for government regulatory action existed, the resistance to industrial safety laws was palpable. Evasion of the Factory Acts was common, because the laws themselves were vaguely worded, containing language like "securely fenced" rather than specifying particular materials to be used or measures to be taken.[15] The Factory Acts also did not apply to many nontextile industries in which children might injure themselves on machinery, potentially leaving an injured child with no means of redress.[16] The power differential between employer and employee made it particularly easy for factory owners to flout the law. The *Ten Hours' Advocate* noted that hundreds of workers were compelled by their employers to come back to work immediately after such accidents, and to sit all day by their machinery, so that their accidents would not be considered reportable.[17] Manufacturers saw no option for increasing profits besides cutting labor costs, including through the use of illegal child labor—and so many were content to incur token fines on a regular basis. When cases were brought, the issue of willfulness or motivation was purposely elided by holding the employer "strictly liable," in a sort of no-fault liability that blurred the blame.[18]

As W. G. Carson pointed out, the whole system of prosecutions under the Factory Acts was structured to permit evasion by mill owners. Inspectors who were from the same social class as manufacturers generally preferred to coerce and warn rather than prosecute them, and discretion became an important buffer between the law as written and its execution. The Appleton case noted in the previous chapter is one example that shows just how much forbearance the factory inspector displayed with an employer before finally taking action. The case of Edwin Lee is also illustrative. Seventeen-year-old Lee was at work on September 22, 1854, in the cotton waste spinning factory of Peter Bailey at Stockport. He was putting a strap on a pulley eight feet from the floor when the strap slipped, wrapped around his arm, and drew him to the shaft. Lucky for him the strap broke, and he escaped with a broken arm.[19] After the accident, mill owner Peter Bailey wrote to Factory Inspector Charles Trimmer proposing a settlement. Bailey, who had only fifteen employees, claimed that a prosecution under the Factory Acts would ruin him. He never thought that the horizontal shaft would be a problem, considering it was so high from the floor. He proposed to fence the shaft, pay Lee 9s. per week in wages and £2 compensation, and to pay all medical expenses for having the arm reset.[20] Trimmer had forwarded this letter to Factory Inspector Howle, who wrote to the Home Office. Howle could see two courses of action: prosecution against Bailey would ruin the man's business, which was unacceptable. The other option, summary proceedings before the Stockport magistrates under section 60 of the Factory Acts, would probably fail.

> A large proportion of these Borough Justices are themselves occupiers of factories, and none of them have fenced any such shafts, or adopted any of the precautions suggested by your Lordships for prevention of accidents from such shafts being unfenced; it therefore is highly improbable that these gentlemen would convict Peter Bailey of an offence which they themselves are daily committing, especially since by declining to convict in his case they would establish a precedent useful to themselves whenever a similar accident shall occur in one of their own factories.[21]

Given that neither of these options was optimal, the Home Office agreed to take the settlement. Nor was Lee's case an isolated instance. Factory Inspector Alexander Redgrave refused to prosecute under the Factory Acts any mill owner who promised to pay compensation to an employee privately. As a result, there was an alarming spike in factory accidents on Redgrave's watch, something that he explained as due to the briskness of trade.[22]

Factory Inspector Leonard Horner faced opposition to the Factory Act not just from manufacturers, but also from the government. In 1851, in the wake of a successful Factory Act prosecution, Home Secretary Sir George Grey warned Horner against sending a general warning to mill owners about the nature of the offending machinery. Grey feared that doing so would put ideas in the heads of workpeople—he feared, then, that they might be fully informed of their right to bring a prosecution under the Factory Acts! But Horner would not be moved, noting that he felt responsible for protecting working people from the "fearful" accidents to which they were exposed and also for warning factory owners about the risks to which they exposed themselves.[23] Factory inspectors continued to send mill owners periodic warnings about dangerous machinery, incorporating their knowledge of new sources of accidents.[24]

The government also showed its ambivalence on the issue of the moving horizontal shafts that powered much mill machinery. Before 1854 these shafts had been out of the reach of legislation as long as they were at least seven feet above the ground. Nonetheless, a seventeen-year-old boy was caught by one and killed, impelling Horner to press the issue. While the then Home Secretary Palmerston at first supported the initiative to regulate the placement of shafts, he wondered whether it would create too great an expense for mill owners. Throughout 1854, deputations of mill owners—from Belfast and Glasgow as well as Lancashire and Yorkshire—visited Palmerston, applying pressure. Finally, Palmerston cracked, telling Horner to

> say to inspectors that strong representations have been made to me by numerous deputations of Millowners and Master Manufacturers that to case all the horizontal shafts in mills would occasion a very great expense and that as those shafts are generally near the ceiling or at all events at some height above the heads of the workpeople there can be little danger to be apprehended from those shafts to any persons who use common Prudence and Care.[25]

Clearly, there was a balance to be struck between achieving worker safety and putting employers out of business.

On March 2, 1854, the factory inspectors wrote to Palmerston enclosing a circular that they had prepared to counter some of the allegations being made by the mill owner deputations. They listed accidents from horizontal shafts, including the age or status of the injured party, how the accident happened, and its aftermath. One adult, who climbed to the top of his machine to put the strap back on the drum and had his smock wrap around the shaft, had "both arms torn out of the shoulder joints, abdomen lacerated, the intestine protruded, both legs broken, head contused, and *death*." In another case, a young person called out to a fellow worker, "watch me do a trick," and got up on a stool and put his arm around the shaft. The strap locked onto his arm and carried him around the main shaft. His leg was cut off and fell into the room, his right arm was broken in several places, his ankle was fractured, his head was cut, and he was "dashed and mutilated in a shocking manner."

A third young person died when he was holding a belt which the master had been sewing, and the belt suddenly caught onto the shaft, carrying him with it at 120 revolutions per minute, "striking him against the ceiling and reducing his bones almost to powder." He was killed instantly. Other workers suffered amputations and fractures of the arm, bruises, scalpings, and lacerations. The use of these gothic details was a political tactic; only in this way could factory inspectors bring home to Palmerston the true human impact of unfenced shafts.

> To the objection that the workpeople ought to take care of themselves by understanding the dangers to which they are exposed and taking due care to protect themselves—it is sufficient to answer that persons are employed in factories from the age of eight and that death or maiming for life is a punishment too severe for heedlessness or incaution, and that accidents occur from which no caution on the part of the sufferer can guard him, as from a ladder slipping, being pushed by another person, stumbling, or the like.[26]

A handwritten extension of the roster of horizontal shaft accidents was compiled, and there had been sixteen between October 1853 and the end of February 1854. The youngest victim was a boy of ten.

The attempt by the factory inspectors to recast factory workers in dependent mode, by noting the early age at which they entered the mills, was a good gambit, but it failed. Given the constant obstructionism waged by mill owners, both actively and passively, it was no surprise when, in 1856, Parliament modified the Factory Acts to make employers less responsible for the fencing of dangerous machinery than they had been in 1844. Despite the futility of doing so, Factory Inspector Leonard Horner continued publicly to expose the limitations of the system. He argued that the Factory Acts were one of the few instances in which it was both just and appropriate to depart from the general principal of laissez-faire. From Horner's perspective, unless legislation were tightened, no amount of watchfulness on the part of workers would prevent accidents. The very proliferation of fatalities due to unguarded belts was a demonstration of this. In the meantime, £10,563 had been spent on investigations since 1844.[27]

Although women, children, and young persons working in factories received the most legislative attention, the occupational safety of railway laborers was also a concern early in the Victorian period. In 1846, a Select Committee of the House of Commons was convened to study the many work-related grievances of the navvies, the men who worked in railway track and tunnel construction.[28] The Select Committee noted in its overall report that there had been a large number of accidents to life and limb among the railway laborers. Not only were these accidents dangerous to the public economy, but they also transformed otherwise fit and strong adult men into lesser beings who were dependent on public charity:

> In estimating the harm thus occasioned, not merely must the actual suffering inflicted on the subjects of these accidents and their relatives be taken into account, but also the fact, that society, if the sufferer dies, is deprived of a useful, industrious, and productive member, in the prime of life and efficiency; or, if he survives, he lives a wretched cripple, a mendicant, or a pauper, to be maintained, with those who were dependent on his labour, at the public expense.[29]

Again, those who favored the idea that society had some responsibility for the alleviation of workplace accidents conjured up the notion of widespread dependency to support their view. The committee, rather uniquely, also sought to shift the burden of proof, noting that the companies involved in railway labor accidents should have to prove that legislation would *not* alleviate the accidents, rather forcing the government to prove that legislation would be helpful.

The free agency argument functioned in the case of railway workers not only in prospect—because they were likely to be turned into "wretched cripples"—but also because their particular system of working made it difficult for workers to assess and avoid risk. Railway laborers often worked for subcontractors, alongside the workmen of other subcontractors, about whose safety record and trustworthiness they knew nothing. "In a system of combined labour, the greater the subdivision of employment, the less control has each labourer over the general conduct of the operation; and it is to acts or defaults in this conduct, that your committee believes one portion of the accidents occurring may undoubtedly be traced."[30] In fact, the laborer, as the weaker and less educated party, was actually the one least likely to recognize or provide against danger and yet he was the only sufferer. The suffering of the worker certainly caused him to learn a lesson, but the employer took away no lesson for himself.

The Select Committee proposed a new set of arrangements that, if adopted, would have inaugurated a new legal principle: that the party with the greatest power to prevent an injury, and the greatest means to repair it, should bear the greatest burden for such accidents. "Your Committee cannot but feel convinced, that what is called accident, too often arises from a neglect of precautionary arrangement, of improved instruments or methods of working, the recourse to which lies entirely in the power of the employer."[31] The committee also put forth the radical notion that even overseeing fellow servants so that they did not, in their incautiousness, injure each other, was properly the responsibility of the employer. By stating this, the committee called into question the prevailing legal doctrine, that men working in the same industry, even if hired by different subcontractors and working in different departments, had a responsibility under the fellow-servant rule to monitor each others' conduct.

The Select Committee was presented with a "French" option to the prevailing system, having been told by an expert that compensation under French law was a certainty after a short legal proceeding.[32] Witnesses were then called who either endorsed, or rejected, the proposition that Britain follow the French example. Edwin Chadwick proposed moving in the direction of no-fault compensation. He noted that the laborer's ability to sense and avoid danger had been overstated. Like factory workers, who were already protected by law, railway construction workers had little control over the work process. Guaranteed compensation would be beneficial practically as well as ethically, as it would act as a wage premium to interest workers in the more dangerous subsets of the industry.[33] Chadwick suggested that railway companies pass the charge for workers' compensation insurance on to their contractors, who would then have a good motivation to safeguard the lives of their men. "It is observed that employers and contractors do lose, and suffer stoppages and inconveniences, by most accidents. No doubt they do, but not enough. An unexpected charge of £10, or £20, or £30, will not, in such works, put parties out of their way, when a £100 or £200 charge would arrest serious attention, and stimulate exertion for prevention." Chadwick objected to the existing policy that the cheapest bidder won the contract, even if he used inhumane or dangerous methods.[34]

Another witness, M. G. Dowling, the chief of the Liverpool police force, pointed out that part of the problem was the way in which the railway construction work was structured. Paying subcontractor teams by the square foot completed rather than by hours worked gave them only a motivation to work as fast as possible, not necessarily to be safe. Subcontracting also gave companies and contractors the opportunity to wash their hands of accidents that did occur.[35]

Although witnesses and members of the committee showed in this way that they were capable of really revolutionary thinking about the reasons for workplace accidents and possibilities for their amelioration, they confronted tough opponents. British railway executives rejected guaranteed compensation schemes out of hand, arguing that they would rob the independent British workman of initiative and independence. Isambard Kingdom Brunel noted that guaranteed compensation

> would, I think, inevitably alter the present position of things, by which every department, from the highest to the lowest, is sublet to men, who are free agents, and seek to execute the work in the cheapest way. Some risks, I admit, are run in consequence; but I do not think that the results of those risks are at all to be compared with the advantage attained in our manufactures generally by that system, the independent efforts of the workmen, and of every class of men employed in manufactures.[36]

Brunel himself had had to pay a heavy deodand that had been levied against the Great Western after the death of a worker, but said that the Queen's Bench had excused the company from paying.[37] The Select Committee resulted in a fruitful discussion, but Brunel's ideas and those of other railway magnates won the day, and the existing structure of compensation—lack of compensation—remained in place.

While railroad workers remained unprotected, the 1840s saw real progress in the direction of worker safety through mine inspections. An explosion in early 1847 at the Oaks colliery in Ardsley, that seemed to be due to insufficient ventilation, had renewed the sporadic public outcry for government inspection of mines; and the debate that surrounded the lack of safety legislation pertaining to work underground illustrated ongoing disagreements about the site of responsibility for workplace accidents. The editors of the *Mining Journal,* normally not noted for their excitability, proclaimed,

> We have so often had occasion to remark upon the wholesale sacrifice of human life in our collieries—upon the inefficient direction to which the works are intrusted, and the shamefully-neglected state in general of the ventilation—that the task has become an irksome one and the impossibility of bringing forward new arguments on the subject renders it also a difficult one . . . Private charity will no doubt be called in, and will be prompt to answer and relieve, to some extent, the dire calamity; but such relief can be only evanescent, and as but a

drop in the ocean to the years of accumulated misery which the sufferers must endure. Since all the endeavours of the press, of philanthropic and scientific men, have utterly failed to bring the coal owners to adopt the necessary means for the safety of their men, it now becomes an imperative duty for the Legislature to take up the subject, and enforce stringent regulations for proper supervision and ventilation, however objectionable the public interference with private enterprise may be considered.[38]

A letter to the editor by "a miner" pointed out that coroners' juries invariably focused their attention not on the dangerous gases present underground, but rather on whether some workman had opened his lamp or had a naked light underground. The dangerous state of the ventilation, the miner argued, was really to blame, leaving the lives of hundreds of working men and boys in the hands of perhaps their youngest workmate.[39]

As they had done in the factories and discussed doing for the railroads, so some members of the House of Commons sought legislation that would hold mineowners more responsible for the lives of the men in their employ. A group of miners had petitioned Thomas Slingsby Duncombe to introduce a bill for the safety of miners:

> Your petitioners desire to direct the attention of your Honourable house to the many deaths continually happening from bad ventilation in the mines, and also to the distressing accidents which still more frequently occur from the same cause, and from which your petitioners are put to heavy expense and lose their work for long periods of time . . . Your petitioners admit that many of your petitioners have been neglectful and overconfident, but they are many of them very poor, and their position with their masters does not often allow them to speak freely of facts as they really are.[40]

In response, Duncombe and his colleagues in 1847 introduced a Mines and Collieries Bill that would have set up a system of inspection and even mandated that all injuries should be reported to a subinspector, who would come and investigate each accident. An inspector, with the permission of the secretary of state, could also maintain an action against the proprietor of the mine in cases of accident, as was the case in factories.

When his bill came up for a second reading, on June 30, 1847, Duncombe argued that mine owners would take no steps toward greater mine safety without pressure from the government. Despite the fact that the mining magnate Lord Durham had been his mentor, Duncombe politely insisted that it was the government's responsibility to protect the miners through legislation. Duncombe was joined in his call for change by Thomas Wakley, the radical coroner and founder of the *Lancet*. Wakley noted sardonically that the interests of the poor were always staved off, but if one noble lord had been blown out of a coal pit, there would have been legislation passed the very next day. Other speakers claimed to support the idea of a bill, but noted that such an initiative should properly come from the government rather than out-of-doors. The most vociferous opponent of the bill, Mr. Forster, denied that the government had a right to interfere, since "nineteen out of twenty accidents that occurred were imputable to the carelessness of the men themselves, and did not arise from any causes which it was in the power of the coal owners to remove."[41] The Mines and Collieries Bill was opposed by the Home Secretary Sir George Grey, who made half-hearted promises to consider the measure but urged Duncombe to withdraw the legislation.

While Duncombe did withdraw his first bill, he introduced the subject again the very next day, having been informed by express mail of a large colliery explosion near Wigan. The news contained the kind of horrific information that Duncombe often used to buttress his parliamentary speeches—that six of the men killed in the pit had been left there under the particular instructions of the mine owner, despite the offer by two volunteers to go down and attempt a rescue. Duncombe demanded that the government send an inspector to the scene, but the home secretary refused, noting that the coroners' jury process and local government were responsible for finding the facts in the case.[42]

Now the gloves were off. Still fuming, Duncombe introduced an amended Mines and Collieries Bill, which came up for a second reading two weeks later, on July 14. The new bill applied only to the most volatile Lancashire and Staffordshire collieries, where safety lamps had to be used but gunpowder blasting was commonplace. Patterned after the Factory Acts, the bill would even have provided for prosecution of mine owners who failed to take safety measures. In support of his bill, Duncombe specifically invoked the free agency argument, noting that although factory workers had been protected through safety legislation, mine workers were in an even worse situation, since they were "bound down by stringent contracts for a twelvemonth, and therefore had not the opportunity of escaping from danger."[43] Despite all the eloquence Duncombe could muster, he had little support—and in fact, his long history of support for the Chartists, and of criticism of the government over the question of the secret opening of his mail, positioned him poorly to wrest gains from the government. He was even criticized by Thomas Wakley, who disapproved of the bill's implications for private property and noted that Duncombe should have left the legislative initiative to the government. Mr. Forster denounced the bill as the "most absurd and useless Bill that ever was laid upon the Table of the House," and alleged that it was the work of Chartist attorney W. P. Roberts.[44] When the time came for a vote, the bill was defeated fifty-six votes to twenty-three.[45]

Although specific legislation for mine inspection disappeared in 1847, the issue was not altogether dropped. An 1849 Select Committee of the House of Lords revealed some of the abuses and horrific working conditions suffered by miners underground. Asked about the state of the Jarrow colliery, Dr. John Hutchinson testified that men died of suffocation. He noted that there was hardly any movement of air in the mine, "like as if it were a man gently breathing upon you . . . When I was going toward that mine, I asked a miner, 'Which is the way to the Jarrow colliery?' and he said 'Sir, I do not know of any colliery, but there [pointing me in the direction of the colliery] is a butcher's shop.'"[46] In addition to tabulations showing the rate of accidents in British coal mines to be about 1 in 130, Select Committee members received a petition from the coal miners of Northumberland and Durham calling for legislative protection.

The language of the Select Committee report was noncommittal; they were willing to endorse small improvements in safety as long as they would not put mine owners to substantial expense, but feared that government inspection would alienate mine owners. The Committee argued that mine safety was more ambiguous than factory safety, since fencing machinery was relatively inexpensive.[47] The Select Committee did recommend in favor of inspectors. "When it is considered that, if on the one side, the endeavour may involve some objections, and possibly some obstacles, there is, on the other, to be considered the reasonable protection of the lives and limbs . . . of a great and valuable portion of the population, exposed at the best to many unavoidable dangers "[48]

A spate of mine accidents followed in 1849, finally pushing Parliament to pass the 1850 Mines Inspection Act. Seymour Tremenheere, who investigated the Darley Main colliery explosion in 1849 (which killed 75 of the 101 workers at work on the day), commented, "there can be no manner of doubt that had this colliery been subject to inspection by a properly qualified Government officer, the glaring defects of its ventilation would have been so forcibly represented to the owner, that in all human probability those lives would have been saved. In several contiguous cottages near the scene of the disaster only one male was left alive."[49] For the men who had died at Darley Main, the Act was too little, too late.

The 1850 Mines Inspection Act provided for the appointment of three mine inspectors and a number of subinspectors, who were supposed to tour every mine in their districts four times a year. Once an inspector had informed a mine owner of anything unsafe, if the owner failed to fix the problem, he might be assessed a £100 fine. In the case of a death in the mine, within twelve hours of the death the mine owner had not only to notify the subinspector but also to tell him when and where the inquest would be held, and the coroner was supposed to give two days notice of same to the subinspector. The inspectors were asked to attend these inquests and were allowed to subpoena whomever they wanted to testify.[50] While the level of inspection mandated in the legislation was wholly inadequate, it is significant because it marks the destruction of an important ideological barrier against safety regulation in an industry whose workers were overwhelmingly male.

Coroners' Inquests

While the mining inspectorate was clearly an advance over the system of absolutely nothing that had come before it, the 1850 Mines Inspection Act's dependence on the inquest system did not provide much justice for injured workers. First of all, there was some question about whether the job of a coroner's jury in any given inquest was simply to find the proximate cause of a violent death or to look further at systemic causes. Even in cases in which a piece of faulty equipment seemed to have led to a workers' death, juries were likely to note that a chain had broken, resulting in death—rather than looking at whose responsibility it might have been to provide properly functioning equipment.[51] A second major flaw in the system was that those witnesses who knew what had caused an accident tended to be dead. As a result, the evidence was collected from interested parties.[52] Employers might resort to "treating" members of the workforce in order to elicit positive testimony, or blacklisting recalcitrant witnesses.[53] In 1877, union leader Alexander Macdonald quarreled with the foreman of one inquest jury about Macdonald's failure to turn over the names of miners who had informed him before the mine exploded that it was in a dangerous state. While the jury claimed to want to interview the miners about what they had known, Macdonald feared—probably not without justification—that the real purpose was to blacklist the miners in question.[54]

Working people had little confidence in inquests. According to Martin Jude, miners themselves thought coroners' juries "nearly a farce;" Jude called for juries composed of local men familiar with mining.[55] Mine union leaders noted that coroners were doctors or lawyers and thus unacquainted with the jargon and work practices of the mines.[56] Furthermore, the same men who served on coroners' juries were the taxpayers who would have to foot the bill for an assize trial if they recommended a manslaughter conviction—a financial conflict of interest. David Swallow of the Lancashire miners' union recommended that a practical miner, someone like an ex-mine inspector, serve as a special colliery coroner. "We have had too much law," Swallow noted, "we now want some justice."[57] But even a coroner with practical mining experience did not necessarily ensure justice; one coroner went on at length about the recklessness of the miners with whom he was personally familiar, and the way in which their dangerous practices made accidents unavoidable.[58] James Darlington, the proprietor of several mines, admitted that coroners' juries tended to be charitable to proprietors because they had lost great sums of money from explosions. Proprietors made promises about improvements they were going to make and then failed to make them.[59]

Although it was a commonplace that coroners' juries were biased toward the viewpoints of employers, especially when it came to mining accidents, they became effective sites for political theater. At the 1844 Haswell inquest, an argument broke out among three parties: Chartist attorney William Prowting Roberts, the owner of the Haswell Colliery, and the coroner.[60] Roberts called for the appointment of an independent mine inspector to view the mine; the mine owner objected to the name that Roberts had put forth. Roberts began to grandstand: "Justice would not be done; the ends of fair inquiry even would not be answered if the owners refused to allow Mr. Dunn to examine the pit."[61] In response, the coroner interrupted angrily and would not let Roberts use such confrontational language.

Later on in the same inquest, the coroner and Roberts got into another sparring match. Thomas Forster, the viewer or in-house inspector of the mine in question, reported that he had a personal objection to having Matthias Dunn inspect the pit because Dunn hated him and might use the opportunity to do the mine owners a disservice. Referring to the fact that Foster had had a couple of serious accidents at the collieries to which he had been connected, Roberts responded, "A burnt child dreads the fire." The coroner replied, "You have no right to make such an observation." Roberts shot back, "I have such a right.

You take me up too sharply." The coroner responded, "I do not sir. You shall ask any question you please, but you shall not make such observations." Replied Roberts, "It is a very fair observation. I have a right to expect judicial courtesy." At this point Roberts was threatened with being turned out of the court.[62]

Throughout the inquest, Roberts tried to elicit testimony from witnesses in favor of a more rigorous system of government inspection. He also presented a viewpoint on the workplace that would anticipate twentieth-century attitudes toward removing danger from the workplace: if a necessary act in the workplace could not be done safely, it should either be done by machinery or else with only essential personnel present.[63] But the inquest was not the proper forum for such observations, and on its last day the coroner chided him for making the inquest into a Select Committee meeting. While the workers in this particular case did not have their say within the inquest room, it is worth nothing that they did have a form of comeuppance. Roberts's testimony was highlighted in a pamphlet that was subsequently sold for 3d., cheaply enough so that someone curious about the inquest could read about it and come to his own conclusions. Both Roberts's involvement in the inquest and the subsequent pamphlet were a way for workers to contest the authoritative narrative of the accident. Public exhibitions like Roberts's also seem to have had an impact, since, after 1851, government inspectors attempted to protect workers' interests by attending inquests and playing the confrontational role that Roberts had played at Haswell.

It was extremely rare, although not unheard-of, for someone to be charged with manslaughter in the wake of a mine accident. If anyone were charged, it was more likely to be a manager or other underling rather than the mine owner himself. At the inquest after one rope-breaking incident near Bristol, the jury was shown the broken rope, which had been spliced together in many places with iron, and they heard testimony from many colliers that they suspected the rope was deficient.[64] Testimony was given that several miners had been so afraid of the rope that they walked off the job, until literally driven back to work by fear of starvation. Other miners on the site demanded that the number of men allowed to travel below on the strength of the rope be reduced. The coal owner claimed not to be responsible because he had delegated that responsibility, including superintendence of materials, to a manager.[65] Because they had deliberately used an unsafe rope—and worse, had dismissed miners for complaining about the lack of safety at the mine—the manager of the pit and one of the foremen were committed to trial for manslaughter. The mine owner, on the other hand, escaped unscathed, his defense about delegating power having been accepted.[66]

As noted in Chapter 2, the common law suggested that a worker had some recourse if his employer provided him with faulty tools and equipment. Nonetheless, even when this fact was proven at an inquest, a judgment against an employer was not automatic. A mine elevator operator named Joseph Dudley was brought up on manslaughter charges even though the winding engine at the mine where he worked lacked an indicator to show when the cage or elevator had reached the pitbank. "One of the jurors asked if the law did not require colliery proprietors to have an indicator to their engines. To this the Coroner replied that that was a matter for the Government Inspector to see to, and it was for him, if he saw fit, to proceed against the proprietors." Dudley was found guilty of manslaughter while his employers, who had supplied the faulty equipment, were found guilty of nothing.[67]

Mine owners were insulated from the judgments of coroners' juries not only by coroners' constructions of the law, or the ability to use delegation as a legal defense, but also because they earned sympathy from juries of similar social composition. In one such case, six miners were killed when the Westwood Colliery, near Sheffield, exploded. The colliery agent, Edward Beachar, admitted that he allowed the men to work with open flames although the mine was known to be volatile. Beachar insisted that the ventilation was sufficient even though the government mine inspector testified that when he went down there with an anemometer the device would not even turn—that there was literally no air circulation. The government inspector further said that he had received numerous anonymous letters from pitmen complaining about the state of things in the mine. "The coroner said [there] had been great negligence on the part of Beachar, and although it might not amount to manslaughter . . . if it depended on him, he would commit Beachar." Despite all this evidence, and despite these strong words from the official government representative, the jury returned a verdict of accidental death, along with the comment that it was not safe to work in that mine with naked lights.[68]

It is clear that in the field of coal mining, the decision to make coroners' juries the main forum for addressing workplace accidents was unsatisfactory for workers. Although the 1850 Act had represented an improvement by providing an inspectorate whose members could attend inquests, the inspectors were no match for the problems inherent in the institution. Coroners' juries were plagued by multiple biases, had a very circumscribed legal role (to identify the immediate rather than structural causes of workplace danger), and in al-most every case found a verdict of "accidental death." At best, the inquest could serve as a kind of theatrical space for workers' advocates, like Roberts or like various government inspectors, to point out the glaring inconsistencies in the system.[69]

In contrast with coal mines, where coroners' inquests were guaranteed by law, in other industries the coroner might not call a jury, particularly if he did not hear the circumstances of a violent death on the job.[70] In some areas of the country, "routine" accidents to individuals were not thought to merit a coro-ner's inquest.[71] If a coroner's jury was impaneled, jurors were rarely drawn from the same social ranks as injured workers. Robert Lowe, a member of the Select Committee investigating accidents on railroads in 1857, argued that coroners' inquests were of little use with regard to railroad accidents, because "the coro-ners very often have a very good understanding with the company, and they use their office for the purpose of misleading the public as to the real nature of the accident."[72] The verdicts of these juries were depressingly uniform—they usually found accidental death, unless the evidence of negligence was over-whelming. As in mining inquests, only the immediate overseer or workman who had caused the accident would be brought to trial—the company that hired an incompetent man could not be touched. In Scotland, an even worse situation prevailed; there, where there was no coroner, the procurator-fiscal, a criminal-law officer, was only alerted to sudden or violent death when there was reason to suspect manslaughter or murder.[73]

Just as at coal mine inquests, the tribunes of labor who represented other fields of work used the public platform of the inquest to draw attention to the injustices inherent in the system. An inquest was held in 1862 on the body of a fifteen-year-old, Richard Durkin, who was killed while working on a scaffold. He was a plasterer's boy, and fell from a ladder, dying when he struck his head on the ground. At the inquest,

a slater said the lives of the men were in constant danger . . . Persons used to stop and look up in wonder that the workmen were able to cling on to the roof. The deceased's life would have been saved if there had been a plank along the edge of the scaffolding, as there would have been if it was necessary to save bricks from falling off. But the fact was, greater precautions were taken to save property than to prevent the loss of life. When a workman was killed, an investigation into the circumstances took place, but nothing was done to prevent a recurrence of the mischief. Witness was himself within an inch of being killed on the preceding day. Numbers of dreadful accidents were occurring every week that might be prevented if as much trouble was taken as was used to save even bricks.

The coroner replied to the brave slater by saying the men should complain to their employers. The slater noted in response that the workmen had complained, but that their employer would say, "If you don't do it others will." The slater's testimony was corroborated by another witness, but a verdict of accidental death was found.[74]

For working people, the institution of the coroners' inquest became a tangible expression of government failure to protect their interests. The *Beehive*, published by trade unionist George Potter, kept up a running commentary on inquests and their results. A mine exploded in Barnsley, and the jury's verdict was accidental death. The *Beehive noted,*

> Another fifty or sixty lives lost; and, as usual, no one in fault. We beg pardon; the *Times*, as usual, by both letter and leader, on Thursday week, throws the whole blame upon the men. And so, with a great deal of pity, but no real help, the risks and danger of the British miner will probably continue for some years longer to increase and be fatal . . . until the idea be formed that the British miner is a man, and has both a body and a soul to be cared for, or that life and limb are of *equal* value as wealth and works.

On the free agency theme, the *Beehive* noted that the miner was treated as less valuable than a horse.[75]

In another case, a pub collapsed, killing construction workers, and a jury composed entirely of members of the middle classes failed to censure the builder and owner.[76] The widow of one of the workers pursued the case in court and lost, leading the *Beehive* to lament the lack of representation of workers in Parliament, and to urge them to seek manhood suffrage.[77] Wondering why in the last few colliery accidents the proprietors had not had to pay compensation to the families, the *Beehive*'s editors noted in 1864 that

> The only answer we can give appears in the act that these gentlemen had been allowed to trespass on the public pocket, and to destroy the lives of husbands, fathers, and brothers, with impunity, because of their monetary power and the influence it exerted on the institutions of the country. Juries have been packed, coroners biased, and witnesses cooked by the magic power of the money bag and the brandy bottle, and therefore, generally the result of all inquiries

into the cause of colliery casualties has been the old stereotyped verdict of "Accidental Death."[78]

The editor suggested a court of arbitration be set up to handle matters of compensation, and he thought that such a system would have been in place long before, had working people had any political representation.[79]

The Impact of the Hartley Disaster

While the battle over the political nature of coroners' juries both in and out of mining continued at mid-nineteenth century, investigation into the causes and frequency of mining accidents continued. Successive Select Committees were convened to consider the problem of accidents in coal mines.[80] The Committees' findings show that a discourse of employer responsibility for injured employees was constantly present, but that it was a minority position, not accepted by government representatives. An 1852 Select Committee considered, but rejected, a proposal that after a worker was killed in a mine his family be supported by the mine proprietors.[81] During the 1854 Committee proceedings, miners' spokesman David Swallow suggested that mining be subject to the same rules as the Factory Acts, wherein inspectors could institute proceedings on behalf of injured workers or the families of those killed. He was asked, "You think that the burden should not fall on the working people?' and his reply was "Just so."[82] Despite Swallow's call for change, the 1854 Select Committee rejected workmen's calls for legal remedies, recommending only sufficient ventilation and inspections. The Committee was happy to report that benefit schemes for widows and orphans of miners were already widespread, illustrating that the presence of a system of compensation, no matter how haphazard and dependent on public charity, helped to allay official concern.[83]

While the reigning notion of who should bear the responsibility for workplace accidents had not appreciably shifted by 1860, the establishment of a recognized process for improving workplace safety had resulted in appreciable incremental gains. For example, hard-rock mining had been exempt from the inspection laws levied on coal mining, but by the 1860s concern about accidents in the industry prompted a Select Committee hearing on the travails of hard-rock miners. Unlike the coal miners, so often taken by exploding gases, hard-rock miners were prone to slow deaths from "miner's disease," recognized today, but not in the nineteenth century, as silicosis:

The first symptoms of failing health amongst the miners are weakness in the limbs in climbing the ladders and beating the borer, shortness of breathing, giddiness, and pains in the head; their appetite fails, they are unable to take or to digest an adequate amount of food, and often suffer from sickness and vomiting. These symptoms are followed by harassing cough, much expectoration, sometimes of mucus, occasionally of blood, tightness of the chest, and failure of general strength. These affections precede total disability to work, followed by premature death. [84]

Hard-rock miners were also susceptible to death by blasting, falling off ladders, roof falls, or boilers bursting.[85] The 1864 Committee noted that most hard-rock miners subscribed to clubs that only paid off in case of "visible hurts" or accidents, leaving individual families to pay the cost of death by lingering illness. In addition to calling for increased ventilation, the Committee made a couple of suggestions that showed the persistence of thinking about free agency. They sought to bar boys under fourteen from working underground and recommended the adoption of mine clubs to afford the men sufficient maintenance during sickness, as well as when suffering the effects of an accident.[86]

While Select Committees met intermittently throughout the 1850s and 1860s to address various concerns in the field of mining, it took a major disaster to shift the reigning paradigm on compensation for all injured workers. In 1862, the plunge of the heavy beam engine into the single shaft at the Hartley Colliery brought the question of workplace safety to the forefront of the popular imagination. The fact that the story of the trapped miners was ongoing—that reporters, like miners' families and the general public were held for so long in hopeful suspense, as rescuers dug to help the men—helped to create sympathy between the miners and their families and those who had never before stepped into a mining district. Immediately after the accident, public meetings were held in the mining district, and ordinary miners and experts like James Mather alike questioned the validity of a single-shaft system that killed people. The exasperation felt locally was contagious. The *Times,* which had for many years failed to delve very deeply into mining conditions (past stolid assurances that the miners had always been careless), snapped out of that posture and began to advocate not only for the digging of second mine-shafts at all mines, but also for a tax to be added to every ton of coal in order to pay compensation to the families of deceased miners.[87]

The editors of the *Mining Journal* called the tragedy a wholesale slaughter and lamented that 215 lives had been lost for the want of a thousand pounds to build a second shaft.

Were we living in an age when science was neglected we could understand the frequent recurrence of avoidable accidents, but in the nineteenth century, it certainly seems marvellous that paltry scruples about the unconstitutional character of Government supervision should be permitted to have such influence as to prevent the enactment of laws compelling the best known preventives of accidents to be adopted in every colliery in the kingdom, and making the colliery proprietor criminally responsible for accidents resulting from neglect.[88]

The Newport *Reformer* was even more damning in its indictment of the system of mining and that of inquests. A leader article concluded that "two hundred and fifteen human beings have been sacrificed, and, we seriously fear, to the cupidity of the wealthy owners of the pit." Regarding the verdict of accidental death, the editors noted that "these coroner's juries are the greatest possible sham, and the sooner the better the false pretence of enquiry into the cause of deaths at collieries was abolished, unless the inquests could be conducted with something like common decency. The juries are as a rule designedly packed, and they do the work of the colliery lords with shameless connivance." Unlike horses working below, who could only be replaced by an outlay of capital by the pit owner, men destroyed underground could be replaced at no cost. As a result, the editors alleged, mine owners were quite willing to take dangerous shortcuts in ventilation and safety.[89] By May 1862, seventeen thousand miners had signed a petition calling for more safety and increased mine inspections; this was forwarded to the House of Commons.[90]

At the same time that popular indignation about single shafts was churning, a bill was introduced into the House of Commons to provide injured workers with some recompense. The bill would have provided that whenever a workman or servant was injured on the job, through any action or omission of the employer or anyone else in the same employ, the injured workman was entitled to recover damages from the employer through legal action. The one exception to this rule was to be any willful misconduct on the part of a fellow servant which resulted in injury to a workman. The Act would also have provided that, in case of wrongful death, a worker's relatives could sue under Lord Campbell's Act of 1846.[91]

The bill was introduced into the House of Commons by Acton Smee Ayrton, Liberal MP for Tower Hamlets, on February 11, as an attempt to clarify the existing common law. Ayrton, who was Commissioner of Works, accepted the rule laid down in *Priestley*. He agreed that, historically, masters had not been responsible for any injuries that happened to their workpeople. Ayrton argued that the relationship between employers and workpeople had changed, impelling him to write many exceptions into the common law. The bill's introduction was seconded, but there was no further discussion at that time.[92]

Shortly after Ayrton introduced his bill, editorials in the *Colliery Guardian* came out firmly against it, arguing that as free agents, miners had to accept responsibility for the dangers inherent in their employment. "If workmen are to be treated, not as children needing constant protection, but as rational men, able to make bargains for themselves, they ought to abide by any arrangement which they deliberately accept." The mine owner provided a safe working atmosphere and equipment, and "the working collier knows the risks of his vocation, accepts them on condition of his receiving the wages usually paid in the district." If any accident happened due to poor equipment provided, he might have recourse against his employer, but "on the other hand, he and his fellow workmen are to a certain extent independent of their employer."[93] The editor explained that in contravention of these rules, Ayrton's bill would have allowed the relatives of injured or killed workmen to pursue the employer for damages no matter who had caused the accident, as long as it had not been willful. The editor also warned that colliery owners would not be the only employers "victimized" by the bill and encouraged employers of all types to band together and defeat it. "Like many other foolish and pernicious schemes, it is pushed forward under the pretext of philanthropy, and no doubt its promoters will secure some degree of respect and attention from the House of Commons, by representing it as merely an extension of a principle acknowledged in other cases to the protection of the working classes." In reality, he argued, it would be doing the working classes a disservice, by preventing investment in risky enterprises—without which enterprises, working people would not get paid.[94]

The mine owners drew up a circular against Ayrton's bill, to inform railroad company directors and other large employers of labor. A second editorial in the *Colliery Guardian* explained the mine owners' thought process. They argued that if employers were to be responsible for their workmen, it was only logical that they should also be able to control them—prevent them from drinking in order to make them calm and sober workers, for example. Did colliers want to be serfs or Negro slaves? With the Civil War raging in the United States, this was a portentous question: "When men attain to the dignity of freedom, they must accept the blessing with all its concomitants, if they claim to exercise their mental faculties and use their bodily organs without control or restraint, they must provide for their own subsistence, and defend themselves against the casualties to which they are exposed in pursuing their avocations." The editors of the *Colliery Guardian* also attacked what they called "amateur legislation," noting that any important bills ought to be brought in by the government.[95]

When the bill came up for its second reading on March 19, 1862, Ayrton was harsher in his language and had modified the justification for the bill. He noted that the *Priestley* case had taken the judges totally by surprise, and as a result they had created a law based on expediency rather than jurisprudential principles.[96] Ayrton referred back to the Elizabethan Statute of Artificers, which had made it the responsibility of the master to keep paying the wages of a servant who had been injured, and noted that in more recent times master-servant disagreements had been adjudicated by justices of the peace. Ayrton also mined the common law for help, claiming that the *Priestley* case created an untenable exception to the rule that each man was responsible for his own negligence, by allowing the employer to escape responsibility. Finally, Ayrton came to the hub of the issue, which was that under the common law workmen were treated differently from bystanders simply because they were workmen. "All he proposed was that the workmen should be enabled to recover an amount of compensation limited precisely to the degree of injury sustained—the loss of wages and the expenses of a doctor consequent on the injury."

While Ayrton made strong arguments in favor of a compensation bill, he was unwilling to bring popular pressure to bear on the House of Commons, and his idea was quickly rejected. The Attorney General Sir W. Atherton suggested that the House reject the bill, because in his interpretation the doctrine of employer nonresponsibility was ancient law, not created by the *Priestley* case. He argued that such a law would increase the liability of masters to an untenable extreme, and that in any case it was unfair, since workmen received higher pay because they had to assume the risks of dangerous employments. Finally, in a rather obvious appeal to the manly self-reliance of the working classes, the attorney general said he "objected to a scheme by which Parliament was asked to defend men who ought rather to be left to rely on their own intelligence and energy."[97]

Other MPs representing business interests quickly chimed in to prevent what would have been a disastrously costly change in the law. Sir William Bovill, Conservative MP for Guildford, cited some cases in which a master would be more responsible for the safety of his servant than for that of his own family. Henry Austin Bruce, Liberal MP for Merthyr Tydvil, argued that, if the bill had passed, the owners of the Hartley colliery would have been responsible for damages to every widow and orphan caused by the accident. In a comment which belied the attorney general's vision of the workman as self-reliant, Sir Morton Peto noted that, while employers were extremely concerned for the welfare of their workmen, "the greatest difficulty the masters had was to make the men take even the most ordinary precautions for their own safety." He gave examples of miners sticking naked lights to the wall while blasting or failing to use patent safety tubes because to do so wasted time. Faced with this sustained opposition, Ayrton was unable to prevent the postponement of the bill's second reading, a move which condemned it to death.

Although the 1862 compensation bill failed, the Parliamentary discussions of that year and the high-profile mining accidents energized labor's cause. The editors of the *Beehive* and the *British Miner and General Newsman* campaigned for an end to the noninterventionist attitudes that condemned workers to unsafe work conditions and lack of compensation for accidents. After the Edmund's Main colliery exploded in December 1862, the editor of the *Beehive* noted that that the explosion was due to the use of gunpowder in a fiery mine, and the only reason that the proprietors did this was because the miners were free agents and there was no pecuniary loss to their employers if they died. Had they been bought slaves, the proprietors would have been more careful, "Strong men sell in the Southern States even at present for £200 to £250 each; and more than sixty men and boys were destroyed at Edmund's Main on Monday . . . [if] we reckon [they were worth] £160 [each] or £9000, and if that sum had been risked by the proprietors from the use of gunpowder, they would have ordered their men to 'pick' their way."[98]

The *Beehive* contended that even though the men were free, and thus their financial value could not be calculated, their lives should have been valuable to the nation. "Discharging from consideration for a moment the higher interests of humanity and of life, on the lowest possible ground of money, and therefore of political economy, the state is interested in conserving life, and preventing all needless risks."[99] The editors of another working-class newspaper, *The Commonwealth,* similarly rejected the analysis of working people as free agents responsible for the consequences of risky employment. They looked at the danger-producing fatigue level of railway workers and asked, "Can no Act of Parliament for the Prevention of Cruelty to Animals be made to apply to the companies who thus overwork their men?" [100]

For the editors of the *Beehive,* each accident and inquest following the rejection of Ayrton's bill was visible testimony of the injustice of Britain's system of political representation. After a construction accident in which a workman had been killed and the coroner's jury had found a verdict of accidental death, the workman's widow had attempted unsuccessfully to sue the employer and the owner and architect of the fallen building. The *Beehive* lamented that the law had left this poor widow no recourse. "Why was such a bill [that is, Ayrton's] not accepted? Simply because the working classes are not represented in that house, and this measure only affected the interests of that class. Honourable members pay little attention to the complaints of those who have no votes to dispose of." The *Beehive* asserted that the situation was only made worse by trade unions that claimed to be apolitical.[101]

Once Ayrton's bill failed, a full ten years passed before another compensation bill was attempted, but discussion of the liability issue did not completely disappear. Working-class newspapers continued to call for a resolution to the issue, sometimes presenting a broadening of the electorate as the answer. The editors of the *Commonwealth* again rejected the free-agency argument, asking,

> If in addition to a proved knowledge of the neglect the agents of the proprietor shall be induced to bribe men with additional pay to hazard their lives, in order that the net profits of the mine may be increased, shall such an act be allowed to go unpunished? It is one thing to allow men free scope in the eager pursuit of riches, and another to see that in their eagerness they do not fill the nation with sounds of woe and lamentation.

The editors argued that provision for disablement and loss of life should form part of operating expenses of risky businesses. Instead, "the proprietors of mines are allowed to go on from year to year shirking their just responsibilities, and trusting to a benevolent public to make good their deficiencies."[102]

Salvos continued to be fired from the opposite side as well. Barrister Joseph Brown in 1870 produced a tract advocating against a master or a railway company's liability for accidents to employees, couching his argument specifically in class terms. "Unless something be done to check the present tendency of things, it will not be long before the courts are wholly engrossed in trying to shift the accidental misfortunes of life from those who meet with them to other people," he complained.[103] Lord Campbell's Act had already made masters responsible to the families of people who were killed on the job. Brown claimed that the shift in liability had resulted in a great deal of judicial uncertainty and in injured workmen constantly suing their masters to see if they could get anything out of it.

The systemic reforms Brown suggested all put workers at a disadvantage. He proposed that negligent servants stand as codefendants in accident cases and have liens put on their wages to pay any fine laid on their masters. As far as rail travel was concerned, there had always been accidents and always would be. "Every man who embarks in a ship for a distant voyage knows that he must risk his life in so doing, and so does every man who gets into a railway train ... he becomes a partner in the risk, and must share the loss when it happens." If the assumption-of-risk doctrine was fair for workers, he explained, it should be fair for railway passengers, who knew what they were getting themselves into.[104] Brown saw such accidents as largely the result of worker misconduct:

> Whether I may succeed in opening the eyes of the public to the injustice of a law which puts every master's fortune in the power of his porters, carmen and labourers—into the hands of men who were never trusted with a 2ol. note— I don't know; but, at least, I have had the satisfaction of lifting my voice against a system which daily ruins innocent men; which encourages rogues and impostors; and which makes judges, counsel and attornies the ministers of injustice and oppression.

While few employers were as candid as Brown in their antipathy toward working men, his rhetoric demonstrates how heated and class centered the issue of workplace liability was becoming.

Unions and Reform in the 1870s

The expansion of the electorate under the 1867 Reform Act acted to repair part of the problem that workers had identified with the existing accident regime. With the enfranchisement of about a million and a half additional people, working men were better represented than they had ever been, and of course competing to provide services to this new electorate would become a major focus of both the Conservative and Liberal parties.

The foundation of the Amalgamated Society of Railway Servants, with their professed dedication to solving the problem of workplace safety, was also significant. John Baxter Langley, former editor of the *Newcastle Chronicle* and a longtime crusader for mine reform, and M. T. Bass, the MP for Preston, supported the foundation of the union and its drive for workplace protection. The union's newspaper, the *Railway Service Gazette,* presented railway workers with the forum in which to argue for compensation for workplace accidents. Its editors insisted that accidents were not due to worker carelessness, but rather to structural factors, including too many engines and too few hands.[105] Railway workers were particularly incensed about the differential treatment afforded to railway passengers in contrast with workers.

Railway passengers have a slight check on the carelessness of the companies, but railway servants have none at all. The former can at least obtain pecuniary compensation, but the latter are not allowed by law to claim any damages whatever . . . this is a cruel, partial, and most unjust condition of the law, and one which the President of the Board of Trade has more than once admitted . . . calls loudly for amendment.

The editors called for a petition of one hundred thousand signatures to support a compensation law.[106]

With compensation one of its top objectives, the railway union took concrete steps to hasten legislation. The union sent representatives to inquests, to ensure that accidents that had been caused by faulty equipment were not somehow blamed on worker inattention instead. They encouraged union workers to resist the introduction of unsafe work practices, like coupling cars while the cars were moving, that had been introduced in order to save time and avoid fines for working too slowly.[107] The union also used the legal weapon. Emma Preston, whose husband, a brakeman, was killed on the job, initiated an action for damages, supported by the solicitor for the Amalgamated Society of Railway Servants. Preston was killed at a station, hit by a train operated by a different railroad company from the one that employed him, thus bringing the fellow-servant defense into question. Preston was a respectable employee, who earned 30s. a week, and Emma Preston, as the young and bereaved mother of five boys, including an infant, was a sympathetic plaintiff. In the end, the jury awarded £350 in damages—£100 to the widow and £50 to each of the boys.[108] Nor would Preston be the last plaintiff to be able to wring a large award from a jury in such a case; in 1876, a mother of four received an award for £600. The railroad was temporarily able to escape the award on the ground that a contract between two companies at the site created a common-employment scenario between the dead man and the workman who had killed him. Finally, the law lords reversed the chancellor of the exchequer's decision, so that the marriage of convenience struck between two railway companies did not prevent the dead man's family from receiving his settlement.[109]

Changes in the collection of data in the 1870s also began to reveal to the public the alarming extent of workplace deaths and injuries related to the railroads. Until 1870, the Board of Trade had required British railroads to compile a return of all of their serious personal injuries to the public. By categorizing railroad servants as not part of "the public," railroads had been able legally to understate the extent of injuries to their workers. Starting in November 1871, railroads were directed to list all accidents occurring to servants. As a result, under the old method of counting in 1871, there were just four injuries to railroad servants in ten months, but under the new method of counting, there were sixty-five injuries in two months.[110] Finally, the creation of the Trades Union Congress furthered the compensation issue by providing a forum for the discussion of workplace safety among multiple trades. By 1874 and 1875, the Parliamentary Committee of the Trades Union Congress was actively discussing the issue of a Compensation Bill.[111]

As a result of the combined emphasis on the issue by new unions and by labor representatives in Parliament, bills to increase the liability of masters for employee injuries were introduced almost every year during the 1870s. A bill introduced in 1872 would have held employers responsible for injuries to workmen when such injuries were caused by the failure to use any safeguards or materials required by law, or when the injury or death was due to negligence by any superintendent, from a worker's immediate supervisor to the owner of the company. The bill was introduced but then withdrawn without discussion.[112]

The second major bill to be introduced on this issue helped both sides to develop and sharpen their arguments. Introduced in 1874, it would have eliminated the doctrine of common employment as a bar to collecting damages under tort law and specified that work injury cases be taken before county court judges within a three-month window of the injury. While this sounds generous, since the doctrine of common employment was the most formidable bar to the workingman's family collecting damages, the law would have forbidden the court to grant a greater sum than one year's wages or salary from the year preceding the date of the injury or death. In addition, employers of fewer than fifty workpeople would have been excluded from the operation of the law. The law was introduced by Sir Edward Watkin, who was no friend of the workingman; his personal opinion was that unions and combinations had destroyed the natural amicable feelings between masters and men. He explained that he was introducing the legislation in order to forestall a more sweeping law and to foster out-of-court settlements.[113]

The Amalgamated Society of Railway Servants quickly heard about Watkin's bill, and attempted to meet with him to discuss its provisions, but he refused to fill them in on any of the details. When they finally did see the bill, on its introduction, they were alarmed at its provisions. The cap on compensation meant that medical expenses alone might eat up the total to which a man might be entitled, leaving lost wages uncompensated. More gallingly, since many railwaymen belonged to mutual benefit societies and sick clubs, they resented that their awards would be proportionally offset by any payout from these.[114] By the end of May, Watkin had postponed a second reading of his bill, and at the end of June the union's Parliamentary Committee was urging him to drop the bill on the grounds that there was too much wrong with it for the bill to have their support.[115]

The next year, 1875, Watkin reintroduced substantially the same bill, with an additional caveat that the ceiling for compensation be £200.[116] Like his 1874 bill, this one provided that in assessing the amount of compensation in case of injury, the court take into account any monies already paid to the injured worker or his family from any sick or provident society contributed to by the employer.[117] The Trades Union Congress opposed Watkin's measures, as did the railway union. The railwaymen noted in particular that anyone who had been contributorily negligent was barred from collecting anything, yet all railway servants were required to violate the "rules" of their employers in order to comply with printed schedules. In district meetings, workers objected to the limitation on compensation, insisting that only a jury was capable of setting this amount, and continued to disagree with the proposal to subtract from any amount collected the amount due a worker from a benefit society.[118] Despite its faults, the editors of the *Railway Gazette* supported Watkin's bill, but it too was dropped.

In 1876 the railwaymen were joined by the miners. Alexander Macdonald, president of the Miners' National Association and the Liberal MP for Stafford, introduced a bill that more accurately reflected workers' demands.[119] Macdonald's bill attacked the triumvirate of legal doctrines that had so long hampered workers in court, by eliminating the common employment defense. It did not, however, specify where these cases should be heard.[120] When the bill was read for the second time, on May 24, 1876, Macdonald forcefully and warmly supported it by arguing that without it, the workingman was left without any legal recourse.[121] He was supported by Mr. Dodson, Liberal MP for Chester, who noted that the rationale behind *Priestley* had been lost sight of, and that men should only be considered to be in common employment if they could judge against, and be a safety check upon, each other. Dr. Cameron backed Macdonald's position by referring to the much more ancient principal of Scottish law that an employer was always responsible for workplace injuries. Cameron particularly hoped that when the bill became law it would encourage mine owners to be more careful.

On the opposite side, the attorney general made the most extreme statement of the employers' position. He restated the idea of assumption of risk and illustrated with an example what a hardship it would be for a mine owner when a reckless miner went down the mine and killed fifty of his colleagues. Why, a jury might award a huge sum! "There were many dangers connected with mines, and miners got much higher wages than other operatives did. We had heard of miners who enjoyed all the luxuries of life, and whose favourite daily beverage was champagne." That the argument against the bill was couched in terms of mine accidents is unsurprising, considering that a deputation of mine owners had visited the home secretary to lobby against the bill. The deputation of mine owners claimed that "the bill could only be calculated to encourage that recklessness which was proverbial among people employed in mines, who would know that if any accident happened, they would be kept in idleness until they were better and, if killed their relatives would be supported by the mine owners."[122] As the MP for Preston, cotton magnate Edward Hermon denied knowing any workmen who supported a change in the law.

Most of the discussion of how the bill would impact specific industries centered on mines. Just as Macdonald and Burt represented the mining interests in the debate, so the mine owners were their most vocal opponents. Thomas Knowles, MP for Wigan and himself a mine owner, described an accident which had recently happened to him. Although he ventilated his mine at five times the rate prescribed by the Mines Act, it had exploded, killing everyone in the mine—the best employees he would ever have—and inflicting £100,000 worth of damage. "He had lived long enough to know that those masters were most successful that took the greatest care of their men. He would go so far as to say that men ought to have good wages, they ought to be well fed, well clothed, and well housed," but added that this bill would encourage carelessness and idleness. Behind his position was a patronizing profession of belief in the importance of personal responsibility among the working classes. Again, the "free agency" contrast was invoked; choose protection and be numbered among children and slaves; choose "personal responsibility" and be numbered among men:

> Instead of introducing Bills of this kind, he thought that the Hon. Member for Stafford would do better to give the workmen good advice—advise them that they were thinking and responsible beings—that they were best capable of discovering danger and could prevent it far sooner than their employers, and that they should rather for societies to make provision for themselves in case of accident, than rely upon legislation of this kind, which treated them as children and slaves more than as persons capable of taking care of themselves.[123]

Many of the employers' advocates professed to see doom in the future should the bill pass; they struggled mightily to hold to a more paternalistic and deferential vision of the workplace. Despite the huge extent to which manufactories and mines had grown and workplaces had become more complicated since 1837, several advocates for the employers' position cited examples from *Priestley v. Fowler* as situations that might still actually occur. Joseph Whitwell Pease, Liberal MP for Durham, warned that workmen's wages would go down, since they were no longer eligible for compensation for risk; that the law would be an endless source of litigation; and that all employers would cease all voluntary contribution to provident societies. Furthermore, Pease noted, there was little evidence that Macdonald's bill was a popular measure, since all of the petitions presented on behalf of the workers contained a mere thirty-four thousand signatures.

By the end of the discussion, it was clear that the employers' advocates had the upper hand, commanding as they did an overwhelming majority in the chamber. Nonetheless, miners' advocates were able to use the House of Commons as a theatrical platform, just as William Prowting Roberts had done in coroners' courts years before. Former miner Thomas Burt, who supported Macdonald, was one of the last members to speak. He noted that he had devoted his entire life to helping miners to be provident; they were hardly looking for a handout. He was unwilling to let some of the more egregious statements which had been made during the debate lie unchallenged, arguing that, "with respect to the statements of wages earned by miners within the last few years and the claptrap that had been sent about the country alleging that they lived extravagantly or drank champagne, he pointed out that, when wages were at their highest, miners did not, even in the best paid districts of the country, average more than £2 10s. per week." Up against an iceberg of apathy and dissent, Macdonald reluctantly agreed to withdraw his bill and allow a Select Committee to examine the question of compensation.

The press organs of employers reacted gleefully to the Commons debate. The *Mining Journal* accused Macdonald of pandering to a low class of workmen and of displaying little legal acumen in his arguments before the House:

> Mr. Macdonald made no attempt to disguise the fact that the object of his Bill and the whole tenor of his speech was to make the colliery proprietor responsible for every accident which should occur in his colliery, no matter by whom or how caused. One would imagine from the observations of Mr. Macdonald that the colliery proprietors of this country are altogether indifferent to the

interest of their men, and scarcely bestow a thought upon the safety and lives of those in their employ.[124]

The *Journal* reiterated the popular argument that explosions and other large accidents were more painful and disastrous for the mine owner than for anyone else concerned and that as a result mine owners would stop at nothing to protect the safety of their men. Finally, rejoicing that "the exaggerated and unwarrantable statements made by Mr. Macdonald have been completely refuted," the *Mining Journal* claimed that mine owners were already compensating miners for the increased danger of their jobs by paying them better wages than were received by any other category of unskilled laborer.[125] The *Colliery Guardian* concurred, noting that the best thing that could have been done with Macdonald's bill was to refer the matter to a Select Committee.

> An outcry has been raised in the true fashion of the class of agitators to which Mr. Macdonald prides himself on belonging, and the wisest thing now is promptly to take the matter up, and once and for all time have it settled . . . a Select Committee of the House of Commons is not in danger of being taken with the stale bait of trades unionism, or drawn from the direct course of justice by false issues.[126]

The decision to refer the question of compensation to a Select Committee can be seen as a conservative step, meant to remove any taint of demagoguery from the whole discussion of workplace accidents and move it to a more serious and dispassionate forum.

Select Committees and the Compensation Issue

The Select Committee empowered in 1876 took as its major responsibility to find out whether a conflict really existed in the law. Did the doctrine of *respondeat superior* make an employer liable to compensate a stranger for an injury inflicted by one of the employer's workers, but bar him from compensating a fellow worker for the same injury?

The legal experts could not agree with each other.[127] While the committee and the barristers wrangled with the historical question of whether or not a contradiction existed in the law, the trade unionists brought to testify before the committee were more interested in the practical implications of the law for their constituents' survival and prosperity. Henry Broadhurst, the secretary of the Trades Union Congress Parliamentary Committee and a stonemason, argued that amending the law would reward workers' thrift, since the Operative

Stonemasons paid a large sum annually—about £800—for accidents which might have been avoided.[128] Frederick Evans, the general secretary of the Amalgamated Society of Railway Servants, gave several examples of cases in which injuries had occurred proximately through fellow workmen, but originally through poor management or the failure to enforce safety regulations. He trotted out the familiar allegation that the life of a railway servant was worth less than the life of a horse, because in a situation in which both were killed, the railroad would at least have to replace the horse.[129] Neither these appeals to practical justice, nor a flood of petitions engineered by the railway union, could sway the Select Committee into making a recommendation in favor of Macdonald's bill.[130] The Committee issued no report, and asked instead to reconvene in the following session.

By 1877, the leadership of the Amalgamated Society of Railway Servants was beginning to demonstrate its frustration with trying to get a bill passed to cover all workmen and began engaging in special pleading, motivated by expediency, to get a bill passed that would cover railwaymen alone. The union claimed that railway workers' deaths were more cut-and-dried than those of miners or other workers. As the *Railway Service Gazette* noted, it was possible for a mine owner to take every precaution and yet,

> some scores of miners may be swept away in a moment by an accident not distinguishable in its origin from one due to neglect of precautions. Such a loss might ruin the employer entirely . . . The case of railwaymen is totally different. Proper precautions are not taken; they are killed, in isolated cases, to an appalling extent; nearly all the accidents are clearly preventible; their employers are rich, and well able to afford to employ proper precautions.[131]

Special pleading aside, the railwaymen were correct in one aspect—that in terms of economic calculations, railway companies had much less to gain than did mine companies from maintaining safe workplaces, since a mine accident was more likely to block the infrastructure and slow productivity than was an accident involving a railway worker.[132]

When the Select Committee met again in 1877, the committee narrowed its focus to look primarily at the ways in which the current law operated on master and man. William Crawford, the secretary to the Durham miners' union, altered traditional ways of looking at free agency by arguing that, although workmen were theoretically free agents, the law of compensation did not take into account the great disparity in power between the master and the individual workmen. Social distance made attempts to demand compensation as a right rather than a privilege almost impossible. This meant that the economic burden of accidents was falling disproportionately on other workers. In Yorkshire between 1874 and 1877, men had been compensated out of the miners' own pockets to the amount of £29,000 in grants, donations, and weekly payments to widows.[133] Benjamin Pickard of the Yorkshire miners' union called for the mine owners to be responsible for the economic impact of all mine accidents except those in which contributory negligence could be proven.[134]

Miners were not alone in standing before the Select Committee to complain about the impact of the law on workers' pocketbooks. John Burnett, of the Amalgamated Society of Engineers, said that since 1851 that society had paid out £26,000 in benefits to members disabled from their employment by accident or disease. He cited examples of a number of cases in which he thought the employer should have been liable for compensation; none of them had come to trial, since recent court decisions had discouraged the men from even attempting to sue. Burnett called for the doctrine of common employment to be completely eliminated, and he would have held masters completely responsible for warranting the safety of their machinery.[135]

The workers also discussed legal issues. Robert Knight, general secretary of the Boiler Makers' and Iron Shipbuilders' Association, attacked the doctrine of assumption of risk directly. Since the risk of the workplace changed every day as people are hired and fired, how was a man who had been on the job for a long time to assess the ever-changing level of risk?[136] Knight had support on this issue from Lord Justice of Appeal Sir William Balliol Brett, who denied that there was any such thing as an implied contract between employer and employee by which the employee assumed the risks of the job. He thought it very doubtful that workers entered into employment knowing that they were running the risk of being injured by some fellow workmen whom they did not even know. Nonetheless, Brett called the fellow servant rule a "bad exception to a bad law," because he didn't think the doctrine of *respondeat superior* was a good idea in the first place. He could not see any reason why a master should be liable, either to a third party or to a fellow workman, for the negligent acts of his workmen.[137]

If the trade unionists were by now united in the call for a change in the law, representatives of the major industries that would have been affected were just as stalwart in their opposition.[138] The way in which their arguments had become institutionalized can be seen through the testimony of John Bell Simpson, representing the United Coal Trade Association of the North of England. Contradictions became obvious as Simpson made every possible argument to protect the mine owners' interests. At one moment he said that most accidents were the fault of the workmen, but at another argued that large coal owners could be ruined if they were made responsible for the negligent acts of their own managers. He finished with a threat; mine owners currently gave £29,300 per year to their workers in the shape of accident compensation and also hired doctors and endowed hospitals. All of this paternalism might end if the bill under discussion was passed and made them legally responsible. Simpson's arguments made it seem as though all mine owners offered paternalism as long as they received deference, but as Alexander Macdonald pointed out in a particularly bitter line of cross-examination, the lobbying organization Simpson represented contained plenty of mine owners who had been brought up on charges of violating the Mines Act.[139]

When the Select Committee finally issued its report the following year, it recommended against any change in the law. The Select Committee believed that it was inappropriate to categorize workmen with servants and children under the rubric of *respondeat superior,* because workmen were free agents, able to choose or reject employment and having to take into consideration all of the attendant risks. The Select Committee also recommended against changing the existing law because there were already certain ways in which a master might be held responsible for injuries to his servant: if it could be shown that the employer failed to provide proper materials or chose incompetent workers when he should have known better, for example. The Select Committee did, however, recommend that a workman be able to sue particular directors when the directorship of a company attempted to slip out of all responsibility for negligence by delegating all of its authority to its agents. Finally, the Select Committee opined that the doctrine of common employment had been carried to a poor extreme in the case of workmen hired by contractors.[140]

The intellectual battle of the 1877 Select Committee was carried out over the ground of free agency. The Select Committee had relied on testimony of men like Lord Justice of Appeal Sir George W. W. Bramwell, who stated the classical definition of "free labor" when he denied that a man had no recourse if he found himself in a dangerous workplace. The recourse, of course, was to leave and find other employment; and to claim that economic need forced a man into a particular situation was no excuse.[141] By distinguishing between "workmen" and domestic servants (predominantly female) and children in their final report, the members of the Select Committee refused to acknowledge that class, as well as gender and age, could produce unequal distributions of power. Instead, they chose to pretend that all workers subsumed under the legal rubric "workmen" were adult males and that all adult males stood on an equal footing before the law. In fact, a draft final report suggested by Robert Lowe (but rejected by the Committee) would have put this view into still stronger terms:

> It seems strange to extend a disability which is attached to lunatics on account of their infirmity, to children on account of their tender years, and to sailors by a very questionable policy on account of their notorious imprudence, to men who are the very strength and mainstay of the country, to whom more, perhaps, than to any other class England is indebted for her wealth and her greatness.[142]

Throughout the Select Committee's hearings, Alexander Macdonald strove to point out that, regardless of all the rhetoric of "free agency," mining was governed by regulations such that a man could be fined or prosecuted for meddling where he did not belong or leaving his place underground. This made it impossible for him to supervise, or even to know about, the conduct of employees elsewhere in the mine as the fellow-servant rule seemed to assume.[143]

The negative report of the 1877 Select Committee did not inhibit Macdonald from submitting another bill the following year.[144] This bill was designed to eliminate both the fellow-servant rule and the assumption of risk defense. When the bill was brought for a second reading in April, Macdonald introduced the bill by ignoring the conclusions of the 1877 Select Committee.[145] He attacked the arguments made by employers directly, denying that workmen were to blame for most accidents—and maintaining that, even where they were to blame, lax employer vigilance was also implicated. Employers threatened that they would find workforces abroad if forced to comply with expensive labor laws, but Macdonald ridiculed the idea that British capitalists would take their business elsewhere if made responsible for employee injuries, since many other major countries had laws that were even more restrictive on the subject.[146]

Despite two successive Select Committees on employers' liability, the trade unionists in the House of Commons had failed to convert either the majority of the House of Commons or the public to their position. Benjamin Disraeli's Conservative government also failed to take any legislative initiative on the issue or even to show any interest.[147] At the second reading of Macdonald's 1878 bill, Attorney General Sir John Holker made an arrogant speech, stating that just because the workmen seemed to be clamoring for something did not mean that it had to be granted to them. Holker refused to commit the government to a course of action beyond giving vague promises that the government was at some point planning to introduce a bill on the subject.[148]

Most letters written to the *Times* in 1878 disparaged the idea of employers' liability as an expensive sop for notoriously negligent workmen. A judge from Scotland wrote in to argue that it was inexpedient, in a capitalist economy, to make a master liable for the injuries his fellow servants did to each other, since that would chase all of the small and poorer masters out of business.[149] George Bowyer opined that it was unfair to make a master responsible for his servant's injurious behavior and called for laws to make servants more liable for damage they inflicted to their master's property. "Any one with any experience knows the recklessness not merely of workmen but of all undisciplined minds. I do not suppose that a man will risk his life or limb because his widow or he will have a remedy, but I think it as well to give him as little encouragement that way as possible."[150] An employer, "H. B.," wrote in about a servant of his who had on some impulse let the water out of a boiler and caused an explosion which killed himself and a fellow servant: "I had to bear the whole cost of replacing the boiler, which was hard enough, but it would surely have been a grievous injustice if I had been required to compensate the families of either or both of these men, or of the many others who might have been injured." H. B. argued that the proper remedy for workplace accidents was Victorian thrift in the form of an insurance fund subscribed for by the workmen themselves.[151]

Unions were not ready to let the matter drop; the issue was becoming an endurance test both for the unions and for a Conservative government that sought the support of working men. During the 1878–79 session of the House of Commons, three different bills were introduced. The first, essentially a reintroduction of Macdonald's bill, would have eliminated the defense of common employment in all cases.[152] It was read once and withdrawn on the second reading.[153] The second bill was more complicated and would have made the employer liable for personal injuries to workmen when caused by defective works, machinery, plant, or stock. In addition, the employer would have been liable for injuries caused by the negligence of supervisors under his command, when these supervisors were able to give a worker nonnegotiable instructions or commands. The bill provided that the worker or his surviving relatives "shall have the same right of compensation and remedies against the employer as if he had not been a workman of, nor in the service of, the employer," as long as there was no contributory negligence.[154] The second bill was read only once.[155]

In an attempt to cut off at the pass any discussion of these more radical measures, the government introduced its own bill in March 1879. The government offered as little as possible. Its bill, introduced by Sir John Holker, would simply have changed the common employment defense to exclude so-called "servants in authority," including mine managers, railway managers, and mill managers.[156] The short debate in Parliament over the measure showed that members on both extremes of the question were beginning to move toward a compromise. Alexander Macdonald gave his tentative support to the bill but called for an even stronger measure.[157] Sir Henry Jackson, who would have preferred to make every man responsible for his own negligence, admitted that changes in tort law were unlikely to happen and also supported the government's bill.[158]

With both extremes reluctantly moving toward the center, the stage was set for the final, great discussion of negligence and liability which led to the passage of the Employers' Liability Act in 1880. In 1880, two bills were on the table: Macdonald's bill, which would have gotten rid of the common employment defense, and the more comprehensive bill, which had been the second introduced in the 1878–79 session. The bill which was finally adopted originated from the second bill. It made an employer responsible when a worker was injured under any of five conditions: by reason of any defect in the ways, works, machinery, plant, or stock in trade connected with or used in the business of the employer; by reason of the negligence of a superintendent; by reason of the negligence of any person in the service of the employer whose orders or directions the workman at the time of the injury was bound to and did obey; by reason of any act or omission by any person in obedience to the employer's bylaws or specific instructions; or, finally, by reason of the negligence of any workman in charge or control of any signal, points, locomotive engine, or any train upon a railway. Under all these circumstances, the workman, or in case of death his survivors, "shall have the same right of compensation and remedies against the employer as if the workman had not been a workman of, nor in the service of the employer, nor engaged in his work." The worker also had some responsibility; he could not collect anything if he knew about defective equipment but failed to give information about it to a superior. Finally, compensation for injury was limited to three years' wages earned by a person at that same post or a similar post.[159]

At this stage of the negotiations, pressure from outside Parliament increased in a way that would have been impossible before the founding of the TUC. Railway workers from all the railway lines running into London, plus the chief officers of the National Plasterers Union, the Iron and Steel Workers, London Carpenters, Sheffield Trade Council, London Trade Council, bricklayers, cabdrivers, cabinetmakers, printers, and a host of workingmen's and political clubs formed a deputation of 150 to meet with Liberal Party leader William Gladstone. Many petitions were also presented. Both the *Times* and the *Scotsman* supported the bill as a just measure.[160]

Employers warned darkly that any worker who sought compensation from an employer was guilty of an immense breach of trust and should not think of being able to find work in the future; "Surely the most contemptible cur that ever lived would not go back to seek again work of an employer whom he had so grievously insulted."[161] Companies sent petitions representing the shipping industry, the textile industry, and the coal industry, warning that the bill would result in incessant litigation and a rise in prices that would be passed onto the consumer. The managing director of the Sheepbridge Coal and Iron Company warned that "It would do away with complete graduated supervision, encourage carelessness on the part of the workpeople, at once abolish the accident fund, close the Chesterfield Hospital and all kindred institutions, and substitute instead continual vexatious legislation."[162]

Despite the fact that the issue of employers' liability had seen two Select Committees and multiple debates in the House of Commons, the 1880 Employers' Liability Act was not passed without a major revisiting of all the issues which had surrounded previous bills. When the bill was recommitted in July, representatives of the employers' interest who had long been silent or had had no constructive ideas suddenly became creative. In one of the more extreme statements of the case, Arthur Balfour spoke out in favor of changing the law to make the general public on a par with workmen—that is, unable ever to collect money for negligence from a third party.[163] Thomas Knowles, mine owner and MP for Wigan, suggested a scheme of compulsory insurance, to be contributed to by both employers and workmen.[164] Sir Hussey Vivian, also a mine owner, argued against the bill on the grounds that it would engender endless litigation, while a compulsory insurance system would cover more accidents with less divisiveness. "The community of feeling between employer and employed was of a sacred character, and cognate with the relations of a family; and unless master and man pulled heartily together success would not be attained. They must not suppose that any man would be so inhuman as willfully to endanger human life."[165] Workmen in turn objected to these insurance schemes, seeing them as conservative backpedaling designed to allow employers to avoid their full social responsibility.[166]

A recent explosion in the Risca colliery in Wales was on every mind as the MPs discussed the impact that the proposed bill would have on mine owners.[167] Mr. Hussey Vivian invoked the good of the country, warning that if the mine industry were overregulated it would falter, and it was the product upon which all of the welfare of other industries was based.[168] Charles Bradlaugh responded with an impassioned speech:

> He thought that when so much was said about the rights of property, that something should be said on the other hand with regard to human life. There was absolute ruin to the wives and families of the 250 miners instantaneously destroyed by the horrible explosion the other day. There was often life-lasting ruin to the miner, and misery to his family, when an accident permanently disabled him. Those who pleaded so strongly for the rights of property should remember that something ought also to be said for the rights of life.[169]

By the end of the first week of August 1880, both sides were proposing amendments with the idea that the legislation might actually be passed. An amendment which would have put government shipyard workers on a footing with other workers was rejected on the grounds that it would trespass on the rights of the Crown.[170] Another amendment, which would have instituted mandatory self-insurance, was rejected with the argument that it would have relieved masters of all responsibility to provide adequate plant and supervisors.[171] Lord Randolph Churchill proposed a popular amendment which would have exempted those employers who contributed one-third of a mutual insurance fund for their injured workers. Several mine owners spoke in favor of the amendment, but it was defeated.[172]

Having finally passed the House of Commons with no disabling amendments, the bill faced more opposition in the House of Lords.[173] The Lord Chancellor introduced its second reading with an ironic little dig. He reassured the Lords that they need have no fear that the bill would have an adverse impact on great industries like mining, because, as employers had shown, most of the accidents there were due not to supervisory problems or to the provision of insufficient plant, but to negligence on the part of the workmen.[174] On the opposite side of the question, employers continued to lobby, even beseeching the bishops to hold it up on the grounds that compensation was a moral question—"a question of the disturbance of social peace and faith, and the introduction of elements of hatred and uncharitableness, which lays upon the shoulders of our Legislature a responsibility so grave and so closely allied with religious and moral wrong, that they should, in duty to their own peace, pause before accepting such a responsibility."[175]

Buoyed by the support of some large employers of labor who opposed the bill, Lord Beaconsfield, whose government had toyed with the idea of employer's liability legislation for so long without taking action, alleged that the government had not taken the time to craft a proper bill. He insisted on saddling the bill with an amendment that made it a two-year, temporary measure.[176] Once the idea of a time limit had been introduced, the House of Commons had trouble removing that element from it, even though some of its proponents claimed it was tantamount to killing the bill. In the end, a seven-year time limit was adopted, and the bill became law as a temporary and experimental measure.

Like parliamentary reform in 1832, employers' liability in 1880 marked a turning point. In both cases, despite the fact that working people were underrepresented in Parliament, conservative interests were forced to concede a little in order to save other, major parts of a regime that was under attack. During the debate over employers' liability, employers' interests had warned that any changes to the compensation scheme would break down the ties of paternalism that had for so long connected master and man. By 1880, however, with strong labor unions representing highly complex modes of workplace organization as on railroads and in mines, this argument about the cost of compensation outweighing the benefit was no longer compelling.

Working people understood that, although the 1880 Employers' Liability Act was gained with major compromises that severely weakened it, it was still a substantial victory. The Operative Stonemasons, who had documented so many injuries with lasting consequences to their own members since the 1830s, welcomed the new legislation.

> Although it will not affect us as a trade to anything like the extent to which it will affect many other trades and callings of a more dangerous character than ours is, such as the Railway Servants, Miners, etc., it will place us, in common with all other trades and callings, on a level with the general public with regard to suing an employer for damages in case of accident through defective machinery and plant, or through the negligence of an employer or of some other person in the position of manager or foreman, and does away with the plea which has hitherto stood as a bar to action by a workman against an employer, that of "Common Employment."

The stonemasons also expected that the Act would have a domino effect, encouraging employers to provide better machinery and plant in an attempt to keep their costs down. The Operative Stonemasons advised their membership not to "contract yourselves out of the Act by accepting any scheme of insurance that the employers may offer you in place of it, but do your utmost to support Bro. Broadhurst and Messrs. Macdonald and Burt." Finally, the stonemasons noted that the fact that such an Act could make its way through a Parliament in which employers were five-hundred times better represented than labor was little short of a miracle.[177]

The workers of Great Britain had had much to overcome in the struggle for employers' liability legislation. Although discussion of the issue had originated in the 1830s among the utilitarians, who espoused a European, no-fault model of compensation, and the issue had resurfaced again during discussions of railway contractors in the 1840s, the idea of predictable compensation was suffocated again and again by the free agency doctrine and by powerful industry advocates. Even a disaster as great as the Hartley colliery cave-in, despite all of the national attention in attracted, was insufficient to unite labor or to defeat employer opposition and government apathy. Only after the major unions had united in the TUC, and only after Alexander Macdonald had been elected to Parliament specifically as workers' representative, was momentum maintained on the issue.

The rehearsing and re-rehearsing of the arguments for and against an Employers' Liability Act, through repeated introductions of legislation and two separate Select Committees, helped to routinize the arguments for and against intervention. Workers emphasized the financial impact of accidents, not only on individual families but on their communities as a whole. Employers made apocalyptic threats about the probable effect of such legislation on business, and warned that it would doom the good relationships between employers and employees. By introducing a temporary measure, the government managed to placate both sides and to reap the political reward while simultaneously limiting the transformation of the existing compensation regime.

Epilogue:
The Anglo-American Aftermath

THE REALLOCATION OF THE SOCIAL RESPONSIBILITY for workplace accidents from workers and the charitable public to employers was a project that accompanied other changes in thinking about social welfare. In the United States, where factory mechanization came later and "progressivism" and the idea of the social collectivity caught hold later than in England, the first workers' compensation laws were not passed until more than twenty years later than in England.

Some of the reasons are cultural. As Jennifer Clark has pointed out, in the United States technology was too closely identified with national independence and progress to permit any kind of critique of its impact on working people.[1] In the post-Civil War period, the almost unbroken succession of Republican presidents, none of whom was a particular friend of the worker, blocked the consideration of workers' issues and used federal troops to put down strikes. The concept of "free labor"—a founding construct of the Republican party—had a great impact on the making of American policy.

American workers seem to have bought into these arguments. In contrast with workers representing Britain's dangerous industries, American trade unions failed to press workplace safety issues until employers' liability legislation had already been laid on the table by the Progressives. By pressing for higher wages instead of on-the-job safety, American workers hewed to the interpretation that the best way to provide for workplace accidents was through individual thrift.

The legal culture of the United States also played a role. Not until the twentieth century did American legislators look to the example of Europe and consider a no-fault workers' compensation scheme, as the Utilitarians had done in England as early as the 1830s. In contrast with England, where the application of common-law rules regarding collecting anything in court for workplace injuries was somewhat uniform, many exceptions were developed in American states—a fact that buffered the harshness of the American regime for compensating workplace accidents.[2] Individual states—beginning with Massachusetts in 1887—also adopted employers' liability laws, limiting employer use of the trio of common-law defenses and making it more likely that injured workers or their families would triumph in court.[3]

The much greater decentralization in the United States had created marked differences in the degree to which workers in various parts of the country could expect to be routinely protected or compensated. For example, the states and territories of the West, where many kinds of government regulation were shunned or ill-funded, were also home to many mines. The mine companies had complete social and political control.[4] Until the U.S. Bureau of Mines was created in 1910, the initiative for safety legislation lay with the several states; thus, devastating mine accidents were commonplace, particularly in territories like Oklahoma and New Mexico.[5]

Given these differences between England and the United States, why did the regime for compensating workplace accidents change at all? Looking at the American context helps to clarify not only the American, but also the English case. The first issue in both countries was a change in the location of responsibility. In the English case, a long history of devastating workplace accidents in mines and on railroads, combined with newspaper commentary, public charitable activity, and political discussion, helped focus attention on the human toll of workplace accidents. Workplace accidents were ideologically reconstituted, from individual human tragedies into a social problem that could only be solved by government intervention. By the early twentieth century, the Progressives were making it impossible for Americans to ignore workplace accidents, as Americans were exposed to Crystal Eastman's muckraking journalism, Lewis Hine's photographs of the victims of workplace accidents, and President Roosevelt's advocacy of the issue.[6] As John Witt has noted, in the aftermath of the carnage of the Civil War, the government agreed to assume some of the responsibility for the welfare of injured veterans. This marked a turning point for Americans. As the toll of industrial accidents was likened to wartime, it became harder for the government to shrug off any responsibility for reallocating the social costs of workplace accidents.[7]

Changes in the size and complexity of some of the most dangerous work-places also clearly gave the lie to the concept of common employment in both Britain and the United States. Workers faced with Byzantine systems of sub-contracting, with the collaboration of several railroad companies in a single effort, or with the collapse of factory buildings or giant beam engines, clearly could not monitor their own safety effectively in the way that the law claimed. Looking at the United States, John Witt has identified a shifting of responsi-bility in the workplace itself, as the factory floor became more complex and hierarchical, and workers were deprived of the opportunity to work in their own customary ways. With the advent of Taylorism and the streamlining of the workplace, any semblance of worker control was completely surrendered. The result of this rethinking of workplace control was an acceptance of re-sponsibility for workplace accidents and safety by large employers, and a view of workplace accidents as not accidents at all, but rather the inevitable toll of industry. Subscribing to this view, companies like U.S. Steel implemented the first no-fault compensation programs in America.[8]

Structural changes in the legal regime in the two decades before 1900 had made the playing field between injured workers and American corporations more lopsided. By allowing corporations to remove lawsuits against them from their states of origin into federal courts largely perceived as probusiness, federal diversity jurisdiction gave an edge to corporations. In contrast with individuals, who approached corporations with little knowledge of the legal system and in financial distress, incorporated companies, including and espe-cially railroads, had entire legal departments, doctors on staff who might be ready to testify in the company's favor, and economies of scale when it came to the delivery of legal services.[9] The net effect of this was to discourage work-ers' claims and promote a bureaucratized out-of-court settlement as the usual path in the case of workplace injury.

Greater awareness of safety problems was also a factor in both Britain and the United States. In Britain, whether or not the accident rate was truly increasing, the appointment of factory and mine inspectors and attempts to collect more accurate statistics about railroad deaths and injuries resulted in greater attention to the problem. In the United States, state bureaus of labor statistics began to collect statistics created explicitly with the labor vote in mind. The bureaus were the first governmental entities to inspect workplaces and try to enforce labor laws, and in this they anticipated the creation of a more active state as early as the 1870s.[10] The amassing of statistics related to the living and working conditions of the working classes providing a scientific foundation for the work of Progressive reformers, helping to establish the authority of an alternative ideology to laissez-faire economics.[11] Bureaus of Labor Statistics could also craft factory laws along the English model. In New York, an 1886 factory law was passed to regulate the workplaces and working hours of women and young people under twenty-one. Factory inspectors were empowered to enter workplaces to search for safety violations and to require factory owners to report accidents as they occurred.[12]

This chapter has documented a long history of government oversight and consideration of the workplace safety issue in Britain beginning in 1830. In the United States, government oversight of firms also increased incrementally over time, although the process started later. For example, Anthony Wallace describes 1870 as a key moment for American miners. In that year, in the immediate wake of the Avondale explosion, Pennsylvania mine safety law was expanded, prohibiting boys under twelve from working underground and specifying two shafts 150 feet apart.[13] John Eltringham was chosen as the first mine inspector in the United States, and he set a standard (an inadequate one) for ventilation based on the ventilation in his own Pioneer Colliery mine. An 1876 act in the Maryland legislature provided for a mines inspector who had to report annually to the governor on both conditions and accidents, and who was also to attend inquests. Section 4 of the act provided that if a mining death were fully proven to be caused "by any violation of this act, or any wilful failure to comply with its provisions," the widow or heirs might bring suit for damages. Despite the passage of this act, there were widespread allegations that nothing was done to temper the bad air in the mines; this is only logical since the act set no standards either for specific volumes of air or for specific systems of ventilation.[14]

In railroads and other large, mechanized operations alike, the late nineteenth and early twentieth century saw the rise of a safety technocracy charged with the responsibility of crafting safer workplaces.[15] In the railroad industry, as C. Clark describes, state legislators began to shift responsibility for safety to the employer in the 1880s. Legislation not only specified the accountability of management for safety, but also guided the selection process of safe couplers and brakes. Finally, prompted by requests from employee unions, state railroad commissioners, and President Harrison, Congress in 1893 passed safety appliance legislation that split responsibility for accidents between the employer and the federal government.[16] Ultimately, all of these kinds of attempts at prevention were seen as uneven and insufficient, prompting state governments to turn to legislation.[17]

Greater tolerance for government intervention in business was accompanied in both Britain and the United States by the erosion of the doctrine of free agency—the doctrine that it was the responsibility of each worker to deal with the vicissitudes of a market economy by making his or her own provision for disaster. As this chapter has shown, British employers hammered home the discourse of free agency to the bitter end, wondering aloud why adult male workers were unwilling to take responsibility for their actions and warning of horrible disruption to the social order. In the United States, in contrast, the influx of new immigrant groups helped give the lie to the assertion that the workforce was full of "free agents."

Britain and the United States resembled each other in their passage from a free-agency regime to a more predictable and bureaucratic one in stepwise fashion, by first codifying exceptions to the three common-law defenses. The first employers' liability in New York in 1902 excepted management from the status of fellow servants, thus simply codifying the "vice-principal" rule which had been in effect in American courts for the previous thirty years. A law conferring management status on all railroad signalmen followed in 1906. Both of these laws, combined with the development of contingent fee representation by attorneys specializing in such tort suits, encouraged a rise in the number of lawsuits, as did the increasing perception of danger in the world due to streetcars, traffic, and railroads.[18] The existence of factory inspectorates and bureaus of labor provided injured workers with additional ammunition to use in cases against their employers, increasing the likelihood of jury awards and thus increasing employers' desire for a more predictable system.[19]

One major difference between the achievement of workers' compensation in Britain and in the United States was the willingness of legislators in each place to look to European models of no-fault compensation. Wisconsin, whose courts had been fairly hard-line in their interpretation of the barriers to workers' compensation, was unique in the willingness of its Progressives to look at German models.[20] But even in liberal Wisconsin, the rigid legal regime had first come under attack between 1880 and 1910 due to the growing number of accident suits in the courts and their diversification from the railroad industry to a number of industrial mill-based industries.[21] Judges and juries in lower courts found for the workers, only to have their decisions reversed on appeal when cases reached the state Supreme Court.[22] Revision of the workers' compensation regime was a way to remove uncertainty from this system.

As this study has shown, the workers' compensation regimes in Britain and the United States were similar throughout most of the nineteenth century.

In Great Britain and the United States, the perception that the workplace was becoming more dangerous coexisted with highly voluntaristic regime for the amelioration of accidents. Luck and individual circumstances played a role in determining the impact of a workplace accident on a worker and his or her family: was a worker injured in a highly publicized disaster or as part of the routine workings of a factory or mine? Was an employer paternalistic or penny pinching? Did a worker have generous co-workers who might participate in a whip-round, or was he thrifty enough to belong to a field club or mutual aid society? Was a worker able to be hired again by the same company in some lesser capacity, or was he, like Phineas Gage, destined by his disability to drift from one short-term job to another?

The age, gender, and condition of servitude also helped to determine the path that a worker might follow to compensation. Women and child workers injured on the job might pursue justice through Factory Act prosecutions or have an easier time prevailing in court. While slaves injured on the job collected nothing personally for the pains of their injury, theoretically their masters would be compensated in a way that would cover the cost of their medical care. But white, male workers were often sidelined by arguments about "free agency" that left them bearing the largest burden of contributory negligence and assumption of risk.

In both Britain and the United States, the shifting of the workers' compensation regime from one supported by the triumvirate of workers, employers, and the public working together, to a more bureaucratic model, had its costs and benefits. As Fishback and Kantor have argued, taking as their basis a quantitative, econometric group study of the achievement of workers' compensation in several states, compensation laws were ultimately passed in the United States because all three groups, employers, workers, and insurers, could see that they would reap a financial benefit. Although workers would receive a relative wage reduction, they would be better insured for injuries on the job through workers' compensation. Employers would find more predictability in a system that had begun to break down under the pressure of unpredictable jury awards. Insurers would find a net benefit in those states—the majority of states—which did not create a monopolistic state fund for workers' compensation insurance.[23]

There are other sacrifices and gains that Fishback and Kantor's econometric models cannot measure. In both Britain and the United States, the move toward a more predictable workers' compensation regime meant that members of the general public were largely excused from thinking about the individual toll of workplace accidents or from contributing directly to their amelioration. The system of compensation may have been more unsystematic than it is today in both countries, but public awareness of the existence of workplace accidents was acute. In labor and middle-class newspapers alike, readers were exposed to stories of familial destruction and worker heroism, religious redemption and attempts to outguess Providence. While few of these stories focused on the economic burden faced by workers, they did provide consumers with an opportunity to process some of the guilt about the workplace's inevitable toll.

The evolution of the workers' compensation regime also had an ambivalent result for workers' families. They were relieved of a burden that might become intolerable or entail the shifting of the responsibility for wage earning from fathers to mothers and children. On the other hand, friendly societies, a key feature of working-class sociability, became relatively less important— especially in Britain, as the role that these had played was assumed by the National Health Service.

No one who understands the history of workplace accidents and injured workers would argue for a return to the culture of poverty and uncertainty that plagued working families; but it is unfortunate that the close tie between our commodity culture and the harsh impact on the bodies of workers—once so well-understood by the reading public—has left our collective consciousness, except on rare occasions. Even then, our reactions are different than they were 150 years ago: a chicken-processing plant may burst into flame, a chemical works explode, or a group of miners suffocate in West Virginia, but the idea that one should then send something to the families of the workers left behind is no longer as common. The issue of fault has also been obscured. Businesses are free to take calculated risks with workers' lives; workers are free to take advantage of the system by filing claims for occupational illnesses that they might never have filed. While compensation for workplace accidents is a more secure process today, there is less public awareness of the toll of workplace accidents or even of their existence. Death on the job has become the subject of the occasional documentary or front-page exposé, rather than being a feature of almost every issue of every newspaper. The worker is safer, but the potential hazards of employment have largely been forgotten.

Notes

Notes

Introduction

1. Gage's story is chronicled in Malcolm Macmillan, *An Odd Kind of Fame: Stories of Phineas Gage* (Cambridge, MA: MIT Press, 2000).

2. P. W. J. Bartrip and S. B. Burman's excellent book *The Wounded Soldiers of Industry* (Cambridge, UK: Cambridge University Press, 1983) concentrated on the legal and social history aspects of workplace accidents. Elizabeth Cawthon examined some of the cultural attitudes toward workplace accidents in her Ph.D. dissertation, "Occupational Accidents and the Law: The Role of Coroners' Inquests in England, 1830–1850," University of Virginia, 1985.

3. Arthur F. McEvoy, "The Triangle Shirtwaist Factory Fire of 1911: Social Change, Industrial Accidents and the Evolution of Common-Sense Causality," *Law and Social Inquiry* 20 (1995): 621–51.

4. Arthur F. McEvoy, "Working Environments: An Ecological Approach to Industrial Health and Safety," *Technology and Culture* 36 Supplement (1995): S145–S172.

5. The idea that free labor was specific to the American accident regime is one of the three major arguments in John Witt's *The Accidental Republic: Crippled Workingmen, Destitute Widows, and the Remaking of American Law* (Cambridge, MA: Harvard University Press, 2004).

6. Eric Foner, *Free Soil, Free Labor, Free Men: The Ideology of the Republican Party Before the Civil War* (New York: Oxford University Press, 1970), pp. 11–39.

Chapter 1

1. See, e.g., Norris Pope, "Dickens's *The Signalman* and Information Problems in the Railway Age," *Technology and Culture* 42:3 (2001): 436–61; Raphael Samuel, "Mineral Workers," in Raphael Samuel, ed. *Miners, Quarrymen and Saltworkers* (London: Routledge & Kegan Paul, 1977), p. 47.

2. Clive Emsley, *Crime and Society in England, 1750–1900* (New York: Longman, 1987), Chapter 2.

3. James Riley, "Ill Health During the English Mortality Decline: The Friendly Societies' Experience," *Bulletin of the History of Medicine* 1987 61(4): 563–88. Friendly societies made no distinction between workplace accidents and illness for the purposes of paying out benefits, but in his monograph *Sick, Not Dead*, Riley shows that accidents accounted for 15.78 percent of cases among members of Odd Fellows' lodges and friendly societies whose records he surveyed for the period between 1896 and 1919. The average duration of sickness due to accident was 33.4 days. For the Great North of Scotland Railway employees between 1902 and 1913, accidents accounted for 21.3 percent of sicknesses, and caused on average 20.6 days of absence. James C. Riley, *Sick, Not Dead: The Health of British Workingmen during the Mortality Decline* (Baltimore: Johns Hopkins University Press, 1997), pp. 192–93.

4. Edward A. Purcell, Jr., *Litigation and Inequality: Federal Diversity Jurisdiction in Industrial America, 1870–1958* (New York: Oxford Unviersity Press, 1992), p. 19.

5. *Papers Read Before the Statistical Society of Manchester on the Demoralisation and Injuries Occasioned by the Want of Proper Regulations of Labourers Engaged in the Construction and Working of Railways* (Manchester, UK: Simms and Dinham, n.d.), pp. 10–12.

6. Parliamentary Reports, Reports from Committees, *Report from the Select Committee on Railway Labourers* 1846 (530) XIII.425, p. x.

7. Ibid., p. 67.

8. Ibid., pp. 118–19.

9. Ibid., p. 120.

10. Pope, "Dickens's *The Signalman*," p. 452.

11. Parliamentary Papers, Accounts and Papers, *Return of the Number and Nature of the Accidents and the Injuries to Life and Limb which have Occurred on all the Railways Open to traffic in England, and Wales, Scotland and Ireland, from the 1st of July to the 31st December, 1855,* 1856 (0.6) LIV: 297, pp. 15–23. The number of railroad workers, excluding track layers and other laborers, was computed from Parliamentary Papers, Accounts and Papers, *Return of the Number and Description of Persons Employed on Each of the Railways in England and Wales, Scotland and Ireland, Respectively, on the 30th Day of June, 1856,* 1856 (409) LIV: 659, p. 40.

12. P. W. Kingsford, *Victorian Railwaymen* (London: Frank Cass & Co., 1970), p. 47.

13. Walter Licht, *Working for the Railroad: The Organization of Work in the Nineteenth Century* (Princeton, NJ: Princeton University Press, 1983), pp. 183–85.

14. C. Clark, "The Railroad Safety Movement in the United States: Origins and Development, 1869 to 1893," Ph.D. dissertation, University of Illinois, 1966, pp. 59–60.

15. Robert C. Reed, *Train Wrecks: A Pictorial History of Accidents on the Main Line* (Seattle, WA: Superior Publishing, 1968), p. 60.

16. John Phillips, *Report on the Condition of the Ventilation of Mines and Collieries* (London: William Clowes, 1850), pp. 27–29.

17. Parliamentary Papers, Reports from Committees, *Select Committee on Accidents in Coal Mines* (1852–1853), vol. 20. no 13, pp. 177–79.

18. James Mather, *The Coal Mines: Their Dangers and Means of Safety* (London: Longman, 1853), p. 4.

19. Parliamentary Papers, Reports from Committees, *Select Committee on Accidents in Coal Mines* (1854), p. 84.

20. This analysis is based on a database of all accidents reported in the *British Miner and Workman's Advocate* between the first issue of September 13, 1862, and n.s. 20, July 18, 1863. Another analysis, of ninety-four deaths reported in 1840, revealed a similar distribution of causes of death. For the seventy cases in which a cause of death was listed, wagons and rolleys accounted for approximately 21 percent of the deaths. Another 20 percent of the unfortunates were crushed by coal, and another 20 percent died from falls. Explosions only accounted for 10 percent of deaths, if after-damp and choke-damp deaths are included in that total. The information in this section was compiled using the table printed in Parliamentary Papers, *Reports on Gases and Explosions in Collieries* by Sir Henry T. De La Beche and Sir Lyon Playfair, 1847 (815) vol. XVI, pp. 40–41.

21. John Benson, *British Coal Miners in the Nineteenth Century: A Social History* (New York: Holmes and Meier, 1980), pp. 39–40.

22. The information in this section was computed using the tables printed in Parliamentary Papers, Reports from Committees, *Select Committee on Accidents in Coal Mines* (1854), Second Report, pp. 24–28.

23. Parliamentary Papers, Reports from Commissioners, *Commission for Inquiring into the Employment and Condition of Children in Mines and Manufactories,* Appendix to First Report, Part I, 1842 vol. XVI (381): 552, 554.

24. Anthony Wallace has argued that American coal bosses were emotionally invested in admitting no safety problems at any of their mines, since the discovery of some safety problem that they should pay to fix might be the thin end of the wedge and deprive them of all their profits. This view of the world was reinforced by the American myth of the industrialist as hero. Anthony F. C. Wallace, *St. Clair: A Nineteenth-Century Coal Town's Experience with a Disaster Prone Industry* (New York: Alfred A. Knopf, 1987), p. 53.

25. Thomas Knox, *Underground: Or, Life Below the Surface* (Hartford, CT: J. B. Bin, 1875), pp. 580–81.

26. Ibid., p. 256.

27. Christopher Baer, "The Miner as Market Victim: 1840–1860," Unpublished Research Reports, Hagley Museum (1979), in possession of Museum Director. No pagination.

28. Benson, *British Coal Miners*, p. 37.

29. The information in this section was compiled using the table printed in *Reports on Gases and Explosions in Collieries* 1847 (815) vol. XVI, pp. 40–41.

30. Benson, *British Coal Miners*, p. 37.

31. T. Boyns, "Work and Death in the South Wales Coalfield, 1874–1914," *Welsh Historical Review* 12 (1985): 514–37.

32. *Ferndale Colliery Explosion: The Single Shift System of Working Collieries in England and Wales, the Cause of Nearly Double the Loss of Life* (Cardiff, UK: The Chronicle Office, 1867).

33. Edward Headlam Greenhow, *Third Series of Cases Illustrating the Pathology of the Pulmonary Disease Frequent Among Certain Classes of Operatives Exposed to the Inhalation of Dust* (London: J. E. Adlard, 1868–69); Franz Oppert, *On Melanosis of the Lungs, and other Lung Diseases Arising from the Inhalation of Dust* (London: John Churchill and Sons, 1866).

34. *Blue Hen's Chicken*, vol. 4 no. 37, April 27, 1849.

35. J. T. Arlidge, *The Hygiene, Diseases and Mortality of Occupations* (London: Percival and Co., 1892), pp. 259–60. See also Parliamentary Papers, *Return of the Number of Accidents to Men, Women, Young Persons and Children Caused by Shuttles Flying from Power Looms*, 1890–91 (197) LXXVII, 343.

36. *Ten Hours' Advocate*, no. 24, March 6, 1847, p. 188.

37. Parliamentary Papers, Reports from Commissioners, *Report of the Royal Commission on the Employment of Children in Factories*, 1833 (450) XX: 99–1119.

38. Ibid., pp. 596–99.

39. Parliamentary Papers, Accounts and Papers, *Reports of the Inspectors of Factories to Her Majesty's Principal Secretary of State for the Home Department for the Half Year Ending 31 October 1848*, 1849 (1017) : 131, p. 17, 103, 149.

40. Arlidge, *The Hygiene*, p. 364.

41. P. W. J. Bartrip and P. T. Fenn, "The Measurement of Safety: Factory Accident Statistics in Victorian and Edwardian Britain." *Historical Research* 63 (1990): 58–72.

42. *Blue Hen's Chicken*, vol. 3 no. 27, February 25, 1848; vol. 3 no. 28, March 3, 1848; vol. 3 no. 43, June 9, 1848; vol. 4 no. 18, December 15, 1848; vol. 4 no. 25, February 2, 1849; vol. 4 no. 36, April 20, 1849.

43. Printed letter from Leonard Horner, dated November 1859, HO 45/6756, Public Record Office.

44. "Return of Persons Killed and Injured by Steam Boiler Explosions from the Year 1863 to 1868 Inclusive," Document 3656/70, HO 45/7605, Public Record Office.

45. Peter Way, *Common Labor* (Cambridge, UK: Cambridge University Press, 1993).

46. Randolph Emil Bergstrom, *Courting Danger: The Evolution of Tort Liability in New York, 1870–1910* (Ithaca, 1992), p. 82.

47. Keith Krawczynski, "A Note on Accidental Death in Colonial New Jersey," *New Jersey History* 100:3 (1992): 63–70.

48. *Commonwealth,* no. 223, June 27, 1867, p. 3.

49. *Blue Hen's Chicken,* vol. 3 no. 4, September 10, 1847, p. 2.

50. *Blue Hen's Chicken,* vol. 3 no. 5, September 17, 1847.

51. *Times,* no. 17198, November 13, 1839; no. 21272, November 13, 1852.

52. *Blue Hen's Chicken,* vol. 3 no. 18, December 24, 1847; Maurice B. Dorgan, *Lawrence Yesterday and Today* (Lawrence: Dick and Trumpold, 1918), p. 54; *London Mercury,* no. 29, April 2, 1837; *Newcastle Courant,* no. 8638, June 13, 1835.

53. *Times,* no. 2348, July 1, 1792.

54. *Newcastle Chronicle,* no. 5123, September 13, 1862.

55. *The Times,* no. 2154, October 15, 1791, p. 3. col. c; *Blue Hen's Chicken,* vol. 4 no. 6, September 15, 1848; *Newcastle Chronicle,* no. 3685, March 7, 1835; *Commonwealth,* no. 181, August 25, 1866, p. 2.

56. *Reformer* (Newport), vol. 1 no. 22, February 7, 1862.

57. C. Calvert Holland, *Diseases of the Lungs from Mechanical Causes* (London: John Churchill, 1843), p. 25; see also Thomas Peacock, *Notes on a Case of Millstone-Makers Phthisis. Siliceous Matter Found in the Lungs* (London: J. W. Roche, 1861); Thomas B. Peacock, *On French-Millstone-Makers' Phthisis* (London: G. Rowland Brown, 1862).

58. Charles Parsons, *On a Form of Bronchitis (Simulating Phthisis) Which Is Peculiar to Certain Branches of the Potting Trade* (Edinburgh, UK: Maclachlan and Stewart, 1864), p. 21.

59. *British Miner and Workman's Advocate* no. 13, December 6, 1862.

60. *British Miner and Workman's Advocate* n.s. 7, April 18, 1863; no. 23, February 14, 1863; no. 11, November 22, 1862; n.s. 16, June 20, 1863; no. 9, November 8, 1862; n.s. 12, May 25, 1863; n.s. 7, April 18, 1863; no. 20, January 24, 1863; no. 14, December 13, 1862; no. 10, November 15, 1862; no. 4, October 4, 1862; no. 11, November 22, 1862; n.s. 12, May 25, 1863; no. 12, November 29, 1862; n.s. 14, June 6, 1863; no. 6, October 18, 1862; n.s. 18, July 4, 1863; n.s. 14, June 6, 1863.

61. *British Miner and Workman's Advocate* no. 23, February 14, 1863.

Chapter 2

1. Laura Peebles, Tanya Heasman, and Vivienne Roberts, *Analysis of Compensation Issues Related to Health and Safety Claims* (London: HSE Books, 2003).

2. Benefit Tables for 2003, U.S. Department of Labor, Employment Standards Administration, Office of Workers' Compensation Programs: http://www.dol.gov/esa/regs/statutes/owcp/stwclaw/stwclaw.htm.

3. Peter Karsten, *Heart vs. Head: Judge-Made Law in Nineteenth-Century America* (North Carolina, 1997).

4. Michael Ashley Stein, "Priestley v. Fowler (1837) and the Emerging Tort of Negligence," *Boston College Law Review* vol. 44 (2003): 689–731.

5. In fact, as Michael Ashley Stein argues convincingly, the *Priestley* case was not understood in England to have created a doctrine of common employment until 1850, when Lord Abinger's dicta were first cited as having created a fellow-servant rule. Stein argues that *Priestley* was nothing more than a failed attempt to extend the concept of negligence to the employer-employee relationship. See Stein, p. 714. Bartrip and Burman agree that the importance of the *Priestley* case has been overstated. As they have pointed out, had *Priestley v. Fowler* been seen as an important test case, it would have received more press comment at the time. P. W. J. Bartrip and S. B. Burman, *The Wounded Soldiers of Industry* (Oxford, UK: Clarendon Press, 1983), pp. 24–25.

6. R. G. Gammage, *History of the Chartist Movement* (London: Merlin Press, 1976), first published 1894, pp. 240–41. See also Elisabeth Cawthon, "Occupational Accidents and the Law," Ph.D. dissertation, University of Virginia, 1985. p. 478.

7. Thomas Beven, *The Law of Employers' Liability for the Negligence of Servants Causing Injury to Fellow Servants* (London: Waterlow Brothers and Layton, 1881), p. 22.

8. *Farwell v. Boston and Worcester Railroad Company*, 4 Met 49.

9. Ibid., at 56.

10. Leonard Levy, *The Law of the Commonwealth and Chief Justice Shaw* (New York: Harper and Row, 1957), p. 172.

11. *Farwell v. Boston and Worcester Railroad Company*, 4 Met 49, at 62.

12. Beven, *Law of Employers' Liability*, p. 22.

13. Christopher Tomlins, *Law, Labor and Ideology in the American Republic* (Cambridge, UK: Cambridge University Press, 1993), p. 362; Levy, *Law of the Commonwealth*, p. 172.

14. Levy, *Law of the Commonwealth*, p. 176.

15. *Bartonshill Coal Co. v. Reid* (1858) 3 Macq. 266.

16. *Little Miami Railroad Co. v. John Stevens*, 20 Ohio Reports 416, December 1854 (pp. 353–85).

17. Karsten, *Heart vs. Head*, passim.

18. Ibid., p. 216, 246.

19. Jerrilyn Marston, "The Creation of a Common-Law Rule: The Fellow Servant Rule, 1837–1860," *University of Pennsylvania Law Review* 32 (1984): 579–620.

20. Tomlins, *Law, Labor and Ideology*, pp. 382 et. seq.; Paul Bellamy, "From Court Room to Board Room: Immigration, Juries and the Creation of an American Proletariat," Ph.D. dissertation, Case Western Reserve, 1994, pp. 46–52; Robert Asher, "Failure and Fulfillment: Agitation for Employers' Liability Legislation and the Origins of Workmen's Compensation in New York State, 1876–1910," *Labor History* 1983 24(2): 198–222; Beven, *Law of Employers' Liability*, p. 14.

21. *Skipp v. Eastern Counties Railway* (1853), 9 Ex 223, 23 L.J. Ex. 23, cited in Beven, p. 23.

22. In one such case a stripper was charged with manslaughter after causing the death of a thirteen-year-old co-worker. *Manchester Guardian,* no 1934, July 21, 1847. On the master as a fellow servant, see *Ashworth v. Stanwick and Walker,* 3 E&E 701; 30 LJQB 183; 7 Jur N.S. 467, cited in Beven, *Law of Employers' Liability,* p. 48.

23. See, e.g., *Stark v. McLaren* 10 M 31, 44 J 56; *Gregory v. Hill,* (1877) 8 M. 282, 42 J. 132, cited in Beven, *Law of Employers' Liability,* p. 47.

24. *Bartonshill Coal Company v. Reid,* 4 Jur n.s. at 773.

25. See, for example, Morton Horwitz, *The Transformation of American Law, 1780–1860* (Cambridge, MA: Harvard University Press, 1977). Similarly, Leonard Levy did not portray Charles Shaw as antilabor, he did portray him as strongly prorailroad, and a believer in "free labor." See Levy, *Law of the Commonwealth,* pp. 179–80.

26. Robert Steinfeld, *The Invention of Free Labor* (Chapel Hill: University of North Carolina Press, 1991), p. 154.

27. Tomlins, *Law, Labor and Ideology,* pp. 333–38.

28. A. W. B. Simpson, *Leading Cases in the Common Law* (Oxford, UK: Oxford University Press, 1995), pp. 100–134. See also Terence Ingman, "The Rise and Fall of the Doctrine of Common Employment," *Juridical Review 1978:* 106–25.

29. Richard Epstein, "The Historical Origins and Economic Structure of Workers' Compensation Law," *Georgia Law Review* 16 (1982): 777. Epstein's findings are a restatement of the opinion of Justice Pollack in *Vose v. Lancashire and Yorkshire Railway Company, Jurist* n.s. v. 4 at 365 (1858).

30. Bartrip and Burman, *The Wounded Soldiers,* p. 98; Elisabeth Cawthon, "New Life for the Deodand: Coroners' Inquests and Occupational Death in England, 1830–1846," *American Journal of Legal History* 33:2 (1989): 137–47. See also *Newcastle Courant,* no. 8376, August 8, 1835; no. 8638, June 13, 1835; *Newcastle Chronicle,* no. 3703, July 11, 1835.

31. Albert B. Bolles, *The Liability of Employers to their Employees* (Harrisburg: Edwin K. Meyers, 1891), p. 115.

32. *Brydon v. Stewart,* 2 Macq 30, cited in Beven, *Law of Employers' Liability,* p. 25.

33. In *Mellors v. Shaw* (1862), 1 B&S 445, 7 Jur N.S. 845, 30 LJQB 333, cited in Beven, *Law of Employers' Liability,* p. 27.

34. *Clarke v. Holmes,* 7 H&N 937, 8 Jur N.S. 992, 31 L.J.Ex 356, 10 W.R. 405, quoted in Beven, *Law of Employers' Liability,* p. 34.

35. *Britton v. Great Western Cotton Company* L.R. & Ex 130, L.J. Ex 99, 27 L.T 125, cited in Beven, *Law of Employers' Liability,* p. 35.

36. Levy, *Law of the Commonwealth,* p. 173.

37. *Morgan v. Vale of Neath RR Company* (1865), LR1QB 149; B&S 736; 35 LJBQ 23, 13 LTNS 564, cited in Beven, *Law of Employers' Liability,* p. 41.

38. Looking at a later period, Fishback and Kantor have found that some male workers in dangerous industries seem to have received a wage premium, but that women and child workers did not. See *A Prelude to the Welfare State: The Origins of Workers' Compensation* (Chicago, IL: University of Chicago Press, 2000), p. 49.

39. As Bolles pointed out, however, just because a usage was common did not mean it was safe. See Bolles, *Liability of Employers*, p. 52.

40. See, e.g., *Griffiths v. Gidlow*, 3 H&N 648, 27 LJ Exch 404; *Assop v. Yates*, 2 H&N 768, 27 L.J. Exch 156.

41. Beven, *Law of Employers' Liability*, p. 56.

42. Bolles, *Liability of Employers*, pp. 38–41.

43. Bartrip and Burman, *The Wounded Soldiers*, pp. 26–28.

44. Lawrence Friedman, "Civil Wrongs: Personal Injury Law in the Late 19th Century," *American Bar Foundation Research Journal* (1987): 351–78.

45. Crystal Eastman, *Work-Accidents and the Law* (New York: Charities Publication Committee, 1910), p. 188. The politics of delay are spelled out in great detail in Bellamy, "From Court Room to Board Room," pp. 67–69.

46. John Witt, *The Accidental Republic* (Cambridge, MA: Harvard University Press, 2004), p. 58.

47. Friedman, "Civil Wrongs," 351–78.

48. See, e.g., the case noted by Alexander McDonald in *Commonwealth*, no. 157, March 10, 1866, p. 6.

49. On class bias among jurists later in the century, see Michael J. Klarman, "The Judges Versus the Unions: The Development of British Labor Law, 1867–1913," *Virginia Law Review* 75 (1989): 1487–1602.

50. R. W. Kostal, "Legal Justice, Social Justice: An Incursion into the Social History of Work-Related Accident Law in Ontario, 1860–1886," *Law and History Review* 6 (1988): 1–24.

51. Mark Aldrich, *Safety First: Technology, Labor, and Business in the Building of American Work Safety 1870–1939* (Baltimore, MD: Johns Hopkins University Press, 1997), p. 114.

52. J. T. Arlidge, *The Hygiene, Diseases and Mortality of Occupations* (London: Percival and Co., 1892), p. 5.

53. *Colliery Guardian*, vol. 3 no. 62, March 8, 1862, p. 184.

54. Ibid.

55. Matthias Dunn Diary, June 21, 1832, Newcastle Public Library.

56. *Colliery Guardian*, vol. 3 no. 54, January 11, 1862, p. 33.

57. See letters to Messrs. Elder, Gelston, T. J. Roger, and Isaac Cromie, Records of E. I. Du Pont de Nemours & Co., Series I Part II, Acc 500 no. 798, Outbooks, E. I. Du Pont & Co., 1846-7, pp. 443–45. See also letters to Bradford and Coach, and Mr. Kemble, August 27, 1832, Acc 500 no. 787, Outbooks, E. I. Du Pont & Co., 1832, pp. 146–47.

58. Letter dated September 28, 1835, Records of E. I. Du Pont de Nemours & Co., Series I Part II, Acc 500 no. 788, Outbooks, E. I. Du Pont & Co., 1835, p. 317.

59. Letter to William Kemble, September 22, 1843, Records of E. I. Du Pont de Nemours & Co., Series I Part II, Acc 500 no. 794, Outbooks, E. I. Du Pont & Co., 1843, p. 20.

60. Du Pont to A. J. Cazenove, April 19, 1847, , Records of E. I. Du Pont de Nemours & Co., Series I Part II, Series N 5, Acc 500 no. 798, Outbooks, E. I. Du Pont & Co., 1846–7, p. 450.

61. Aldrich, *Hygiene, Diseases and Mortality*, p. 116. See also Gertrude Himmelfarb, *The Idea of Poverty: England in the Industrial Age* (New York: Knopf, 1984); and Seth Rockman, *Welfare Reform in the Early Republic* (New York: Bedford Books, 2003).

62. Edward A. Purcell, Jr., *Litigation and Inequality: Federal Diversity Jurisdiction in Industrial America, 1870–1958* (New York: Oxford University Press, 1992), p. 33.

63. The information in this section was compiled from Parliamentary Papers, Reports from Commissioners, *Royal Commission on the Employment of Children in Factories,* 1834 (167) XX: 799–1080.

64. Parliamentary Papers, Reports from Commissioners, *Royal Commission on the Employment of Children in Factories,* 1833 (450) XX: 252, 286, 297, 308.

65. Ibid., p. 470.

66. Parliamentary Papers, Reports from Commissioners, *Royal Commission on the Employment of Children in Factories,* 1834 (167) XX: 974.

67. P. W. Kingsford, *Victorian Railwaymen* (London: Frank Cass & Co., 1970), p. 152.

68. Ibid., pp. 154–55.

69. *Railway Service Gazette,* no. 60, March 22, 1873.

70. *Railway Service Gazette,* no. 163, March 12, 1875.

71. Walter Licht, *Working for the Railroad: The Organization of Work in the Nineteenth Century* (Princeton, NJ: Princeton University Press, 1983), p. 202; Robert C. Reed, *Train Wrecks: A Pictorial History of Accidents on the Main Line* (Seattle, WA: Superior Publishing, 1968), p. 182.

72. Tomlins, *Law, Labor and Ideology,* p. 362.

73. Mark Aldrich, "Train Wrecks to Typhoid Fever: The Development of Railroad Medicine Organizations, 1850 to World War I," *Bulletin of the History of Medicine* 75 (2001): 254–89.

74. C. Clark, "The Railroad Safety Movement in the United States: Origins and Development, 1869 to 1893." Ph.D. dissertation, University of Illinois, 1966, p. 11.

75. Licht, *Working for the Railroad,* pp. 203–6.

76. Aldrich, "Train Wrecks," p. 269.

77. Parliamentary Papers, Reports from Committees, *Select Committee on Accidents in Mines,* 1835 (603) V, p. 169.

78. *Colliery Guardian,* vol. 3 no. 56, January 25, 1862, p. 69.

79. Failure to pay "smart money" was a cause for grievance. See Colliers of the United Association of Durham and Northumberland, *A Voice from the Coal Mines, or a Plain Statement of the Various Grievances of the Pitmen of the Tyne and Wear* (South Shields: J. Clark. 1825), p. 28.

80. Parliamentary Papers, Reports from Committees, *Royal Commission on the Employment of Children in Mines and Manufactories,* Appendix I, 1842 (381) XVI, p. 550.

81. Parliamentary Papers, Reports from Commissioners, *First Report of the Midland Mining Commission* (South Staffordshire), 1843 (508) XIII, p. li.

82. See *Times*, no. 11390, October 30, 1821.

83. R. M. M. Alloway, *Cheap Coal? If not, What?* (London: Kent and Co., n.d), p. 48.

84. Govan Colliery Journal no. 3, pp. 37, 115, 121, 195, 202. UGD/1/17/1, Glasgow Business Records Center. Workers at the colliery did have some pay deducted for the funeral fund, Royal Infirmary, and the mine surgeon; it is impossible to tell to what extent disbursements were actually subsidized by the employer rather than the workforce. See Govan Colliery Pay Book, November 1855–August 1856. UGD 1/37/1, Glasgow Business Records Center.

85. Govan Colliery Funeral Fund Roll Book, UGD/1/35/1/1841; Funeral Fund Roll Book, 1845, UGD 1/35/2, Glasgow Business Records Center.

86. J. R. Leifchild, *Our Coal and Coal Pits* (London: Frank Cass and Co., 1968), [1853], p. 152–53.

87. John Benson, *British Coal Miners in the Nineteenth Century: A Social History* (New York: Holmes and Meier, 1980), p. 178.

88. Katherine Harvey, *The Best-Dressed Miners: Life and Labor in the Maryland Coal Region, 1835–1910* (Ithaca, NY: Cornell University Press, 1969), p. 48.

89. Antoine Bidermann, E. I. Du Pont's son-in-law, described the promise of a widow's pension as one of the main factors bringing workmen back to work after the explosion of 1815. See Dona McDermott, "E. I. Du Pont de Nemours and Company: The Treatment of Widows Whose Husbands Were Killed in the Powder Mill Explosions, 1815–1880," Unpublished research paper (n.d.) in possession of Museum Director, Hagley Museum, p. 5.

90. John Rumm, "Mutual Interests: Managers and Workers at the Du Pont Company, 1802–1915." Ph.D. dissertation, University of Delaware, 1989, p. 107.

91. E. I. Du Pont de Nemours & Co., Group 5, Series B, Accounts, 1816–1820, Box 37, "Bills and Receipts," Hagley Museum and Library. For the cost of grave digging, see E. I. Du Pont de Nemours & Co., Accession 500 no. 962, Petit Ledgers, 1815–1816, p. 9. Not all of the men had to pay for grave digging; see account of Francis Leonard, p. 14. For individual savings accounts, see E. I. Du Pont de Nemours & Co., Group 5 (1815) Part I, Box 34, "Accounts: Company Ledgers, Records"; Group 5, Series B Accounts (1849–1894), Box 44, Hagley Museum and Library.

92. E. I. Du Pont de Nemours & Co., Accession no. 384, Folder 47, item 34, sketch of the Du Pont family cemetery.

93. Rumm, "Mutual Interests," p. 106.

94. See drawing of Du Pont family graveyard, in Lammot Du Pont Papers, Series B. Technical Papers, Acc 384, Box 32, Folder 47-34.

95. E. I. Du Pont and Company, Accession 500 no. 964, Petit Ledgers, 1820, p. 1.

96. E. I. Du Pont and Company, Accession 500 no. 975. Petit Ledgers, 1848, p. 163.

97. E. I. Du Pont and Company, Accession 500 no. 963, Petit Ledgers, 1818–1819, p. 27.

98. Acc 384, Box 30, Lammot Du Pont papers series B, Technical Papers, Folder 45–45.

99. McDermott, "E. I. Du Pont de Nemours," p. 19.

100. "A Fatal Explosion," loose newspaper clipping, n.d., Acquisitions, Series A, Dealers and Donors A to Du Pont, E. Longwood MSS Box 1.

101. E. I. Du Pont and Company, Accession 500 no. 962, Petit Ledgers, 1815–1816, p. 37; E. I. Du Pont and Company, Accession 500 no. 963, Petit Ledgers, 1818–1819, p. 261.

102. E. I. Du Pont and Company, Accession 500 no. 974, Petit Ledgers, 1847, pp. 20, 380. See also McDermott, "E. I. Du Pont de Nemours," pp. 9–10.

103. Petit Ledgers of the Charles I. Du Pont and Company Woolen Mills, Acc 500 no. 66, WPL-3, p. 26. Smith's connection with Du Pont ceased tragically; he was killed when he asked his wife to bring him some medicine from his closet and she brought him a draft of deadly aconite instead.

104. Receipt from Thomas Mackie Smith to A. Berger, dated Brandywine, Jan. 1 1850, Petit Ledgers of the Charles I. Du Pont and Company Woolen Mills, Acc 500 no. 66, WPL-3, Hagley Museum and Library. See also receipt from Smith, to John Algeo, December 10, 1850, p. 96.

105. Polly Joe Scafidi, "Doctor Pierre Didier and Early Industrial Medicine," *Delaware History* 15:1 (1972): 41–54.

106. TMKS to Eleuthera Smith, March 8, 1838, Group 6, Daughters of E. I. Du Pont, Series C., Box 33 (Thomas Mackie Smith). For another description of Smith's industrial medicine, see TMKS to Eleuthera Smith, March 5, 1838.

107. Eastman, *Work-Accidents and the Law,* p. 128.

108. Fishback and Kantor, *Prelude to the Welfare State,* p. 38.

109. Ibid., pp. 135–40.

110. After a coroner's jury found a verdict of "accidental death" in the wake of a mine accident, local gentry collected £230 for the victims' families. See *London Mercury,* no. 37, May 28, 1837.

111. John Hodgson, *The Funeral Sermon of the Felling Colliery Sufferers* (Newcastle, UK: Edward Walker, 1815), pp. 47–51.

112. *Times,* no. 20097, February 12, 1849.

113. *Times,* no. 20100, February 15, 1849.

114. Alloway, *Cheap Coal,* p. 79.

115. John Elliott McCutcheon, *The Hartley Colliery Disaster, 1862* (Seaham, UK: E. McCutcheon, 1963), p. 101. The *Newcastle Chronicle* estimated that 20,000 disaster tourists had come to see the tragedy, most of them arriving by train. See no 5090, January 25, 1862.

116. See, e.g., the case of the Ferndale Colliery subscription. Alloway, *Cheap Coal,* p. 48.

117. Benson, *British Coal Miners,* pp. 176–77.

118. John Hodgson, *The Funeral Sermon of the Felling Colliery Sufferers* (Newcastle, UK: Edward Walker, 1815), pp. 47–51.

119. Ibid., p. 52.

120. *Report of the Committee Appointed to Administer the Fund Subscribed for the Relief of the Families who suffered by the Burradon Explosion on the 2nd of March, 1859* (Newcastle, UK: Daily Journal Office, 1861), pp. 5–6. For a similar allowance system set up in the wake of a Canadian mine explosion, see James M. Cameron, "Disasters in the Pictou Collieries," *Collections of the Nova Scotia Historical Society* 38 (1973): 138.

121. Acc 146 File 48, Eleuthera Bradford Du Pont Collection, Folder marked "March 23, 1818."

122. Acc 146 File 48, Eleuthera Bradford Du Pont Collection, Folder 17.

123. It is interesting to note that the fall of the Pemberton Mill was quite similar to two other collapsed buildings. In 1844, Samuel Radcliffe and Sons's mill collapsed in Oldham; it was also a long, wide, six-story structure that collapsed when one of its beams fell. Because it fell soon after construction, only construction workers were killed. See *Times,* no. 18759, November 4, 1844. For a similar building collapse, see *Times,* no. 20085, May 19, 1851.

124. [Mason, S. W. and E. B. Haskell, comps.] *An Authentic History of the Lawrence Calamity* (Boston: John J. Dyer, 1860), pp. 10–11.

125. Clarrisse Anne Poirier, "Pemberton Mills, 1852–1938: A Case Study of the Industrial and Labor History of Lawrence, Massachusetts," Ph.D. dissertation, Boston University, 1978, p. 98

126. Ibid., pp. 102–4.

127. Ibid., pp. 93–95.

128. Mason and Haskell, *Authentic History,* p. 35; *Report of the Treasurer of the Committee of Relief for the Sufferers of the Fall of the Pemberton Mill* (Lawrence, MA: 1860), pp. 23–36.

129. Ibid., p. 100.

130. Ibid., p. 109; see also *Report of the Treasurer of the Committee of Relief for the Sufferers of the Fall of the Pemberton Mill* (Lawrence, MA: 1860), p. 16.

131. Ibid., pp. 119, 132.

132. On the subject of charitable giving in this time period, see Seth Rockman, *Welfare Reform in the Early Republic* (New York: Bedford, 2003); Gertrude Himmelfarb, *The Idea of Poverty: England in the Early Industrial Age* (New York: Knopf, 1984).

133. *Newcastle Chronicle,* no. 5124, September 20, 1862.

134. *Reformer* (Newport), vol. 1 no. 21, Jan. 31, 1862.

135. *Ten Hours' Advocate,* no. 14, December 26, 1846, p. 107.

136. *The Miner,* no. 9, May 3, 1863.

137. J. Robson, *Hartley Sacrifice* (Sunderland, UK: R. H. Coleman, n.d.).

138. *Workingman's Advocate,* no. 137, October 21, 1865.

139. John Griffith, *Colliery Explosions* (Merthyr, UK: M. W. White and Sons, 1867).

140. Museum exhibit, National Coal Mining Museum for England, Capstone Colliery, Yorkshire.

141. *Beehive*, no.112, December 5, 1863.

142. Parliamentary Papers, Reports from Commissioners, *Royal Commission on the Employment of Children in Factories, Second Report,* 1833 (XXI), p. 140.

143. Parliamentary Papers, Reports from Commissioners, *Second Report of the Children's Employment Commission, Appendix to the Second report of the Commissioners* (Trades and Manufactures) 1843 (XV), p. Q8.

144. Parliamentary Papers, Reports from Commissioners, *Royal Commission on Children's Employment in Mines and Manufactories, Appendix 1,* 1842 (381) XVI, p. 76.

145. Parliamentary Papers, Reports from Committees, *Accidents in Coal Mines, Session 4 November 1852—20 August 1853, Second Report,* 1853 (13). XX, p. 24.

146. Parliamentary Papers, Reports from Committees, *Select Committee on Railway Labourers* 1846 (530) XIII.425, p. 18.

147. *Railway Gazette,* no. 58, March 8, 1873.

148. See, e.g., the case of the London and Northwestern Railway's friendly society detailed in Kingsford, *Victorian Railwaymen,* pp. 163–64.

149. The families of two dead New Jersey dynamite workers benefited from provident membership in the Oddfellows; the other eight victims of an explosion were both uninsured and destitute. "Ten Victims of Dynamite: Only Small Bits of the Bodies Found," newspaper clipping, dated July 3, 1886, Longwood MSS Group 10—Papers of P. S. Du Pont, File 418-1 to 418-3.

150. *Blue Hen's Chicken,* vol. 3 no. 7, October 1, 1847.

151. Thus, the members of the Glen-Patrick Sick and Burial Society, affiliated with a Scottish carpet works, voted to suspend sickness payments to members as soon as they were actively looking for work again after an illness. Patrick Bank Works Sick Society Minute Book, December 5, 1854, UGD 265/2/28/4, Glasgow Business Records Center. For women and the definition of illness as the inability to work, see Marjorie Levine-Clark, "Engendering Relief: Women, Ablebodiedness and the New Poor Law in Early Victorian England," *Journal of Women's History* vol. 11 no. 4 (2000): 107–30.

152. James C. Riley, *Sick, Not Dead: The Health of British Workingmen during the Mortality Decline* (Baltimore, MD: Johns Hopkins University Press, 1997), pp. 28–31.

153. Amalgamated Union of Foundry Workers (MSS 41) Book #1, MSS 41/FSIF/1/1, Warwick Modern Records Centre.

154. *The Sixteenth Half-Yearly Report of the Friendly Society of Iron-Moulders* (London: G. Harvey, 1845), MSS 41/FSIF/4/2/5, Warwick Modern Records Centre. Subsequent and previous reports in this series contain more detailed information about the types of accidents, injuries, and medical attention that workers received.

155. Operative Bricklayers' Death Book, MSS 78/M8/2/7/1; Monthly Reports of the Friendly Operative Bricklayers' Accident and Burial Society, MSS 78/MB/4/1/1-12, Warwick Modern Records Centre.

156. *The First Half-Yearly Report of the Friendly Society of Iron-Founders, New Series* (London: G Harvey, 1865), p. xv, MSS 41/FSIF/4/2/9, Warwick Modern Records Centre.

157. Workers at the Prestonholm Spinning Mills were required to join its Benefit Society, which provided them with up to two-thirds of their weekly wages, plus access to a doctor and a medicine chest in case of work-related injury. See James Millar, *The Friendly Society Guide* (Dundee, UK: David Hill, 1825), p. 8.

158. *The First Half-Yearly Report of the Friendly Society of Iron-Founders*, p. 85, 94.

159. Ibid., p. 178.

160. *An Abstract of the Rules, Orders and Regulations of the Mutual Insurance Benefit Institution*, (London: Printed for the Institution, 1825), p. 7.

161. *London Journal and Pioneer*, vol. 2 no. 61, April 18, 1846.

162. *The Miner*, no. 7, April 18, 1863.

163. Eastman, *Work Accidents and the Law*, p. 145.

164. David M. Emmons, "Immigrant Workers and Industrial Hazards: The Irish Miners of Butte, 1880–1919." *Journal of American Ethnic History* 5 (1985): 41–64.

165. John Witt, *Accidental Republic*, chapter 3.

166. Ibid., p. 94.

167. Ibid., p. 99.

168. Eastman, *Work Accidents and the Law*, p. 201. For specific examples of occupational friendly societies, see *Rules and Regulations for the Good Intent Society of United Sawyers* (Newcastle, UK: John Marshall, 1825); *Rules and Regulations of the Wallsend Colliery Relief Fund*, (Newcastle, UK: K. Mackenzie, 1832); *Rules of the Wilson's Darton Collieries Club* (Barnsley, UK: G. Harrison, n.d.); *Rules and Regulations to be Observed by the Friendly Society of Joiners* (Newcastle, UK: Preston and Heaton, 1821).

169. Kingsford, *Victorian Railwaymen*, p. 158, 161.

170. Reports from Commissioners, *Royal Commission on the Employment of Children in Factories*, 1833 (450) XX : 1, pp. 195, 380

171. Parliamentary Papers, Reports from Commissioners, *Royal Commission on Children's Employment in Mines and Manufactories, Appendix I Part I*, 1842 (381), p. 13.

172. John Buddle, *The First Report of a Society for Preventing Accidents in Coal Mines* (Newcastle, UK: Edward Walker, 1814), pp. 23–27.

173. *Colliery Guardian*, vol. 3 no. 61, March 1, 1862, p. 168.

174. Reports from Committees (13) Accidents in Coal Mines, Session 4 November 1852—20 August 1853, vol. XX, Second Report, p. 49.

175. *Newcastle Chronicle*, no. 5100, April 5, 1862.

176. *Newcastle Chronicle*, no. 5104, May 3, 1862.

177. Christopher Frank has identified many opportunistic arguments made by employers regarding enforcement of the Truck Act. See "Fighting the Company Store: Resistance to Truck Wages in mid-nineteenth-century Britain," unpublished paper delivered at the Western Conference on British Studies, October 2006.

178. *Newcastle Chronicle*, no. 5106, May 17, 1862.

179. *British Miner and General Newsman*, no. 11, November 22, 1862.

180. *Newcastle Chronicle*, no. 5130, November 1, 1862.

181. *Beehive,* no. 118, January 16, 1864.

182. *Operative Stonemasons' Fortnightly Return,* November 3, 1842, MSS OS/4/1/1, Warwick Modern Records Centre.

183. *Operative Stonemason's Fortnightly Return,* January 20, 1848. MSS78/OS/4/1/10, Warwick Modern Records Centre.

184. *Operative Stonemason's Fortnightly Return,* February 3, 1848. MSS78/OS/4/1/10, Warwick Modern Records Centre.

185. Letter from Dr. Frederick Fry, *The Lancet,* January 18, 1862, p. 87.

186. Parliamentary Papers, Reports from Commissioners, *Royal Commission on Children's Employment in Mines and Manufactories, Appendix I Part I,* 1842 (381), p. 631.

187. J. R. Leifchild, *Our Coal and Coal Pits* (London: Frank Cass and Co., 1968), [1853], p. 214.

188. *Blue Hen's Chicken,* vol. 3 no. 44, June 15, 1849.

189. Jennie Collins, *Nature's Aristocracy* (Boston: Lee and Shepart, 1871), p. 219.

190. B. Franklin Palmer, *Steps Forward* (Philadelphia: n.p., n.d.).

191. Charles Willms Surgical Instrument Co., *Illustrated and Descriptive Catalogue and Price-List* (Baltimore, MD: n.p., n.d.)

192. Parliamentary Papers, Reports from Commissioners, *Royal Commission on Children's Employment in Mines and Manufactories,* Appendix I Part I, 1842 (381), p. 81.

193. Ibid., p. 463.

194. Ibid., pp. 435, 440.

Chapter 3

1. This was one of several poems of sympathy submitted to the *Newcastle Chronicle* after the Hartley disaster. See no. 5091, February 1, 1862.

2. Robert Asher, "Workmen's Compensation in the United States, 1880–1935," University of Minnesota Ph.D. dissertation, 1971, pp. 17–19.

3. Thomas Haskell, "Capitalism and the Origins of the Humanitarian Sensibility, Part I," *American Historical Review* 90: 2 (1985): 339–61.

4. Thomas Lacqueur, "Bodies, Details and the Humanitarian Narrative," in Lynn Hunt, ed., *The New Cultural History* (Berkeley: University of California Press, 1989): 176–204.

5. Haskell, "Capitalism," p. 358.

6. The strategies of the first abolitionist movement are discussed in Leo D'Anjou, *Social Movements and Cultural Change: The First Abolition Campaign Revisited* (New York: DeGruyter, 1996).

7. *Blue Hen's Chicken,* vol. 3 no. 5, September 17, 1847.

8. Thomas Knox, *Underground: Or, Life Below the Surface* (Hartford, CT: J. B. Bin, 1875), p. 586.

9. See, e.g., *The Explosion of Felling Colliery, by which Ninety-Two Persons Lost their Lives, On the 25th of May, 1812.* (Dublin, IR: C. Bentham, n.d.). On the general

issue, see also Elisabeth Cawthon, "Occupational Accidents and the Law: The Role of Coroners' Inquests in England 1830–1850," Ph.D. dissertation, University of Virginia, 1985, p. 12.

10. *Harrisburg Republican,* March 27, 1818.

11. The Greensburg paper is excerpted in the *Miners' Journal and Pottsville General Advertiser,* vol. 19 no. 48, November 25, 1843.

12. *Newcastle Chronicle,* no. 5091, February 1, 1862.

13. Thomas Knox, *Underground: Or, Life Below the Surface* (Hartford, CT: J. B. Bin, 1875), p. 586. Cf. Sam Watkins, *Company Aytch: A Side Show of the Big Show* (New York: Plume, 1999).

14. *Blue Hen's Chicken,* vol. 4 no. 25, February 2, 1849: "We learn that Edmund Wollaston, brother of Joseph Wollaston of this city, who resides near Unionville, Chester County, was accidentally caught in the machinery of his Grist Mill, on Tuesday last, and instantly killed," leaving a wife and six or seven children. See also the *Miners' Journal and Pottsville General Advertiser,* vol. 21 no. 19, May 10, 1845; vol. 21 no. 26, June 28, 1845; vol. 21 no. 29, July 19, 1845.

15. It is not, however, safe to assume that a report that a man's death had left a family destitute would have been understood the same way by all readers. Some may have seen the report as a call for legal or social change, to put the worker on a better footing; others, as a personal call for charitable action toward the family; still others as a criticism of a lack of foresight on the part of the worker who had been killed. Elisabeth Cawthon also discusses the characteristics of accident reporting in "Occupational Accidents," p. 17.

16. *Times,* August 19, 1795.

17. Museum Display, Coalport China Museum, Ironbridge Gorge, England.

18. Parliamentary Papers, Reports from Commissioners, *Commission for Inquiring into the Employment and Condition of Children in Mines and Manufactories, First Report, (Mines)* 1842 (380) XV: 30.

19. Asher, "Workmen's Compensation," p. 55.

20. Asher, "Workmen's Compensation," pp. 50–51.

21. See the explicit connection drawn between gory detail and charitable feelings in Parliamentary Papers, Reports from Commissioners, *Copies of the Report made by Mr. Dickinson, Inspector of Mines, upon the Oaks Colliery Explosion, and with reference to the Prevention of such Occurrences; and of a Report made by Mr. Wynne, Inspector of Mines, on the Explosion at Talk-o'th'-Hill; with the Evidence taken before the Coroner's Inquest,* 1877 (3811) III.241, p. 11.

22. *Harrisburg Republican,* March 27, 1818, quoted in S. Fulton and R. Scott, "Interpretive Packet on Explosions," Hagley Museum and Library, 1990, p. 37.

23. Substantial public subscriptions were raised to support the widows and orphans made by the 1818 explosion. See Memorial from Widows and Orphans, Acccession no. 146 File 48, Folder 17, Eleuthera Bradford Du Pont collection, Hagley Museum.

24. Parliamentary Papers, Accounts and Papers, *Return of Colliery Accident Funds in Great Britain raised by Public Subscription*, 1893–4 (359) LXXIII: 493.

25. John Hodgson, *The Funeral Sermon of the Felling Colliery Sufferers* (Newcastle, UK: Edward Walker, 1815), p. 70.

26. [S. W. Mason and E. B. Haskell, comps.] *An Authentic History of the Lawrence Calamity* (Boston: John J. Dyer, 1860), p. 52.

27. "Local Intelligence," undated news clipping, in Winterthur MSS, Group 10, Series D, Box 15 (Residual Material), Hagley Library.

28. Pat Jalland, *Death in the Victorian Family* (New York: Oxford University Press, 1996), chapter 1.

29. *The Hartley Coal Pit* (London: Religious Tract Society, n.d).

30. Alexander Reid. *A Voice from Hartley: Or, the Recent Catastrophe Described and Improved* (Newcastle, UK: Home Piety Office, 1862), p. 10.

31. *The Hartley Coal Pit* (The Religious Tract Society: London, n.d.), pp. 8–9; Benjamin Beddow, *A Call to Consideration in Prospect of Eternity* (Barnsley, UK: John Elliott, 1847), p. 4.

32. The Author of "Lilian's Talks with Mama about the Stars, Moon and Sun," *Fuel For Our Fires: or Coal-Pits, Colliers, and their Dangers* (London: The Religious Tract Society, n.d.), p. 18.

33. Letter from Thomas Hodgkin, reprinted in T. E. Forster, ed. *Memoir of the Hartley Colliery Accident and Relief Fund.* (Newcastle, UK: Andrew Reid, 1912), p. 111.

34. Rev. Charles, Gutch, *The Sure Judgement of God Upon all Sinners, Especially the Rich, for their Neglect of the Poor* (London: F and J. Rivington, n.d.), p. 42.

35. Excerpts from the sermons are reprinted in *An Authentic History of the Lawrence Calamity*, pp. 42–50. Clarisse Anne Poirer has noted that Baptist, Methodist, and Presbyterian clerics were especially likely to see the collapse as an act of Providence or retribution against mankind as a whole, while Unitarian, Episcopal, and Congregational ministers stressed the importance of physical laws in understanding the disasters. Clarisse Anne Poirier, "Pemberton Mills, 1852–1938: A Case Study of the Industrial and Labor History of Lawrence, Massachusetts," Ph.D. dissertation, Boston University, 1978, p. 188.

36. John Sykes, *An Account of the Dreadful Explosion in Wallsend Colliery* (Newcastle, UK: John Sykes, 1835), p. 27.

37. *The Lamentation of twenty-five poor colliers who were stopped up in a coal-pit four days and four nights, fifteen of whom lost their lives, and ten were brought up alive, at the Haussees Colliery, Shropshire, February 29, 1819* (Birmingham, UK: T. Bloomer, 1819); T. Papworth, *An Appeal for Aid to the Fellow-Workmen of W. Wood and A. Leonox, who have been Incapacitated by Accident.* (n.p., n.d.); William Sanders, *Pontypridd Colliery Disaster* (n.p., April 11, 1877); J. Robson, *Hartley Sacrifice* (Sunderland, UK: R. H. Coleman, n.d.). See also the songs reprinted in Edith Fowke and Joe Glazer, *Songs of Work and Protest* (New York: Dover Publications, 1973).

38. *Full Particulars of the Dreadful Accident with the Loss of Twelve Lives at the Crystal Palace, Sydenham* (London: E. Hodges, 1853). See also Asher, "Workmen's Compensation," p. 57.

39. *Times*, no. 5620, January 17, 1803, p. 3 col. d.

40. *Times*, no. 10736, July 27, 1819, p. 2 col. b.

41. *London Mercury*, no. 42, July 12, 1837.

42. *Blue Hen's Chicken*, vol. 3 no. 25, February 4, 1848.

43. *An Authentic History of the Lawrence Calamity*, p. 17.

44. *Times*, no. 12425, August 24, 1824.

45. *Times*, no. 4390, January 22, 1799.

46. *Times*, no. 5512, September 11, 1802.

47. David P. Hendy, *Wreck of the Princess Alice* (London: Elliot Stock, n.d.); Walter Knight, *the Sunderland Disaster* (July 3, 1883—n.p., n.d.); *Steamboat Disasters and Railroad Accidents in the United States* (Worcester, MA: Warren Lazell, 1846). Slightly more graphic is *Narrative of the Dreadful Accident which Happened in the Parish Church of Kilmarnock, On Sunday the 18th October, 1801* (Glasgow, UK: Niven, Napier and Rhull, 1802).

48. Arthur McEvoy, "Working Environments: An Ecological Approach to Industrial Health and Safety," *Technology and Culture* 36 Supplement (1995): S145–S172.

49. Workers' deaths by machinery are described in the *Times*, no. 5620, January 17, 1803; no. 7138, August 28, 1807; no. 8034, July 14, 1810; no. 8044, July 26, 1810; no. 9358, November 3, 1814; and no. 9895, July 24, 1816.

50. *Blue Hen's Chicken*, vol. 3 no. 27, February 25, 1848.

51. *Newcastle Courant*, no. 3685, March 7, 1835; see also Elisabeth Cawthon, "Apocrypha from the Victorian Workplace: Occupational Accidents and Employee Attitudes in England, 1830–1860," *Victorian Periodicals Review* (1992) p. 57; Cawthon, "Occupational Accidents," p. 148; Mark Aldrich, *Safety First: Technology, Labor, and Business in the Building of American Work Safety 1870–1939* (Baltimore, MD: Johns Hopkins University Press, 1997), p. 81.

52. *Miners' Journal and Pottsville General Advertiser*, vol. 22 no. 4, January 24, 1846.

53. *Harrisburg Republican*, March 27, 1818 quoted in S. Fulton and R. Scott, "Interpretive Packet on Explosions," (Hagley Museum and Library: 1990), p. 34.

54. Robert C. Reed, *Train Wrecks: A Pictorial History of Accidents on the Main Line* (Seattle, WA: Superior Publishing, 1968), p. 163.

55. *Newcastle Courant*, no. 8375, August 1, 1835.

56. "Ten Victims of Dynamite: Only Small Bits of the Bodies Found," newspaper clipping, dated July 3, 1886, Longwood MSS Group 10—Papers of P. S. Du Pont, File 418–1 to 418–3, Hagley Library.

57. L. Simonin, *Mines and Miners: Underground Life* (London: William MacKenzie, 1868), p. 224.

58. *Beehive*, no. 57, November 15, 1862. See also Edward Hedley, "The Lund Hill Colliery Explosion," *Lectures Delivered at the Bristol Mining School* (Bristol, UK: Mining School, 1857), pp. 138; rescuers at the site of the Lund Hill explosion dug for bodies wherever in the debris pile the smell was the strongest.

59. Quoted in John Elliott McCutcheon, *The Hartley Colliery Disaster, 1862* (Seaham, UK: E. McCutcheon, 1963), pp. 172–73.

60. *Times*, no. 12108, February 12, 1824.

61. *Times*, no. 12726, August 8, 1825.

62. *Times*, no. 5736, March 27, 1802.

63. [Mason, S. W. and E. B. Haskell, comps.] *An Authentic History* p. 14.

64. *Wilmington Every Evening*, December 9, 1898.

65. Benjamin Beddow, *A Call to Consideration in Prospect of Eternity* (Barnsley, UK: John Elliott, 1847), p. 14.

66. McCutcheon, *The Hartley Colliery Disaster*, p. 103.

67. *Newcastle Chronicle*, no. 5090, January 25, 1862.

68. *Miner and Workman's Advocate*, no. 15, June 13, 1863.

69. *Times*, no. 15825, June 25, 1835.

70. *American Watchman*, March 24, 1818, in Acc 501, P. S. Du Pont Office Collection, Series D, Business Papers, Notebooks 1–4, Hagley Library.

71. *British Miner and General Newsman*, new series no. 4, March 28, 1863. Thomas Lacqueur has argued that the relationship of gory accident descriptions with calls for reform constituted a "humanitarian narrative" which moved society toward social change. See Thomas Lacqueur, "Bodies, Details and the Humanitarian Narrative," pp. 176–204.

72. Asher, "Workmen's Compensation," pp. 59–60.

73. Parliamentary Papers, Reports from Commissioners, *Midland Mining Commission, First Report*, 1843 (508) XIII: li.

74. *The Lancet*, March 1, 1862, p. 226.

75. *Papers Read Before the Statistical Society of Manchester on the Demoralisation and Injuries Occasioned by the Want of Proper Regulations of Labourers Engaged in the Construction and Working of Railways* (Manchester, UK: Simms and Dinham, n.d.), p. 17.

76. Jennie Collins, *Nature's Aristocracy* (Boston: Lee and Shepart, 1871), p. 164.

77. Anthony Bale, "Compensation Crisis: The Value and Meaning of Work-Related Injuries and Illnesses in the United States, 1842–1932," Ph.D. dissertation, Brandeis University, 1986, p. 39. The trope also impressed Bartrip and Burman, who titled their study of workplace accidents *The Wounded Soldiers of Industry.*

78. *Railway Service Gazette*, no. 102, January 10, 1874.

79. See Paul Fussell, *The Great War and Modern Memory* (New York: Oxford University Press, 1989).

80. T. Longmore, "Observations on the Preliminary Care and Attention Necessary for Accidental Bodily Injuries and Mutilations Occurring in Mines and Establishments

where Many Workpeople are Employed," *Report of the Chapter of the Order of the St. John of Jerusalem in England* (London: Harrison and Sons, 1874), pp. 18–22.

81. Ibid., pp. 155–57.

82. Fred Albert, *The Welsh Miners* (London: H. Pontin, n.d.)

83. Parliamentary Papers, Reports from Committees, *Report from the Select Committee on Coal Mines*, 1852 (509) V: 160.

84. *Newcastle Chronicle*, no. 5090, January 25, 1862. Cf, George Orwell's description of the coal workers underground in *The Road to Wigan Pier* (London: V. Gollancz Ltd., 1937).

85. George H. Gibson, "William P. Brobson Diary, 1825–1828," *Delaware History* 15 (1972), pp. 128–29.

86. *Illustrated London News*, vol. 60 no. 1129, February 1, 1862.

87. The medal is reproduced in the plates of McCutcheon, *The Hartley Colliery Disaster.*

88. Order of St. John of Jerusalem in England, *Descriptive History of Medals and Grants for Saving Life on Land by Special Acts of Bravery* (London: Harrison and Sons, 1876), pp. 7–9.

89. *Railway Service Gazette*, no. 238, August 18, 1876.

90. *An Authentic History of the Lawrence Calamity*, p. 53.

91. Visit to Earsdon churchyard, April 1999.

92. Thomas Knox, *Underground: Or, Life Below the Surface* (Hartford, CT: J. B. Bin, 1875), p. 580.

93. *Miner and Workman's Advocate*, no. 126, July 29, 1865.

94. [Mason, S. W. and E. B. Haskell, comps.] *An Authentic History* p. 28.

95. *Dreadful Colliery Explosion at the Jarrow Pit, with the loss of a great number of lives, on Thursday Afternoon, August 21, 1845.* (Newcastle, UK: Newcastle, 1845); *Explosion and Awful Loss of Life at the West Pit, Murton Colliery, on Tuesday Night* (Newcastle, UK: Crow, 1848); *An Account of the Dreadful Explosion Which took Place at Trimdon Colliery, On Monday Morning, January 26, 1852. Dreadful Loss of Life!* (Gateshead, UK: Robert Rankin, 1852); *An Account of the Melancholy Explosion Which Took Place at Usworth New Colliery, Near Washington, on Monday Night Last* (Gateshead, UK: R. Rankin, n.d.); *Dreadful Explosion* (n.p., 1841); *An Account of that Dreadful Explosion Which Took Place at West Moor Colliery, on Friday, October 31, 1851, Which Was Attended with Loss of Life.* (Gateshead, UK: Robert Rankin, 1851).

96. *An Account of the Dreadful Explosion Which Took Place at Hebburn Colliery on Thursday, May 6, 1852. Dreadful Loss of Life.* (Gateshead, UK: Robert Rankin, 1852).

97. *A Full Account of the Hebburn Colliery Explosion* (Newcastle, UK: John Ross, 1849).

98. *Dreadful Explosion and Loss of Life at Jarrow Pit, on Thursday Afternoon, August 21, 1845* (South Shields, UK: Joseph Ryle, 1845).

99. *An Account of the Coroner's Inquest on the Bodies of the Sufferers at Washington Colliery* (Gateshead, UK: Robert Rankin, 1851).

100. *An Account of that Dreadful Explosion, Which Took Place at Houghton Colliery on Monday Morning Last, the 11th of November, Which Was Attended by a Dreadful Loss of Life.* (Gateshead, UK: Robert Rankin, n.d.).

101. *An Account of an Awful Accident Which Happened at Jarrow Colliery on the Night of Tuesday, the 17th of January, 1826* ... (Newcastle, UK: Boag, 1826).

102. *Dreadful Explosion and Loss of Life at Jarrow Pit, on Thursday Afternoon, August 21, 1845* (South Shields, UK: Joseph Ryle, 1845).

103. *Dreadful Explosion in a Pit Called the I Pit, Near Washington, in the County of Durham, Nov. 20, 1828* (Newcastle, UK: W. Boag, 1828).

104. *Dreadful Explosion and Loss of Life at Jarrow Pit, on Thursday Afternoon, August 21, 1845* (South Shields, UK: Joseph Ryle, 1845).

105. *Terrible Colliery Explosion* (Newcastle, UK: T. Dodds, 1850).

106. Ibid.

107. *An Account of the Coroner's Inquest on the Bodies of the Sufferers at Washington Colliery.* (Gateshead, UK: Robert Rankin, 1851).

108. *British Miner and General Newsman*, vol. 1 no. 1, September 13, 1862.

109. *British Miner and General Newsman*, vol. 1 no. 5, October 11, 1862.

110. *British Miner and General Newsman*, vol. 1 no. 6, October 18, 1862.

111. *British Miner and General Newsman*, vol. 1 no. 9, November 8, 1862.

112. *Ten Hours' Advocate*, no. 11, December 5, 1846, p. 83.

113. Even the collapse of a church during a Sunday service could elicit this reaction. See *Authentic Account of the Dreadful Accident at Kirkcaldy* (n.p.d., n.d., 1828); A Spectator, *A Serious Address to the Inhabitants of Kirkcaldy and Vicinity* (Kirkcaldy, UK: William Gemble, 1828). On Christianity and working people, see William R. Sutton, "Tied to the Whipping Post: New Labor History and Evangelical Artisans in the Early Republic," *Labor History* vol. 36 no. 2 (1995): 251–81.

114. Parliamentary Papers, Reports from Committees, *Report from the Select Committee on Accidents in Mines*, 1835 (603) V: 216.

115. *A Letter from the Dead to the Living: Or the Collier Boy and his Mother* (Newcastle, UK: Great Northern Advertiser, 1841). Twelve miners dying underground at West Virginia's Sago Mine in January 2006 also left messages for their loved ones. See Allen G. Breed, "Miners Wrote Farewell Messages," *Boston Globe*, January 6, 2006.

116. Theophilus Lessey, *A Short Account of the Life and Christian Experiences of John Thompson, One of the Persons Killed by the Explosion Which Took Place in Felling Colliery on Monday, May 25, 1812* (Newcastle, UK: J. Marshall, 1812), p. 5.

117. Ibid., p. 22.

118. Ibid., p. 24.

119. An undergraduate of Cambridge, *The Accident at the New Hartley Colliery* (London: Jarrold and Sons, 1862), p. 15.

120. *The Hartley Catastrophe: Thomas Watson's Narrative* (Newcastle, UK: D. H. Wilson, 1862). *Reformer* (Newport), vol. 1 no. 22, February 7, 1862.

121. Richard Weaver, *A Voice from the Coal-Pit: Seven Addresses to the Working Classes* (London: Morgan & Chase, n.d.), p. 39.

122. Patrick Vance to Robert Miller, June 23, 1826, Lammot Du Pont Papers, Series B. Technical Papers, Acc 384 Box 30, Hagley Library.

123. The message is reproduced in the plates of McCutcheon, *Hartley Colliery Disaster*.

124. Dick Browne, *Tom Downing, Miner: Take of a Staffordshire Colliery Disaster* (Stoke on Trent, UK: Vyve and Hill, 1896). See also, "The Author of 'Lilian's talks with Mama about the Stars, Moon and Sun,'" *Fuel For Our Fires: or Coal-Pits, Colliers, and their Dangers* (London: The Religious Tract Society, n.d.). See also Asher, "Workmen's Compensation," p. 57.

125. Peter Dennison, *A Descriptive Elegy on the Late Unfortunate Sufferers at Heaton Colliery* (Newcastle, UK: J. Marshall, 1816).

126. Thomas Christopher Maynard, *An Authentic Copy of the Investigation taken into the Nature and Causes of the Recent Hetton Colliery Explosion* (Durham, UK: George Walker, 1861), p. 80.

127. *Newcastle Chronicle*, no. 5091, February 1, 1862.

128. *Papers Read Before the Statistical Society of Manchester on the Demoralisation and Injuries Occasioned by the Want of Proper Regulations of Labourers Engaged in the Construction and Working of Railways* (Manchester, UK: Simms and Dinham, n.d.), pp. 10–12.

129. Jim Bullock, *Bowers Row: Recollections of a Mining Village* (Wakefield, UK: EP Publishing, 1976), p. 178.

130. Ibid., p. 178.

131. *The Explosion of Felling Colliery, by which Ninety-Two Persons Lost their Lives, On the 25th of May, 1812* (Dublin, IR: C. Bentham, n.d.), p. 8.

132. See, e.g., Parliamentary Papers, Reports from Committees, *Royal Commission on the Employment of Children in Mines and Manufactories, Appendix I*, 1842 (381) XVI, p. 495, 501, 511, 577, 602.

133. A Miner, "A Trade Union Solitary: A Mid-Nineteenth-Century Miner," *History Workshop* 25 (1988): 152–53.

134. Ibid., pp. 152–53.

135. Ibid., p. 154.

136. Jane Reed to Alfred Du Pont, Richmond, Indiana, March 7, 1842, Longwood Manuscripts, Group 5 E. I. Du Pont & Company Series A—Correspondence in File (1816–1844), Box 13.

137. Letter from Elizabeth MacFarlane, August 6, 1855, Acc 384, Lammot Du Pont Papers, Series B, Technical Papers, Box 30, Folder 45–47.

138. Margaret Greer Wilkinson and Meary Greer Elvin to Du Pont, Letterkenny, 12 April 1836; Longwood Manuscripts, Group 5, E. I. Du Pont & Company Series A—Correspondence in File (1816–1844), Box 13.

139. Bullock, *Bowers Row,* p. 219.

140. Joe Kenyon, "Working Underground," *London Review of Books,* November 27, 1997, pp. 19–21.

141. Colliers of the United Association of Durham and Northumberland. *A Voice from the Coal Mines, or a Plain Statement of the Various Grievances of the Pitmen of the Tyne and Wear* (South Shields, UK: J. Clark. 1825), p. 28.

142. Clipping from unknown newspaper, dated May 11, 1844, in the Pitmen's Collection, D/DZ A31, item no. 55, Wigan Record Office, Leigh.

143. Proposed new bond, 1844, in the Pitmen's Collection, D/DZ A31, item no. 92, Wigan Record Office, Leigh.

144. On the role played by working-class wives, see Christine Stansell, *City of Women: Sex and Class in New York, 1789–1860* (Chicago: University of Illinois Press, 1987); Marjorie Levine-Clark, "Engendering Relief: Women, Ablebodiedness and the New Poor Law in Early Victorian England," *Journal of Women's History,* vol. 11 no. 4 (2000): 107–30.

145. *British Miner and General Newsman,* no. 17, January 3, 1863. It is quite possible that one of the editor's friends was writing in to the newspaper as a woman using a "Silence Dogood" sort of tactic, but even this presupposes a female audience for the newspaper and its safety concerns.

146. Bullock, *Bowers Row,* p. 220.

147. B. L. Coombes, *These Poor Hands: The Autobiography of a Miner Working in South Wales* (London: Victor Gollancz, 1939), p. 92.

148. Ibid., p. 95.

149. *Operative Stonemasons' Fortnightly Return,* January 27, 1842, MSS OS/4/1/4, Warwich Modern Records Centre.

150. *Railway Service Gazette,* no. 8, March 23, 1872.

151. *Railway Service Gazette,* no. 9, March 30, 1872.

152. *Railway Service Gazette,* no. 101, Janaury 3, 1874.

153. *Miner and Workman's Advocate,* no. 43, December 26, 1863.

154. Operative Stonemasons' Fortnightly Return, June 18, 1840, MSS OS/4/1/1, and December 12, 1844 and March 6, 1845, MSS OS/4/1/6, Warwich Modern Records Centre.

155. *Explosion of Felling Colliery,* p. 8.

156. See, e.g., the editorial in *Labour Press and Miner's and Workmen's Examiner,* no. 36, April 25, 1874.

157. Parliamentary Papers, Reports from Committees, *Select Committee on Accidents in Mines,* 1835 (603) V, p. 81.

158. Coombes, *These Poor Hands,* p. 121.

159. Parliamentary Papers, Reports from Commissioners, *Midland Mining Commission, First Report,* 1843 (508) XIII: lix.

160. Parliamentary Papers, Reports from Commissioners, *Midland Mining Commission, First Report,* 1843 (508) XIII: p. 28.

161. Colliers of the United Association of Durham and Northumberland, p. 4.

162. Parliamentary Papers, *Royal Commission for Inquiring into the Employment and Condition of Children in Mines and Manufactories, Appendix to First Report of Commissioners,* Part I, 1842 vol. XVI (381): 13.

163. Parliamentary Papers, Reports from Committees, *Report from the Select Committee of the House of Lords on Accidents in Coal Mines,* (1840) VII: 493.

164. Parliamentary Papers, Reports from Commissioners, *Midland Mining Commission, First Report,* 1843 (508) XIII, p. lxii, cxxxvi.

165. Bullock, *Bowers Row,* p. 183.

166. Sir Henry T. De La Beche and Sir Lyon Playfair, *Report on the Gases and Explosions in Collieries,* 1846 (529) Vol XLIII, p. 21.

167. Winterthur MSS Group 4 Series 6 Box 18, item no. 4988, small notebook listing powdermen working in yards, Hagley Library.

168. Du Pont to Grant and Stone, April 16, 1847, Records of E. I. Du Pont de Nemours & Co., Accession no. 500, Series I Part II, no. 798, Outbooks, E. I. Du Pont & Co., 1846–7, p. 446, Hagley Library.

169. Letter to William Kemble, July 25, 1844, Records of E. I. Du Pont de Nemours & Co., Accession no. 500 Series I Part, B, no. 795, Outbooks, E. I. Du Pont & Co., 1844, p. 56, Hagley Library.

170. J. R. Leifchild, *Our Coal and Coal Pits.* (London: Frank Cass and Co., 1968), [1853].

171. Parliamentary Papers. Reports from Commissioners, *Second Report of the Children's Employment Commissions, Reports from Subcommissioners* 1843 (432) XIV: D43.

172. Henry Bedford, ed., *Their Lives and Numbers: The Condition of Working People in Massachusetts, 1870–1900* (Ithaca, NY: Cornell University Press, 1995), p. 117.

173. James Riley has proposed that the social definition of "illness" is even more important than the physical symptoms of illness in defining who is sick in a given historical period. See James C. Riley, *Sick, not Dead: The Health of British Workingmen during the Mortality Decline* (Baltimore, MD: Johns Hopkins University Press, 1997).

174. J. R. Leifchild noted this obstacle in Parliamentary Papers, Reports from Committees, *Royal Commission on the Employment of Children in Mines and Manufactories, Appendix I,* 1842 (381) XVI: 524–25.

175. *Beehive,* no. 61, December 13, 1862.

176. Aaron Watson, *Thomas Burt, A Great Labour Leader* (London: Brown, Langham and Co., 1908), p. 43.

177. B. L. Coombes, *These Poor Hands,* p. 53.

178. Parliamentary Papers, Reports from Commissioners, Sir Henry T. De La Beche and Sir Lyon Playfair, *Report on the Gases and Explosions in Collieries,* 1846 (529) XLIII: 17.

179. Ibid., p. 64.

180. Jerome Groopman, "The Grief Industry," *New Yorker*, vol. 79 no. 44, January 26, 2004, p. 30. See also Charles Dickens's experience with posttraumatic stress following a railway accident, in Pope, "Dickens's 'The Signalman,'" p. 445.

181. Parliamentary Papers, Reports from Committees, *Royal Commission on the Employment of Children in Mines and Manufactories, Appendix*, 1842 (381) XVI, pp. 487, 553.

182. Similar reticence to talk fully about the causes and consequences of accidents was noted among twentieth century workers in Lillian Trettin, "The Case of the Crippled Blockholer; Miners, Managers and Talk about Early Twentieth-Century Industrial Accidents," *Oral History Review* 18 (1990): 1–27.

183. Twentieth-century mining songs can be much more fierce in their assignment of blame. See, e.g., "The Gresford Disaster," which blames a 1934 explosion on criminal activity by the mine owner, in Jon Raven, ed., *Songs of a Changing World* (London: Ginn and Company, 1972), pp. 33–34.

184. "Polly Parker," n.d., in Raven, ed., *Songs of a Changing World*, p. 23.

185. "The Pitman's Pay," in Roy Palmer, *Poverty Knock: A picture of industrial life in the nineteenth century through songs, ballads and contemporary accounts* (Cambridge, UK: CUP, 1974), p. 38.

186. "Down in the Coalmine," in Raven, ed., *Songs of a Changing World*, p. 29.

187. "Five in the Morning," in Palmer, *Poverty Knock*, p. 38.

188. See "Poverty Knock," and "Talli I O the Grinder!" in Palmer, *Poverty Knock*, pp. 14, 30.

189. *British Miner and Workman's Advocate*, no. 124, July 15, 1865.

190. R. Holder, "The Collier's Appeal to the Country," D/DZ A31 no. 52, Pitmen's Collection, Wigan Record Office, Leigh.

191. Martin Cooper, "The Shocking Colliery Accident," in *Miner and Workmen's Examiner*, no. 107, September 17, 1875. See also *Dreadful Colliery Explosion and Awful Loss of Life, at Oaks Colliery Near Barnsley* (London: Henry Disley, circa 1866).

192. William Johnson, "The Miners' Grievances," D/DZ A31, no. 107, Pitmen's Collection, Wigan Record Office, Leigh. "Mence" is a Northern regionalism meaning "propriety."

193. *A Metrical Tale of the Late Lamentable Occurrence Which Took Place at Wallsend Church Pit* (Newcastle, UK: Newcastle and Shepard, 1835).

194. A popular piece called "The Miner's Doom" was recited by a practical miner at an 1844 concert in Newcastle. See D/DZ A31 no. 90, Pitmen's Collection, Wigan Record Office, Leigh.

195. Reports from Commissioners, Sir Henry T. De La Beche and Sir Lyon Playfair, *Report on the Gases and Explosions in Collieries*, 1846 (529) XLIII: 33.

196. Parliamentary Papers, Reports from Commissioners, *Royal Commission on the Employment of Children in Mines and Manufactories, Appendix*, 1842 (381) XVI: 817.

197. Ibid., p. 854.

198. *Account of the Dreadful Explosion of Fire, Which took Place on Monday, the 19th of July, at Sheriff-Hill Colliery, near Newcastle, in the County of Durham* (North Shields, UK: Pollock, 1819).

199. Bullock, *Bowers Row,* pp. 31–32.

200. Parliamentary Papers, Reports from Commissioners, *Royal Commission for Inquiring into the Employment and Condition of Children in Mines and Manufactories, Appendix to First Report of Commissioners, Part I,* 1842 (381) XVI: 157, 441.

201. Bullock, *Bowers Row,* p. 31.

202. See, e.g, *The Explosion of Felling Colliery, by Which Ninety-Two Persons Lost Their Lives, on the 25th of May, 1812.* (Dublin, IR: C. Bentham, n.d.), pp. 2–8.

203. James Mather, *The Coal Mines: Their Dangers and Means of Safety* (London: Longmans, 1868, p. 12.

204. Kenyon, pp. 19–21.

205. Parliamentary Papers, Reports from Committees, Royal Commission on the Employment of Children in Mines and Manufactories, Appendix I, 1842 (381) XVI, pp. 644, 650, 651; *Railway Service Gazette,* no. 81, August 16, 1873. See also *United States Orthopedic Institute for the Application of Improved Anatomical Machinery to the Treatment of Every Variety of Deformity* (Philadelphia: George W. Yerger and John Ord, 1850).

Chapter 4

1. J. G. Burke, "Bursting Boilers and the Federal Power," *Technology and Culture* vol. 7 no. 1 (1966): 1–23. Peter Bartrip shows that, despite the number of legislative acts to protect workers from the 1830s on, little money or manpower were earmarked for enforcement—calling into question the whole purpose of the legislation. See Peter W. J. Bartrip, "State Intervention in Mid-Nineteenth-Century Britain: Fact or Fiction?" *Journal of British Studies* vol. 23 no. 1 (1983): 63–83.

2. This is not to deny, as Christopher Frank has pointed out, that many workers were subject to legal compulsion of various kinds and that the law was interpreted in ways that favored employers over workers—just the opposite. However, this compulsion coexisted with an official ideology that celebrated the free agency of the white working man. See Frank, "'Let But One of Them Come Before Me, and I'll Commit Him': Trade Unions, Magistrates, and the Law in Mid-Nineteenth-Century Staffordshire," *Journal of British Studies* vol. 44 no. 1 (2005): 64–91.

3. James D. Schmidt provides an excellent review of the legal changes forced by the appearance of waged child labor, and the accompanying rethought of children's position in the "free labor" ideology, in "'Restless Movements Characteristic of Childhood': The Legal Construction of Labor in Nineteenth-Century Massachusetts," *Law and History Review* vol. 23 no. 2 (2005): 315–50.

4. The definitive recent work on these issues is Marjorie Levine-Clark, *Beyond the Reproductive Body* (Columbus: Ohio State University Press, 2004), which teases out

various contradictory modes of thinking and talking about women workers in this period, including within the context of workplace accidents.

5. J. T. Ward, *The Factory Movement, 1830–1855* (New York: Macmillan, 1962).

6. These arguments were recycled again in the United States in the early twentieth century, again by employers, although this time the "free agents" in question were female. Using the freedom of contract line of argument enabled manufacturers who wanted women to work more than ten hours a day to claim that they were just support-ing women's right to equal treatment. In contrast, those who sought protectionist labor laws for women were forced to argue against women's equality. See Nancy Woloch, *Muller v. Oregon: A Brief History With Documents* (New York: Bedford Books, 1996).

7. Reports from Commissioners, *Royal Commission on the Employment of Chil-dren in Factories,* 1833 (450) XX: 1, p. 33.

8. Ibid., p. 52.

9. Ibid., p. 464.

10. Ibid., p. 72.

11. Ibid., p. 869.

12. Parliamentary Reports, Reports from Committees, *Report from the Select Committee of the House of Lords on Accidents in Coal Mines,* 1840 (613) VII: 74.

13. Parliamentary Reports, Reports from Commissioners, *Royal Commission on the Employment of Children in Factories,* 1833 (450) XX: 410.

14. Ibid., p. 414.

15. Ibid., p. 865.

16. *Times,* no. 13068, September 9, 1826.

17. *Times,* no. 19074, November 28, 1846.

18. *Lumsden v. Russell,* 18 Dunlop 468, Feb. 1, 1856. Printed in *Scots Revised Re-ports* 9 Court of Session, Second Series, pp. 949–52.

19. Leonard Horner to Sir George Grey, April 5, 1851, HO 45 OS 3675, Public Record Office.

20. Thomas Beven, *The Law of Employers' Liability for the Negligence of Servants Causing Injury to Fellow Servants* (London: Waterlow Brothers and Layton, 1881), p. 82.

21. 4 *Jur,* n.s. 774 (1858)

22. *James Whitelaw, Pursuer, v. John Moffat and Alexander Pollack, Defenders.* 12 Dunlop 434, 27 Dec. 1849, reported in *Scots Revised Reports* 6 (1848–50), pp. 796–98.

23. *Grizzle v. Frost,* 3 Foster & Fin 623. In a third case, when a thirteen-year-old Scottish girl lost her arm to a toothed factory wheel, it was held that the wheel should have been protected. *Gemmills v. Gourock Ropework Company* (1861) 23 D. 425, 33 *Jur* 216. cited in Beven, *The Law of Employers' Liability,* p. 54.

24. Margo Schlanger, "Injured Women Before Common-Law Courts, 1860–1930," *Harvard Women's Law Journal* 21 (1998): 79–140.

25. *Emory A. Hayden v. the Smithville Manufacturing Company,* 29 Connecticut 538; 1861 Lexis 62, at 6.

26. Anthony Bale, "Compensation Crisis: The Value and Meaning of Work-Related Injuries and Illnesses in the United States 1842–1932," Ph.D. dissertation, Brandeis University, 1986, p. 87.

27. Schmidt, "Restless Movements," at para. 60.

28. Paul Finkelman, "Slaves as Fellow Servants: Ideology, Law and Industrialization," *American Journal of Legal History* 31 (1987): 269–305.

29. Frederick Wertheim, "Note: Slavery and the Fellow Servant Rule: An Antebellum Dilemma," *New York University Law Review* vol. 61 (1986): 1112–48.

30. Thus, in 1859, the Richmond and Danville Railroad paid $1,379.44 to a master whose slave had been killed while in service to the company. See Walter Licht, *Working for the Railroad: The Organization of Work in the Nineteenth Century* (Princeton, NJ: Princeton University Press, 1983), p. 88.

31. Wertheim, "Note: Slavery," p. 1144.

32. The most valuable discussion of the law of slave hires can be found in Thomas D. Morris, *Southern Slavery and the Law, 1619–1860* (Chapel Hill: University of North Carolina Press, 1996), pp. 132–58.

33. See, e.g., the judgment of B. Mills Crenshaw in *Louisville and Nashville Railroad Company v. Yandell* (1856), quoted in Morris, *Southern Slavery and the Law*, p. 156. For a comparison of the five cases in which Southern jurists rejected slaves as fellow servants, see Wertheim, "Note: Slavery," pp. 1131–32.

34. Gary T. Schwartz, "The History of Early American Tort Law," *UCLA Law Review* 36 (1989): 641–718.

35. See Morris, *Southern Slavery*, pp. 354–68, for an extended discussion of the civil liability of masters for the actions of their slaves.

36. See Wertheim, "Note: Slavery," p. 1134.

37. Paul Finkelman, "Slaves as Fellow Servants: Ideology, Law and Industrialization," *American Journal of Legal History* 31 (1987): 269–305.

38. *British Miner and General Newsman*, no. 12, November 29, 1862.

39. Jeanne Boydston, *Home and Work* (New York: Oxford University Press, 1990).

40. The most dangerous work for women workers in the nineteenth century was reproduction. The unpaid labor that is labor was part and parcel of a woman's responsibilities, but its casualties were rarely documented in the public sphere.

41. *Times*, no. 10428, August 6, 1818.

42. Workers' deaths by machinery are described in the *Times*, no. 5620, 17 Jan. 1803; no. 7138, 28 Aug. 1807; no. 8034, 14 July 1810; no. 8044, 26 July 1810; no. 9358, 3 Nov. 1814; no. 9895, 24 July 1816.

43. *Miners' Journal and Pottsville General Advertiser*, vol. 25 no. 23, June 2, 1849.

44. Teresa Murphy, *Ten Hours' Labor: Religion, Reform, and Gender in Early New England* (Ithaca, NY: Cornell University Press, 1992).

45. The applicability to adult women of the clause in the 1844 Factory Act which ordered the fencing of dangerous machinery was tested in 1851, but the judges in that

case ingeniously escaped having to make a decision on its merits. See *Coe v. Platt*, 15 *Jur.* 732. For a factory prosecution on behalf of an injured adult male worker, see James Stuart to Henry Manners Sutton, May 25, 1846, HO 45/1113, Public Record Office.

46. Factory Inspector Saunders to Secretary of State. June 17, 1845, HO45/1119, Public Record Office.

47. R. L. Howells, "Priestley v. Fowler and the Factory Acts," *Modern Law Review* 26 (1963): 367–95. The test case is also described in Parliamentary Papers, Reports from Commissioners, Reports of the Inspectors of Factories (1841 Session 1) vol. 10 (294) p. 161.

48. Parliamentary Papers, Reports from Commissioners, *Reports of the Inspectors of Factories to Her Majesty's Principal Secretary of State for the Home Department for the Half Year Ending 31 October 1848*, 1849 (1017): 119. See also the case of Jean Jones, a fourteen-year-old worker who was scalped in the mill, pp. 148–49.

49. Parliamentary Papers, Reports from Commissioners, *Reports of the Inspectors of Factories . . . for the Half-Year Ending 30th April 1849*, (1084) vol. XXII: 10.

50. Parliamentary Papers. Reports from Commissioners. *Second Report of the Children's Employment Commissions* 1843 XIII: 390: 90–91.

51. Parliamentary Papers, *Special Reports of the Inspectors of Factories on the Practicability of Legislative Interference to Diminish the Frequency of Accidents to the Children and Young Persons Employed in Factories, Arising from Machinery being Cleaned while in Motion, and from Dangerous Parts of the Machinery being left Unguarded*, 1841 (311) X.

52. Robert Baker to Secretary of State George Cornewall Lewis, October 19, 1859, HO45/6753, Public Record Office.

53. William Prowting Roberts to Samuel Appleton, August 18, 1859, HO45/6753, Public Record Office.

54. Samuel Appleton to Robert Baker, August 22, 1859, HO45/6753, Public Record Office.

55. Samuel Appleton to Robert Baker, August 31, 1859, HO45/6753, Public Record Office.

56. Robert Baker to Samuel Appleton, August 31, 1859, HO45/6753, Public Record Office.

57. Robert Baker to Messrs. Woods, August 31, 1859, HO45/6753, Public Record Office.

58. William Woods to Robert Baker, September 5, 1859, HO45/6753, Public Record Office.

59. Samuel Appleton to Robert Baker, September 13, 1859, HO45/6753, Public Record Office.

60. William Woods to Robert Baker, September 15, 1859, HO45/6753, Public Record Office.

61. Robert Baker to William Woods, September 16, 1859, HO45/6753, Public Record Office.

62. William Woods to Robert Baker, September 21, 1859, HO45/6753, Public Record Office.

63. Robert Baker to Secretary of State George Cornewall Lewis, October 19, 1859, HO45/6753, Public Record Office.

64. Petition from Samuel Appleton, dated Seprember 9, 1859, HO45/6753, Public Record Office.

65. Undated letter from James Mile to Robert Baker, HO45/6753, Public Record Office. The Appleton family's census record is located at *Census Returns of England and Wales,* 1861, Class RG 9, Piece: 2773, Folio: 47, Page: 34, GSU roll: 543027.

66. T. Jones Howell to Sir Denis Le Marchant, January 5, 1848, HO 45/1113, Public Record Office.

67. Ibid.

68. *Beehive,* no. 161, November 12, 1864.

69. Copy of Report of Mr. Higson, Inspector of Collieries, on the Death of Ellen Hampson, killed at the Moss House Colliery, Lancashire, 1866 (99) LX p. 23

70. *London Journal and Pioneer,* vol. 2 no. 105, December 5, 1846.

71. See, e.g., Carolyn Malone, *Women's Bodies and Dangerous Trades in England, 1880–1914* (Woodbridge, UK: Boydell Press, 2003).

72. *Times,* no. 11392, November 1, 1821.

73. *Times,* no. 21306, December 23, 1852.

74. J. T. Arlidge, *The Hygiene, Diseases and Mortality of Occupations* (London: Percival and Co., 1892), p. 499.

75. Ibid., p. 27.

76. Ibid., p. 430. As Raphael Samuel has pointed out, little safety training was provided for miners. See "Mineral Workers," in Raphael Samuel, ed. *Miners, Quarrymen and Saltworkers* (London: Routledge & Kegan Paul, 1977), p. 47.

77. Ibid., p. 47.

78. Anthony F. C. Wallace, *St. Clair: A Nineteenth-Century Coal Town's Experience with a Disaster Prone Industry* (New York: Alfred A. Knopf, 1987), p. 273.

79. Crystal Eastman, *Work-Accidents and the Law* (New York: Charities Publication Committee, 1910), p. 59.

80. Ibid., p. 81.

81. Crystal Eastman, *Work-Accidents,* pp. 41, 101.

82. Typescript entitled, "Explosions at Brandywine Mills: (Brief Record Taken from Book of Francis G. Du Pont," folder marked "Explosions," passim, at Hagley Museum and Library.

83. *The People,* vol. 1 no. 18, August 15, 1857.

84. Parliamentary Papers, Reports from Commissioners, *Royal Commission on the Employment of Children in Factories,* Supplementary Report of the Central Board, 1834 (167) XIX: 356–57.

85. Undated news clipping, D/DZ A31 no. 24, Pitmen's Collection, Wigan Record Office, Leigh.

86. News clipping dated May 11, 1844, D/DZ A31 no. 55, Pitmen's Collection, Wigan Record Office, Leigh.

87. Parliamentary Papers, Reports from Commissioners, *Royal Commission on the Employment of Children in Factories*, Supplementary Report of the Central Board, 1834 (167) XIX: 356–57.

88. Parliamentary Papers, Reports from Committees, *Report from the Select Committee on Accidents in Mines*, 1835 (603) V: 215.

89. *Times*, no. 6026, May 18, 1804.

90. Letter from James Allan to John McDonald, June 27, 1843, Glasgow Colliery Records UGD/1/25/3/54, Glasgow Business Records Center.

91. Letter from James Allan to Messrs. R. Newall and Co., December 4, 1844, Govan Colliery Records UGD/1/25/3/102, Glasgow Business Records Center.

92. Letter from James Allan to John McDonald, 16 June 1845, Govan Colliery Records UGD/1/25/3/111, Glasgow Business Records Center.

93. James Mather, *The Coal Mines: Their Dangers and Means of Safety* (London: Longmans, 1868, p. 60.

94. Reports from Committee's *Select Committee on Accidents in Coal Mines, First Report*, 1853 (691) XX: 103.

95. See, e.g., the report of Edward Rymer in *Miner and Workman's Advocate*, no. 115, May 13, 1865.

96. Reports from Committee's *Select Committee on Accidents in Coal Mines, Second Report*, 1853 (740) XX: 88–90.

97. The quest for "smart money" in the 1840s is chronicled in D/DZ A31 # 21, Petition to the House of Commons; # 24, newspaper fragment; # 52, "The Colliers' Appeal to the Country," by R. Holder; #55 is a clipping from an unknown newspaper from May 11, 1844; and #92, proposed new bond 1844, all in the Pitmen's Strike Collection, Wigan Record Office, Leigh.

98. See testimony of Thomas John Taylor, in Parliamentary Papers, Reports from Committees, *Select Committee appointed to inquire into the Causes of the numerous Accidents in Coal Mines, Second Report*, 1854 (258) IX: 23.

99. *Reformer* (Newport), vol. 1 no. 21, January 31, 1862.

100. Colliers of the United Association of Durham and Northumberland. *A Voice from the Coal Mines, or a Plain Statement of the Various Grievances of the Pitmen of the Tyne and Wear* (South Shields, UK: J. Clark. 1825), p. 10.

101. J. Robson, *Hartley Sacrifice* (Sunderland, UK: R. H. Coleman, n.d.).

102. Ibid.

103. *Reformer* (Newport), vol. 1 no. 24, February 28, 1862.

104. *Labour Press and Miner's and Workman's Examiner*, no. 68, December 5, 1874.

105. *The Haswell Colliery Explosion, 28 September 1844, Narrative Report of the Proceedings at the Coroner's Inquest* (Newcastle, UK: M. Benson, 1844), pp. iv–vi.

106. Eileen Yeo, "Some Practices and Problems of Chartist Democracy," in James Epstein and Dorothy Thompson, eds. *The Chartist Experience* (London: Palgrave McMillan, 1982), pp. 345–80.

107. Samuel Smiles, *Self-Help* (London: John Murray, 1859).

108. Sean Wilentz, *Chants Democratic* (New York: Oxford University Press, 1984); David Montgomery, *Citizen Worker; The Experience of Workers in the United States with Democracy and the Free Market in the Nineteenth Century* (New York: Cambridge University Press, 1993).

109. *Ryan v. Cumberland Valley RR Co.* (23 PA 384), quoted in Albert B. Bolles, *The Liability of Employers to Their Employees* (Harrisburg, PA: Edwin K. Meyers, 1891), p. 16.

110. *Railway Service Gazette*, no. 25, March 1, 1873.

Chapter 5

1. On the shift to a more "statist" outlook among unionized workers, see Robert Asher, "Experience Counts: British Workers, Accident Prevention and Compensation, and the Origins of the Welfare State," *Journal of Policy History* vol. 15 no. 4 (2003): 359–388.

2. Compare the argument of William Forbath, in "Law and the Shaping of Labor Politics in the United States and England," in Chris Tomlins and Andrew J. King, *Labor Law in America* (Baltimore, MD: Johns Hopkins University Press, 1992), p. 207.

3. John Witt, *The Accidental Republic: Crippled Workingmen, Destitute Widows, and the Remaking of American Law* (Cambridge, MA: Harvard University Press, 2004), p. 10.

4. Vernon describes the institution of a "technocracy" of nutritionists, industrial planners, architects, and other experts to deal with the question of alleviating school hunger; Mark Aldrich has described a similar trajectory for the development of the field of safety engineering in the workplace. Cf. James Vernon, "The Ethics of Hunger and the Assembly of Society: The Techno-Politics of the School Meal in Modern Britain," *American Historical Review* vol. 110 no. 3 (2005): 693–725.

5. See, e.g., *Times*, no. 4535, July 15, 1799; no. 4564, August 17, 1799.

6. *London Mercury*, no. 2, September 24, 1836.

7. Parliamentary Papers, Reports from Commissioners, *Royal Commission on the Employment of Children in Factories*, 1833 (450) XX: 1, p. 73.

8. Ibid., p. 74.

9. "Descriptive Remarks Relative to Railway Contracts and Railway Workmen," in *Papers Read Before the Statistical Society of Manchester on the Demoralisation and Injuries Occasioned by the Want of Proper Regulations of Labourers Engaged in the Construction and Working of Railways* (Manchester, UK: Simms and Dinham, n.d.), p. 49.

10. Ibid., p. 19.

11. Ibid., p. 21.

12. P. W. J. Bartrip and P. T. Fenn, "The Measurement of Safety: Factory Accident Statistics in Victorian and Edwardian Britain." *Historical Research* 63 (1990): 58–72.

13. P. W. J. Bartrip and S. B. Burman, *The Wounded Soldiers of Industry* (Oxford, UK: Clarendon Press, 1983), p. 55.

14. *Ten Hours' Advocate,* vol. 14, December 26, 1846, p. 106.

15. Ralph Dickson, "Industrial Safety: The Political Challenge," *Journal of Legal History* [Great Britain] 1986 7(2): 188–195.

16. The Reverend Francis Hastings Stuart-Monteath to Sir George Grey, June 4, 1851, HO 45/3716, Public Record Office.

17. *Ten Hours' Advocate,* no. 24, March 6, 1847, p. 188.

18. W. G. Carson, "The Conventionalization of Early Factory Crime," *International Journal for the Sociology of Law* 7 (1979): 37–60.

19. Charles Trimmer to T. Jones Howle, October 9, 1854, in HO45/5217, Public Record Office.

20. Peter Bailey to Charles Trimmer, October 6, 1854, in HO45/5217, Public Record Office.

21. T. Jones Howle to the Home Office, undated, in HO45/5217, Public Record Office.

22. Alexander Redgrave to Home Office, June 6, 1853, and report for January–April 1853, HO45/5497, Public Record Office.

23. Leonard Horner to Sir George Grey, April 5, 1851, HO 45 OS 3675, Public Record Office.

24. Factory Inspectors to Sir George Grey, June 17, 1853, HO45/5497, Public Record Office.

25. Palmerston, undated minute, HO 45/5209, Public Record Office.

26. Factory Inspectors to Palmerston, March 2, 1854, HO 45/5209, Public Record Office.

27. Printed letter form Leonard Horner, dated November 1859, HO 45/6756.

28. Parliamentary Papers, Reports from Committees, *Report from the Select Committee on Railway Labourers* 1846 (530) XIII.425

29. Ibid., p. ix.

30. Ibid., p. ix.

31. Ibid., p. x.

32. Ibid., p. 22.

33. Ibid., p. 148–49.

34. Ibid., pp. 149–50.

35. Ibid., p. 194.

36. Ibid., p. 141.

37. Ibid., p. 142.

38. *Mining Journal*, vol. 17 no. 603, March 13, 1847, p. 116.

39. *Mining Journal*, vol. 17 no. 604, March 20, 1847, p. 130–31.

40. Ibid., p. 119.

41. Hansard's Parliamentary Debates, vol. 93, June 30, 1847, cols. 1071–1078. On Wakley's career and relationship to workplace accidents, see Elisabeth Cawthon, "Thomas Wakley and the Medical Coronership: Death and the Judicial Process," *Medical History* vol. 30 no. 2 (April 1986): 191–202.

42. Hansard's Parliamentary Debates, vol. 93, July 1, 1847, cols. 1090–1091.

43. Ibid., at 312.

44. Richard Fynes, *The Miners of Northumberland and Durham* (Blyth: John Robinson, 1873), pp. 119–31.

45. Hansard's Parliamentary Debates, vol. 93, July 14, 1847.

46. Reports from Committees, *Select Committee of the House of Lords on Accidents in Coal Mines; Together with the Minutes of Evidence, Appendix, Plans and Index.* 1849 (613) VII: 146.

47. Ibid., pp. vii–viii.

48. Ibid., p. viii.

49. Parliamentary Papers, *Reports on the Explosions in Darley Main Colliery*, 1849 (1051) XXII: p. 101.

50. *Coal Mines Inspection Act*, 1850 (595): 357.

51. See, e.g., *Times*, no. 20809, May 23, 1851. The question of coroners' juries and workplace accidents is also discussed in Cawthon, "Thomas Wakley and the Medical Coronership."

52. George Fife, *Critical Analysis of the Evidence Adduced at the Inquest Held on the Bodies of Those who Suffered by the Late Explosion at Wallsend Colliery* (Newcastle, UK: John Hernaman, 1835), p. 4. See also the testimony of Warrington Smith, in Parliamentary Papers, Reports from Committees, *Second Report of the 1854 Select Committee appointed to inquire into the Causes of the numerous Accidents in Coal Mines, with a view of suggesting the best means for their prevention*, 1854 (258) IX: 112.

53. *Sheffield Times and Rotherham Advertiser*, no. 51, March 20, 1847.

54. Parliamentary Papers, Reports from Commissioners, *Copies of the Report made by Mr. Dickinson, Inspector of Mines, upon the Oaks Colliery Explosion, and with reference to the Prevention of such Occurrences; and of a Report made by Mr. Wynne, Inspector of Mines, on the Explosion at Talk-o'th'-Hill; with the Evidence taken before the Coroner's Inquest*, Parliamentary Papers, Reports from Commissioners, 1877 (3811) III: 21–31.

55. Parliamentary Papers, Reports from Committees, *Accidents in Coal Mines*, 1853 XX, First Report, p. 132; Second Report, pp. 16–17.

56. Born in Bolton, Swallow entered the mines at age eight, in 1833. At age seventeen, he became a full-fledged collier. In the sixteen years between his entry into the

mines and his first testimony before a Select Committee, he was involved in a mine explosion that left him partially burned. Reports from Committees, *Report from the Select Committee of the House of Lords on Accidents in Coal Mines,* 1840 VII: 452.

57. Parliamentary Papers, Reports from Committees, *Accidents in Coal Mines, Second Report,* 1853 (13) XX: 45–46.

58. *Times,* no. 21306, December 23, 1852.

59. Parliamentary Papers, Reports from Committees, *Accidents in Coal Mines, Second Report* 1853 (13) XX: 72–80.

60. Christopher Frank provides many other examples of Roberts's use of the law as a form of theater, in " 'Let But One of Them Come Before Me, and I'll Commit Him': Trade Unions, Magistrates, and the Law in Mid-Nineteenth-Century Staffordshire," *Journal of British Studies* vol. 44 no. 1 (2005): 64–91.

61. *Full and Authentic Particulars of the Dreadful Explosion at Haswell Colliery* (Sunderland: Vint and Carr, 1844).

62. Ibid., p. 31.

63. *The Haswell Colliery Explosion, 28 September 1844, Narrative Report of the Proceedings at the Coroner's Inquest* (Newcastle, UK: M. Benson, 1844), p. 71.

64. *Times,* no. 20881, August 15, 1851.

65. *Times,* no. 20882, August 16, 1851.

66. *Times,* no. 20084, August 18, 1851. For similar cases, see *Times,* no. 20904, September 11, 1851; no. 20939, October 22, 1851.

67. *Colliery Guardian,* vol. 3 no. 64, March 22, 1862, pp. 227–28.

68. *Colliery Guardian,* vol. 3 no. 68, April 19, 1862, p. 307.

69. See, e.g., the actions of inspector Herbert Mackworth, in *Times,* no. 21322, January 11, 1853.

70. See the testimony of Richard Smith, in Parliamentary Papers, Reports from Committees, *Report from the Select Committee on Accidents in Mines,* 1835 (603) V: 227.

71. Parliamentary Papers, Reports from Commissioners, *Commission for Inquiring into the Employment and Condition of Children in Mines and Manufactories, Appendix to First Report, Part I,* 1842 (381) XVI: 380.

72. Parliamentary Papers, Reports from Committees, *Select Committee on the Causes of Accidents on Railways,* 1857–58 (362) XIV.555, at 56.

73. Parliamentary Papers, Reports from Commissioners, *Commission for Inquiring into the Employment and Condition of Children in Mines and Manufactories, First Report, (Mines)* 1842 (380) XV: 151.

74. *Beehive,* no. 114, December 19, 1863.

75. *Beehive,* no. 63, December 27, 1862.

76. *Beehive* , no. 114, December 19, 1863.

77. *Beehive,* no. 125, February 27, 1864.

78. *Beehive,* no. 125, March 5, 1864.

79. *Beehive,* no. 139, June 11, 1864.

80. Parliamentary Reports, Reports from Committees, *Accidents in Coal Mines, Second Report* 1853 (13) XX: 50.

81. Parliamentary Papers, Reports from Committees, *Select Committee on Coal Mines,* 1852 (509) V: ix.

82. Parliamentary Papers, Reports from Committees, *Select Committee appointed to inquire into the Causes of the numerous Accidents in Coal Mines, with a view of suggesting the best means for their prevention, Third Report,* 1854 (277) IX: 108.

83. Parliamentary Papers, Reports from Committees, *Select Committee appointed to inquire into the Causes of the numerous Accidents in Coal Mines, with a view of suggesting the best means for their prevention, Fourth Report,* 1854 (325) IX: 7–9.

84. Parliamentary Papers, Reports from Commissioners, *Report of the Commissioners Appointed to Inquire into the Condition of all Mines in Great Britain . . . With Reference to the Health and Safety of Persons Employed in Such Mines,* Part 1, 1864 (3389) XXI: ix.

85. Ibid., p. xx.

86. Ibid., xlv.

87. *Times,* no. 24154, January 28, 1862; no. 24156, January 30, 1862.

88. *Mining Journal,* January 25, 1862, p. 58.

89. *Reformer* (Newport), vol. 1 no. 20, January 24, 1862.

90. *Mining Journal,* March 15, 1862, p. 170; *Newcastle Chronicle,* May 10, 1862, no. 5105.

91. *A Bill to Amend the Law Relating to the Recovery of Damages by Workmen and Servants, and of Compensation by the Families of Workmen and Servants Killed by Accidents,* 1862 (8) I: 1.

92. Hansard Vol. 1865 (1862), Feb. 11, 1862, p. 161–63.

93. *Colliery Guardian,* vol. 3 no. 61, February 29, 1862, p. 141.

94. *Colliery Guardian,* vol. 3 no. 61, February 29, 1862, p. 141.

95. *Colliery Guardian,* vol. 3 no. 61, March 1, 1862, p. 161.

96. The discussion can be found at Hansard Vol. 1865 (1862), March 19, 1862, pp. 1835–50.

97. On the other hand, when it was necessary to do so to advance the goal of maintaining law and order, the government could easily paint working people as helpless dupes in need of protection. See the example of the Chartist Land Company, in Jamie L. Bronstein, *Land Reform and Working-Class Experience in Britain and the United States, 1800–1860* (Stanford, CA: Stanford University Press, 1999), p. 227.

98. *Beehive,* no. 61, December 13, 1862.

99. Ibid.

100. *Commonwealth,* no. 182, September 1, 1866, p. 7.

101. *Beehive,* no. 125, February 27, 1864.

102. *Commonwealth,* no. 198, December 22, 1866, p. 5.

103. Joseph Brown, Esq. QC, *The Evils of the Unlimited Liability for Accidents of Masters and Railway Companies* (London: Butterworths, 1870), p. 8.

104. Ibid., p. 25.

105. *Railway Service Gazette,* no.1, February 3, 1872.

106. *Railway Service Gazette,* no. 41, November 9, 1872.

107. *Railway Service Gazette,* no. 86, September 20, 1873.

108. *Railway Service Gazette,* no. 81, August 16, 1873.

109. *Railway Service Gazette,* no. 227, June 2, 1876; no. 233, July 14, 1876; no. 280, June 8, 1877; no. 318, March 1, 1878.

110. *Railway Service Gazette,* no. 34, September 21, 1872.

111. *Miner and Workmen's Examiner,* no. 75, January 23, 1875; no. 110, October 17, 1875; no. 111, October 22, 1875.

112. *A Bill to Amend the Law Relating to Compensation for Injuries to Workmen and Servants,* 1872 (246) VI: 511.

113. *A Bill to Amend the Law Relating to Compensation for Injuries suffered by Persons in the course of their Employment,* 1874 (91) V.593. Discussion on the bill can be found in Hansard, May 5, 1874, vol. 211, p. 1706.

114. *Railway Service Gazette,* no. 119, May 7, 1874; no. 120, May 14, 1874.

115. *Railway Service Gazette,* no. 125, June 18, 1874.

116. *A Bill to Provide for Compensation to Workpeople Engaged in Common Employment in Cases of Injury by Accidents When Employed,* 1875 (186) I.373.

117. The bill was only read once. See Hansard, May 27, 1875 v. 224, p. 916.

118. *Railway Service Gazette,* no. 175, June 4, 1875.

119. The bill was accompanied by a petition from the Parliamentary Committee of the TUC, praying for its acceptance. *Railway Service Gazette,* no. 216, March 17, 1876.

120. *A Bill to Amend the Law Relating to the Liability of Employers for Injuries Negligently Caused to Persons in Their Employment,* 1876 (15) II.353.

121. Hansard, May 24, 1876, v. 229, p. 1154 et seq.

122. *Railway Service Gazette,* no. 226, May 26, 1876.

123. Interestingly, the 1871 explosion at the Moss Colliery that Knowles described killed seventy workpeople, and then, in a second explosion, killed a number of bystanders, and wounded others, among them Knowles's own son. Due to flooding in the explosion's aftermath, the mine was closed for a year before the bodies could even be evacuated, although it was eventually worked again. Knowles himself ordered a large monument to the dead be planted in the graveyard at Ince, near Wigan. Jack Nadin, "Lancashire Colliery Disasters," http://jnadin.50megs.com/custom3.html.

124. *Mining Journal,* vol. 46 no. 2128, June 3, 1876.

125. *Mining Journal,* vol. 46 no. 2127, May 27, 1876.

126. *Colliery Guardian,* vol. 31 no. 804, May 26, 1876.

127. Parliamentary Papers, Reports from Committees, *Report from the Select Committee on Employers' Liability for Injuries to Their Servants,* 1876 (372) IX: 38–40, 48.

128. Ibid., p. 59.

129. Ibid., p. 68.

130. *Railway Service Gazette,* no. 250, November 10, 1876.

131. *Railway Service Gazette,* no. 265, Feb. 16, 1877.

132. *Railway Service Gazette,* no. 271, April 6, 1877.

133. Parliamentary Papers, Reports from Committees, *Report from the Select Committee on Employers' Liability for Injuries to Their Servants,* 1876 (372) IX: 5.

134. Ibid., p. 9.

135. Ibid., pp. 20–23.

136. Ibid., p. 129.

137. Ibid., pp. 116–18.

138. Ibid., p. 27.

139. Ibid., p. 28.

140. Parliamentary Papers, Reports from Committees, *Report from the Select Committee on Employers Liability for Injuries to Their Servants,* 1877 (285) X: iv–v.

141. Ibid., p. 63.

142. *Report from the Select Committee on Employers Liability for Injuries to their Servants,* 1877 (285) X.551, p. x.

143. Ibid., p. 108.

144. *A Bill to Amend the Law Relating to the Liability of Employers for Injuries Negligently Caused to Persons in Their Employment,* 1878 (11) II.459.

145. Hansard, vol. 239 (1878), April 10, 1878, p. 1042.

146. Ibid., p. 1046.

147. See, e.g., the comments of Shaw-Lefevre, p. 1060.

148. Ibid., p. 1361.

149. Mining Association of Great Britain, *Employers' Liability for Injuries* (Wigan, UK: Wall, 1878), p. 10.

150. Ibid., p. 20.

151. Ibid., pp. 28–29.

152. *A Bill to Amend the Law as to Employers' Liability for Injuries to Their Servants* 1878–9 (80) III.121

153. See Hansard, vol. 245 (1879), Feb. 14, 1879, p. 1282.

154. *A Bill to Extend and Regulate the Liability of Employers to Make Compensation for Personal Injuries Suffered by Persons in Their Service* 1878–9 (75) III.117

155. See Hansard, vol. 243 (1879), p. 1391.

156. *A Bill to Amend the Law Relating to the Liability of Employers for Injuries Sustained by Their Servants,* 1878–9 (103) III.113.

157. Hansard, vol. 244 (1879), March 17, 1879, p. 1140.

158. Ibid., p. 1143.

159. *A Bill to Extend and Regulate the Liability of Employers to Make Compensation for Personal Injuries Suffered by Persons in Their Service* 1878-9 (75) III.117.

160. *Railway Service Gazette,* no 437, June 11, 1880.

161. *Colliery Guardian,* vol. 39 no. 1014, June 4, 1880.

162. *Colliery Guardian,* vol. 39 no. 1015, June 11, 1880.

163. Hansard, vol. 253 (1880), July 2, 1880, pp. 1399-1423.

164. Hansard, vol. 253 (1880), July 7, 1880, pp. 1752-87.

165. Hansard vol. 253 (1880), July 7, 1880, p. 1761.

166. *Railway Service Gazette,* no 437, June 11, 1880.

167. Hansard vol. 225 (1880), August 4, 1880, pp. 224-95.

168. Ibid., p. 266.

169. Ibid., p. 273.

170. Up until that point, W. H. Smith, as First Lord, had to look into every case, decide whether it was the workman's fault or not, and come up with a "compassionate allowance" proportionate to the injury. Hansard, vol. 225 (1880), August 6, 1880, p. 571.

171. Ibid., p. 581.

172. Hansard, vol. 255 (1880), August 13, 1880, p. 1103-28.

173. The bill was read for a third time on August 18, 1880. See Hansard, vol. 255 (1880), August 18, 1880, p. 1478.

174. Hansard, vol. 225 (1880), August 24, 1880 pp. 1955-93.

175. *Colliery Guardian,* vol. 40 no. 1025, August 20, 1880.

176. Hansard, vol. 226 (1880), August 26, 1880, p. 86-87.

177. *Operative Stonemasons Fortnightly Return,* no. 342, Feb. 3, 1881, MSS OS/ 4/1/58, Warwick Modern Records Centre.

Epilogue

1. Jennifer Clark, "The American Image of Technology," *American Quarterly* 39:3 (1987): 431-49.

2. P. Blake Keating, "Historical Origins of Workmen's Compensation Laws in the United States: Implementing the European Social Insurance Idea," *Kansas Journal of Law and Public Policy* 11 (2001): 279-303.

3. Price V. Fishback and Shawn Everett Kantor, *A Prelude to the Welfare State: Compulsory State Insurance and Worker's Compensation in Minnesota, Ohio and Washington, 1911-1919* (Cambridge, MA: National Bureau of Economic Research, 1994). p. 94.

4. James Whiteside, *Regulating Danger* (Lincoln: University of Nebraska Press, 1990).

5. Steve Sewell, "Amongst the Damp: The Dangerous Profession of Coal Mining in Oklahoma, 1870-1935," *Chronicles of Oklahoma* 70:1 (1992): 66-83.

6. Ibid., pp. 1–2, 37, 126–31. See also Fishback and Kantor, *A Prelude to the Welfare State*. Julian Go III has argued that Progressives were successful because they managed to frame the discourse about workers' compensation around the inevitability of accidents, rather than blaming employers as workers had long done. See "Inventing Industrial Accidents and their Insurance: Discourse and Workers' Compensation in the United States, 1880–1910," *Social Science History* vol. 20 no. 3 (1996): 401–38.

7. Witt, *Accidental Republic*, pp. 23–24.

8. Ibid., pp. 113–16.

9. Edward A. Purcell, Jr., *Litigation and Inequality: Federal Diversity Jurisdiction in Industrial America, 1870–1958* (New York: Oxford University Press, 1992), p. 31.

10. Edwin Gabler, "Gilded-Age Labor in Massachusetts and Illinois," *Labor's Heritage* vol. 4 no. 3 (1992): 4–21.

11. Wendell C. Macdonald, "The Early History of Labor Statistics in the United States," *Labor History* vol. 13 no. 2 (1972): 267–78.

12. R. R. Higgins-Evenson, "From Industrial Police to Workmen's Compensation: Public Policy and Industrial Accidents in New York, 1880–1910," *Labor History* vol. 39 no. 4 (1998): 365–80.

13. Anthony Wallace, *St. Clair: A Nineteenth-Century Coal Town's Experience with a Disaster-Prone Industry* (Ithaca, NY: Cornell University Press, 1981), p. 304.

14. Katherine Harvey, *The Best-Dressed Miners: Life and Labor in the Maryland Coal Region, 1835–1910* (Ithaca, NY: Cornell University Press, 1969), pp. 210–22. Anthony F. C. Wallace, *St. Clair: A Nineteenth-Century Coal Town's Experience with a Disaster Prone Industry* (New York: Alfred A. Knopf, 1987), p. 312.

15. Mark Aldrich, *Safety First: Technology, Labor, and Business in the Building of American Work Safety, 1870–1939* (Baltimore, MD: Johns Hopkins University Press, 1997).

16. C. Clark, "The Railroad Safety Movement in the United States: Origins and Development, 1869 to 1893." Ph.D. dissertation, University of Illinois, 1966, pp. 358–59.

17. R. R. Higgins-Evenson, "From Industrial Police to Workmen's Compensation: Public Policy and Industrial Accidents in New York, 1880–1910," *Labor History*, vol. 39 no. 4 (1998): 365–80.

18. On the issue of contingent fee representation and the new cadres of lawyers willing to represent immigrant workers in court claims, see also Witt, *Accidental Republic*, p. 61.

19. Higgens-Evenson, "From Industrial Police to Workmen's Compensation," p. 10.

20. Keating, "Historical Origins of Workman's Compensation Laws," p. 298.

21. Donald Rogers, "From Common Law to Factory Laws: The Transformation of Workplace Safety Law in Wisconsin Before Progressivism," *American Journal of Legal History* 39 (1995), p. 189.

22. Ibid.

23. Fishback and Kantor, *A Prelude to the Welfare State*, p. 198.

Index